THE GOLDEN AGE OF PREACHING

THE GOLDEN AGE OF PREACHING

MEN WHO MOVED THE MASSES

A BRITISH CASE STUDY FOR PREACHERS OF ALL NATIONS

Dr. Robert T. Henry

iUniverse, Inc.
New York Lincoln Shanghai

The Golden Age of Preaching
Men Who Moved the Masses

iUniverse books may be ordered through booksellers or by contacting:

iUniverse
2021 Pine Lake Road, Suite 100
Lincoln, NE 68512
www.iuniverse.com
1-800-Authors (1-800-288-4677)

ISBN-13: 978-0-595-36222-6 (pbk)
ISBN-13: 978-0-595-67353-7 (cloth)
ISBN-13: 978-0-595-80666-9 (ebk)
ISBN-10: 0-595-36222-2 (pbk)
ISBN-10: 0-595-67353-8 (cloth)
ISBN-10: 0-595-80666-X (ebk)

Printed in the United States of America

Dedicated to my wife, Svea,

for her faithful and supportive

contribution to my life and to the

writing of this book.

Contents

Part III: Common Characteristics Which Produced Greatness

Preface

The primary purpose behind the writing of this book is to inspire preachers to ask themselves, not simply how they might prepare a better sermon for this coming Sunday, but rather, *"How can I become a better preacher."* Not just to ask how they might improve their outline, or invent a more novel title for advertising purposes, but *"what fundamental changes to my entire approach to preaching must I make in order to elevate my effectiveness in the pulpit."*

Far better to ask oneself these questions than to have our congregations murmur, "Why can't our pastor improve his preaching?"—or even, "Is it time for us to activate the Search Committee?!"

"Since we have to preach, we ought to learn how to preach well." So said Dr. R. W. Dale of Birmingham. He was a prime example of an already fine preacher and theologian, held in high esteem throughout society, who nevertheless felt compelled to completely re-evaluate his preaching style and take active measures to improve it—at age 58! The author was privileged to have access to five different libraries in London and Oxford, and while studying the 1877 Lyman Beecher Lectures on preaching, delivered by Dr. R. W. Dale at Yale University, Dr. Dale, though dead, yet spoke to my heart and changed the style of my preaching. While seated in Dr. William's Library in Gordon Square, London, he completely convinced me of the superiority of extemporaneous preaching over the use of a full manuscript in the pulpit. Then and there I abandoned my former preaching style after 35 years of carrying a full, carefully prepared manuscript into the pulpit every time I preached. My maiden voyage in extemporaneous preaching was before the faculty and student body of Regent's Park College, the Baptist Study Hall attached to Oxford University. It was an intimidating but wholly rewarding experience. I never looked back since that day.

My purpose in undertaking research into the *"Golden Age of Preaching"* was to improve my own preaching ability first of all, and then to put together a seminar on preaching which would inspire, rather than humiliate, its participants. Instead of preaching trial sermons before colleagues who would then descend like vultures, picking apart their sermon carcasses tissue by tissue, I wanted to lure preachers to higher heights by extolling the preaching prowess of these outstanding pulpiteers of yesteryears. As for myself, though I had already held significant pulpit charges, had been a featured speaker in Keswick conventions throughout Australia for several years, had preached in denominational annual councils and assemblies and in annual mission conferences around the world, and served as a nation-wide evangelist and conference speaker for my own denomination,—yet I knew there was plenty of room for improvement. And I still feel that way and seek to do something about it.

Coupled with this inner motivation to improve, was the ministry of memory. I recalled from the early days of my Christian experience, preachers coming from the British Isles to minister in my home church in Hamilton, Ontario. Later still, such men would preach in our colleges and in our denomination's annual councils. There was something about these men and their preaching—not just their accents—which held us captive to their every utterance. There was something more than dialect, wit and charm, although there was all of that.

Eventually I had opportunity to research the lives, ministries and records of the British preachers who spread their wings and soared during an age of preaching which has been unparalleled in Church history. I speak of the extraordinary preachers who ministered during the reign of Queen Victoria. Some questioned how such a study of men from another century could possibly be relevant to today's requirements. Decidedly to the contrary, I discovered that the principles which shape and guide excellent preaching are perpetual, belonging to all generations with unabated strength and validity.

Truthfully, I never intended to write a book about my findings. Gradually pressures were brought to bear upon me which set me on my present course. The United States Air Force stationed in England organized a leadership training session for its commanding officers and a professional refreshment seminar for its chaplains who were scattered throughout the country. We met at the Royal Air Force base in Upper Heyford. I presented a study on the leadership qualities of Moses to the commanding officers, but in separate sessions with the U.S. Air Force chaplains, I was offered my first opportunity to present the early findings from my research on the great preachers of the

Victorian era—"The Men Who Moved the Masses." The reaction was spontaneous and enthusiastic. Some of the men approached me individually and urged me to commit my findings to writing. That was the very first time I ever began to consider the idea of publishing.

The author's research extended beyond the nine men who were eventually selected. There were other impressive pastors and leaders who left their mark upon society and the church in the 19th century, such as, the Rev. Frederick W. Robertson of Trinity Chapel, Brighton; the Methodist Hugh Price Hughes; General William and Mrs. Catherine Booth of the Salvation Army; Scottish evangelist and writer Henry Drummond; Rev. J. C. Ryle, Bishop of Liverpool, to mention only a few. A study on the influence which the American evangelist, D. L. Moody, had upon the lives of some of the British preachers would make a fascinating study in itself. In the end I narrowed my focus down to the nine men whose lives and preaching are the subject of this book.

In more recent decades the North American church in general has mirrored society's infatuation with fads. We seem to have a thirst for trends. A general perception held by people on foreign shores is that the attention span of the average North American is very short. We lurch from one emphasis to another, from one method to another, from one program to another, from one personality to another, as though the value of each option were mutually exclusive of the value of the others. Most churches have abandoned individual evangelistic campaigns in favour of an emphasis on personal evangelism—as though the two were incompatible with each other. Many pastors retreated from pulpit evangelism when it became popular to emphasize that it was the saints who were to do the work of the ministry. Pastors were to prepare the saints to evangelize and consequently they concentrated upon perfecting the saints' inner life and training them in methods of personal evangelism. Prepare the saints? Good emphasis! Stop preaching evangelistically from the pulpit? Bad decision! The adoption of one does not nullify the validity of the other.

Then the church "progressed" to a downgrading of the prominence of the pulpit ministry to an all-consuming emphasis on worship, and in the process, hymn books gather dust in the pew racks while the saints sing choruses with razor-thin theology, the words of which are projected on screens or walls. In some cases another step "forward" has been taken: preaching has been transformed from proclamation to a form of pre-evangelism—an effort to make Christianity and church attendance more palatable and "user-friendly." This is done to coax outsiders into our warm, inviting nest, and once inside, we then present them with the Gospel. The "offence of the Cross" is thereby made less offensive.

Perhaps we would all agree that there is something positive and valid embodied in each new trend that sweeps over the church. After all, are there any among us who are against worship, who oppose being warm and friendly to outsiders, who think personal evangelism is a bad thing, who believe that choruses have no place in the church's music program? No, of course not! But those among us who decided to downgrade the importance of strong, Biblical preaching, made a strategically bad decision. Hence this book, whereby we add one more voice to the chorus of those who long to see a revival of powerful, New-Testament-style preaching.

With deliberate intention the author has chosen to allow first-hand witnesses to speak for themselves in this book instead of attempting to generalize or characterize their observations. You will read the comments of clergymen, family members, the common man in the street, journalists, and in a few cases, what some of these nine featured preachers had to say about each other. The reader will also gain insight into what these men thought about themselves and their ministries. The language may be 19th century but the value of these accounts is undiminished as we study them in the 21st century.

The author's fond hope is that what the reader absorbs through studying the lives and preaching of these British preachers of the Victorian era will somehow ignite a fiery passion deep within their heart of hearts to return to Bible exposition and Gospel proclamation over the pulpits of our local churches. And if it requires a major renovation of one's preaching style, so be it! To that end I dedicate this humble offering.

Robert T. Henry
Toronto, Ontario, Canada
27 May 2005

PART I
The Historical Context

In order to make a fair assessment of the contribution made by the great preachers of the Victorian era one must gain an intelligent understanding of the times in which these men ministered. How were the living conditions, either enjoyed or endured, by the average man in the pew? What were the defining issues faced by society in their time? What was the moral temperature of the nation? What was the condition of the State church and how did the average man regard its leaders? What was the relationship between church and State and why did the majority of these influential preachers in our study choose to minister outside of the State church as "non-conformists"? Understanding the conditions and history of the times helps to unlock the mystery of the extraordinary impact these preachers had upon the masses.

The contribution to Great Britain and the world made by Winston Churchill cannot be fully appreciated apart from an understanding of the threat of Nazi Germany and the sufferings of Londoners during the blitz. Leaders, secular or ecclesiastical, are not judged by how they handle a flimsy bark on the surface of a placid lake. We evaluate their characters and their performance by observing how they guide a ship upon the turbulent waters of the high seas during a raging storm.

Ben Jonson wrote the following on the 'difficulties of government.'

"Each pretty hand
Can steer a ship becalm'd; but he that will
Govern and carry her to her ends must know
His tides, his currents, how to shift his sails;
What she will bear in foul, what in fair weather;
Where her springs are, her leaks, and how to stop them;
What strands, what shelves, what rocks do threaten her;
The forces, and the natures of all winds,
Gusts, storms, and tempests; when her keel ploughs hell,
And deck knocks heaven, then to manage her
Becomes the name and office of a pilot."

It is incumbent upon us, therefore, to take the time and effort to gain an understanding of the conditions of society and the burning issues of the era in which these men preached. To that end, this first section, *"The Historical Context"* will guide us decade by decade through Queen Victoria's reign to give an abbreviated account of societal and historical developments. We shall thereby gain insight into the "world" of these pulpit giants in order to better qualify us to make a more enlightened assessment of the effectiveness of their preaching and overall ministries.

Chapter One

Queen Victoria's Reign in Tumultuous Times

Long Live the Queen!

It was 12 minutes past 2 on the morning of 20 June 1837 when King William IV drew his last breath. Princess Victoria Maria Louisa of the House of Saxe-Coburg allowed her daughter, Alexandrina, to sleep until 6 a.m.. At that early hour, The Archbishop of Canterbury and Lord Conyngham waited for Princess Victoria Maria Louisa to awaken "Drina", who then slipped into a dressing gown and met the gentlemen in her sitting-room. They informed her that her uncle had died and as a consequence, she was now the Queen. She was only 18 years old.

Victoria's ascension to the throne heralded a new day for the monarchy. Dr. L. E. Elliott-Binns in his book, *Religion in the Victorian Era*, wrote in no uncertain terms as to how the world viewed the British monarchy:

> *"The world had become accustomed to seeing the British crown held by a succession of debauched and disreputable old men, 'a melancholy succession of madness, and vice, and folly' Canon Scott Holland named them."*

Victoria was a breath of fresh air.

In the Providence of God, Victoria was not the only source of refreshing air being breathed into Great Britain. There were giants in the land, or more accurately, in the pulpits. Demanding times required indomitable leaders, not only in Britain's Parliament but also in Britain's churches.

Tumultuous Times

It almost staggers the mind trying to fit together the picture of a tiny, reclusive, long-reigning Queen, on the one hand, with the tumultuous events that took place, nationally and internationally, all throughout her reign. Domestically, Britain was in the midst of a tremendous social and economic transition passing from an agrarian society to an urban industrial age. The Industrial Revolution was in full swing. This revolution had its genesis in Britain due to several factors: Britain was at the cross-roads of world trade; it had an easily negotiated coast and navigable waterways; it had large deposits of coal and iron ore; it did not impose domestic tariffs; and its emerging middle-class, Nonconformist segment of the population, actively promoted thrift and industry. During the 19th century Britain's Gross National Product (GNP) per capita, increased 400% in real terms.

Meanwhile, internationally, Britain was expanding its empire, its trade, and imposing its will upon nation after nation across the globe. Let us confine ourselves to a rudimentary overview of the enormous changes which were taking place during the decades in which Victoria ruled the British Empire, from the 1830's through to 1900.

1830's

Two physicists, Michael Faraday of England and Joseph Henry of the U.S.A. independently discovered how to convert mechanical energy into electricity. They discovered that a moving magnet produced electric current in a wire coil. They found that generators could produce electricity from the turning of a water wheel or from a steam-driven turbine. This phenomenon was called electromagnetic induction.

In the year Queen Victoria ascended to the throne, Britain refused to grant more home rule to Canada which in turn led to the Rebellions of 1837. In that same year British scientist Charles Wheatstone designed an electric telegraph system. The following year, 1838, the Boer (Afrikaners) leader, Andries Pretorius defeated the Zulus at the Battle of Blood River and Scottish blacksmith, Kirkpatrick Macmillan, invented the first pedal-driven bicycle. In 1839 Great Britain and China became engaged in the Opium Wars. It was during the 1830's that steam-driven locomotives and railroads came into use.

1840's

1840: Lord Palmerston, then serving as Foreign Secretary, used force when the Chinese Government tried to stop the import of opium from India. A ban on opium would have dealt a harsh blow to the East India Company. In that same year, Maori chiefs in New Zealand signed over their tribal lands to Queen Victoria in the Treaty of Waitangi, and the Queen married Prince Albert. The following year New Zealand was established as a separate British colony. In 1842 China ceded Hong Kong to Britain and was defeated in the first Opium War. China's ports were opened up for British trade.

1844: settlers in New South Wales, Australia, forced Britain to stop its practice of sending convicts to the colony. In that year the Y.M.C.A. was founded in England and Lord Shaftesbury established his Ragged School Union to help children of the poor. In Ireland, the potato blight of 1845, 1846 and 1848 destroyed the basis of Ireland's economy and population growth. Between 1845 and 1850 upwards of one million people died and two million emigrated between 1845 and 1855. In 1845 the Sikh Wars began in British India and in 1848, Karl Marx and Friedrich Engels published the Communist Manifesto.

1850's

The Great Exposition of 1851, encouraged by Prince Albert, proved to be a monumental event in the history of Great Britain. The Crystal Palace was built in Hyde Park in only six months time. The Exposition thrust Britain on to centre-stage in the eyes of the world, as a nation committed to liberalism and economic progress. The attendance totaled six million. That same year a census revealed that more people resided in towns than in rural areas and that the population was increasingly non-Anglican. In 1854 Britain and France declared war on Russia which set into motion The Crimean War, a war which Unstead declared to be *"one of the most useless, ill-managed conflicts that ever wasted the lives of soldiers."* The war brought into conflict Russia, who was making moves toward Turkey, and Britain and France who were determined to protect Turkey from Russian aggression. In that year of 1854 the Allied troops defeated the Russians in the Battle of Inkerman and Britain granted independence to the Orange Free State in South Africa, and the ill-fated Charge of the Light Brigade took place in the Battle of Balaklava.

In the mid-50's the only positive thing to come out of the Crimean War was the work and example of Florence Nightingale (1820-1910), the *"lady with the lamp"* who assembled a company of volunteer nurses to take care of the sick and wounded. When she eventually returned home in ill-health, though constantly confined to her bedroom, for 43 years she led a revolution in health care establishing hospitals and putting a new foundation underneath the nursing profession. 1855: Lord Palmerston became Prime Minister for the first time and David Livingstone discovered Victoria Falls in Africa. 1856: A new Opium War began between China, Britain and France and the Crimean War came to an end with the signing of the Treaty of Paris. In that same year, Sir Henry Bessemer developed a process for converting pig-iron into steel. The Indian Mutiny erupted in 1857 when Indian troops rebelled against the British at Meerut and was put down the following year by the British Army and loyal Indian troops. In that year of 1858 the Government of India was transferred to the British Crown from the East India Company, and Britain and France imposed the Tientsin Treaty upon China. Years later, in a message preached on 19 January 1906, G. Campbell Morgan thundered his disapproval of his own government's *"unspeakable crime against China."* Also, in 1858, Cyrus W. Field laid the first trans-Atlantic telegraph cable, and the Fenians (Irish Republic Brotherhood) was founded with the express purpose of over-throwing British Rule. In 1859 Charles Darwin published *On The Origin of Species by Means of Natural Selection.*

1860's

Jean Joseph Etienne Lenoir, a French inventor, built one of the first workable internal-combustion engines in 1860. In this same year the Chinese resisted the Tientsin Treaty whereupon Peking was occupied by Anglo-French forces. In New Zealand, Maori Wars broke out against the British. In the United States, the American Civil War got underway in 1861 and lasted for four devastating years. Through the wise action of Prince Albert in that same year, war between Britain and the U.S. was averted, in what was to become the Prince's final official act before his death. He had carefully recrafted and softened the language of a note from the Foreign Office before sending it off to the Americans. Only two weeks later he died of typhoid fever at Windsor Castle on December 14th, 1861. In 1864 a Chinese army commanded by

Gordon recaptured Nanking and ended the Taiping Rebellion. 1867: The Dominion of Canada was established by the British North American Act. 1868: The British labour unions formed the Trade Union Congress and liberal William Gladstone became Prime Minister for the first time. 1869:The Suez Canal was opened in Egypt. The 1860's also saw the ascendency of Scientific Anthropology.

1870's

The Modoc Wars began in India in 1872. The following year, back in England, lawn tennis was invented by Major Walter Clopton Wingfield. In 1874 Benjamin Disraeli became the Conservative Prime Minister. Queen Victoria assumed the title of Empress of India in 1876 and in 1877 Britain annexed Transvaal in South Africa. In 1878 the second Anglo-Afghan War began.

1880's

Gladstone again became Prime Minister in 1880, replacing Disraeli. That year the Boer uprising began against the British in Transvaal, South Africa. 1882: The British took control of Egypt by suppressing uprisings against Tawfiq Pasha. 1883: The Fabian Society was founded in London with the mission to spread the teachings of socialism. The first successful steam turbine was designed by the English engineer, Charles A. Parsons, in 1884. General Gordon was killed in 1885 by Mahdist forces at the siege of Khartoum in the Sudan, and a German engineer by the name of Karl Benze, built one of the first gasoline-powered automobiles. The following year Britain made Burma a province of India after winning the Anglo-Burmese War, Gladstone introduced an unsuccessful Home Rule Bill for Ireland, and Arthur Conan Doyle published his first Sherlock Holmes story. In 1888 Britain united its colonies of Trinidad and Tobago. In the late 1880's, Heinrich Hertz, a German physicist, detected invisible radio waves which eventually led to the development of radio, TV and radar.

1890's

As Britain crossed over into the 90's, the British South Africa Company occupied Zimbabwe in 1890 and Zanzibar became a British Protectorate in the same year. In 1893 Gladstone's second Irish Home Rule Bill was vetoed by the House of Lords. Britain established a protectorate over Buganda in 1894 and conquered the rest of Uganda. Mrs. Fawcett's National Union of Women's Suffrage Societies was established in 1897. In 1898 Britain signed a 99-year lease for Hong Kong with the Chinese, the Boxer Rebellion broke out in China, and Kitchener defeated the Mahdists in Omdurman, Sudan. 1899: Young Winston Churchill escaped from Boer captivity; the British, under Robert Baden-Powell, was besieged by Boers at Mafeking; and the South African War began, pitting the Afrikaners against the British.

1900's

As Britain drew to the sunset of Queen Victoria's reign, in 1900, British politician Keir Hardie helped to establish the Labour Party; an international force lifted the Boxer siege of Peking; and the British forces defeated the Boers and occupied Pretoria. On January 22nd, 1901, Queen Victoria died at Osborne.

The breathtaking scope of the British Empire and its blatant imperialism leaves one somewhat astounded. By the time history crossed over into the 20th century, the British Crown ruled over 1/4 of the world's surface and 1/5 of the world's population according to the reckoning of R. J. Unstead. in his book, *England: Book 4, A Century of Change.*

Chapter Two

The Condition of the State Church and the Queen's Influence

The Influence of Queen Victoria upon Church Life in Great Britain

Queen Victoria always regarded herself as the recognized head of the Church of England and by all accounts, this was a responsibility which she took quite seriously. Sometimes she exceeded her authority in the matter of church leadership appointments and she stood as a protective barrier against any possible move to bring the Church of England back under the authority of the Papacy or back into the beliefs and practices of the Roman Catholic Church. She was zealous for the doctrinal purity of the church and supported new laws which would safeguard that purity. She was opposed to what she regarded as extremes on either end of the spectrum. She was wary of Evangelicals on the one hand, and Tractarians, High Churchmen, on the other. She favoured moderate courses of action and moderate people to carry them out. Churchmen who paid too much attention to the poorer classes were held in suspicion in her way of thinking and she had a particular dislike of Salvation Army uniforms and ranks! Believing that highly educated men would lean in the direction of moderation and tolerance, she gave the nod to them when choosing Church leaders as opposed to persons whom she would regard as strong-minded evangelicals. Even though Henry Parry Liddon, Canon of St. Paul's Cathedral, was very well educated, she felt that his strong convictions would make him a disaster as a bishop. The Queen was so adamantly opposed to politically motivated appointments to bishoprics that in the end such appointments came to be regarded as disreputable.

Church historians may look back and judge Queen Victoria in a positive light as being a monarch who safeguarded the Church of England in all sincerity. Others, particularly evangelicals, will question whether her efforts to protect the church did not in fact limit the spiritual impact of the church in a society which desperately needed the Gospel in the midst of fast changing times which were accompanied by deteriorating living conditions for the less fortunate masses.

The Church and Religious Sentiment

The 19th century saw the growing influence of liberal thought, with Non-conformists leading the way. There was a commensurate call for social action to help the poor who lived in appalling conditions. The Church of England was perceived to be against liberal thought and progress in society, regarding urbanization and modernization as threats to the welfare of the Church. The Oxford Movement cried out for reform within the Church of England. This movement was ignited by John Keble's famous Assize Sermon of 14 July 1833, a message which was, in effect, a protest against national apostasy. Keble was joined by such notables as John Henry Newman, and Richard Hurrell Froude who shared his outrage over the lamentable moral condition of the Church. They promoted a rediscovery of the significance of the "Holy Catholic Church", the belief in apostolic succession, and the separation of Church and State. They held that the powers with which God had endowed the Church were sufficient to meet her needs and that all extra-ecclesiastical interference, such as the interference of the State, was both unnecessary and presumptuous. The Oxford Movement's use of tracts—hence the title ascribed to those involved, "Tractarians"—was most probably copied from the methods of Bishop Hobart of New York who established a tract society in 1815. He once dined with John Henry Newman at Oxford in the month of March, 1924, and over dinner they discussed Hobart's use of tracts to disseminate knowledge.

The 1851 census conducted in Britain revealed the growing numbers of dissenting non-conformists. The following numbers reflect church attendance: 5.2 million Anglicans; 4.5 million Protestant dissenters; .3 million Roman Catholics; and 4.25 million who stayed at home.

Meanwhile, other changes were taking place at Oxford University which gave defenders of the faith serious concern. In the 1850's, after Max Muller was established at Oxford, there was a rising interest in the study of comparative religions. Monier Williams took the Sanskrit Chair in Oxford in 1860. In the decade of the 60's monumental challenges to faith took centre-stage in the halls of higher learning and throughout society. 1859 saw the publication of Darwin's *Origin of the Species*, which in turn led to the much publicized debate on Evolution vs. Creation between Huxley and Wilberforce in 1860. *Essays and Reviews* was published that same year in an attempt to reconcile Christianity with modern thinking and theory by debunking traditional creationism, inspiration of the Scriptures, and miracles. Between 1861 and 1865 lawsuits over the Bible were adjudicated in the courts and in 1865 *Ecce Homo* was published in an attempt to provide a fresh account of the life of Jesus Christ. Also, in 1865, William Booth established the *CHRISTIAN MISSION* in East London renaming the movement *THE SALVATION ARMY* in 1878. Booth's Methodist origins accounted for the organization's evangelical and Arminian theology.

In 1865 the Church of England created "lay readers" and in 1866 Henry Parry Liddon gave his powerful Bampton Lectures at St. Mary's in Oxford, on the subject, *The Divinity of Our Lord and Saviour Jesus Christ*. 1870 was the year which witnessed the admission of nonconformists into Oxford University for the very first time and throughout the 70's women's colleges were established in London, Oxford and Cambridge. It was also in this decade that the Sunday School movement began to go into decline. In 1871 Parliament voted to disestablish the Church of Ireland, and the book, *The Descent of Man*, was published, while in Africa Stanley was having his renowned meeting with Livingstone. As part of a temperance campaign, the use of unfermented wine was introduced in communion services beginning in 1873. Dwight L. Moody and Ira D. Sankey crossed the Atlantic in 1874 and 1875 to conduct evangelistic meetings which not only garnered unexpectedly large numbers of converts but had a profound impact upon the lives and ministries of a goodly number of the preachers who are the subjects of our consideration in this book. In 1875 the Keswick conferences promoting the deeper Christian life got underway with the establishment of annual conventions. The momentum of Nonconformist church growth was such that between 1875 and 1885 their growth kept pace with the rate of growth of the nation's population overall.

The decade of the 1880's found the Church in the throes of self-doubt within the context of a society which was enamoured with free thought. Urbanization was diminishing country parishes and creating a widening rift between country labourers and their parsons. Westcott's and Hort's Revised Text of the Greek New Testament was published in 1881, and Edersheim's *The Life and Times of Jesus The Messiah* came off the press in 1883. In 1882, Charles Darwin died, as did Pusey, who was one of the most respected and scholarly Tractarians.

Lux Mundi was published in 1889, challenging the infallibility of the teachings of Jesus Christ and promoting a very low view of the inspiration of the Scriptures.

By the time the 1890's rolled around, over the objections of such notable church spokesmen as Spurgeon, Liddon and Parker, the church at large began to accept Biblical criticism. The battle over Old Testament criticism reached its zenith during the years 1889 to 1892. In 1890 General Booth published his book, *In Darkest England and the Way Out*, in which he tried to lay out a practical plan to alleviate the plight of the impoverished masses. He died in 1912. In 1896, Frederick Temple, an evolutionist, became the Archbishop of Canterbury.

By 1902 and 1903, only 19% of the population of London attended church. The well-meaning efforts of Queen Victoria to safeguard the church and to ensure its robust health, were less than successful.

The Condition of the State Church and its Clergy

In the early part of the 19th century the condition of the State Church and its clergy had sunk to a very low ebb. Elliott-Binns judged that the clergy was *"...too much at home in the world, too much at ease in Zion."* One of the main bones of contention among the populace was the wealth of the Bishops and the abuses which produced that wealth. Lord Bryce in a letter to Thomas Hughes described how the Bishops were regarded:

> *"Forty or fifty years ago they were usually rich, dignified, and rather indolent magnates, aristocratic in their tastes and habits, moderate in their theology, sometimes to the verge of indifferentism,*

*quite as much men of the world as pastors of souls. Now and then
eminence in learning or literature raised a man to the bench; there
were the 'Greek play' bishops, such as Monk of Gloucester, and The
Quarterly Review bishops like Copleston of Llandaff...They were
respected as part of the solid fabric of English society, more than for
personal merits. But they were often a mark for political invective or
literary sneers."*

John Carlile, in his biography of Alexander McLaren quoted Professor
Wakeman describing the English clergy in the days leading up to
Queen Victoria's reign:

*"A few of them hunted, shot, fished, and drank or gambled during
the week like their friends in the army or at the bar, and mumbled
through a perfunctory service in church on Sunday. Some of them,
where there was no residence in the parish, lived an idle and often
vicious life at a neighbouring town, and only visited their parishes
when they rode over on Sundays to conduct the necessary services."*

Thomas Arnold wrote in 1833: *"The Church as it now stands, no human
power can save."* The abuse of office which most outraged the public
was the Bishops' strategy to accumulate wealth by assuming various
appointments to which annual income was attached, whether they
tended to those responsibilities or not. In many positions they were
altogether absent and yet they continued to collect the stipends. These
abuses were referred to as pluralism and absenteeism.

A *Sunday Times* article published on 11 September 1831 contended
that *"16 bishops held 61 preferments including their Sees, viz.: 16 bishoprics,
6 deaneries, 1 chancellorship, 3 archdeaconries, 2 cathedral treasureships, 8
cathedral prebends, 21 rectories, and 4 vicarages."*

In 1811, according to a report furnished to the House of Commons,
out of 10,261 parishes for which the report was made, only 4,421 had
resident incumbents.

Cathedrals were a scandal. Bentham called Cathedral Chapters
"nests of acknowledged idlers." At Canterbury the dean and six canons
divided an income of 8,000 pounds, and in addition, members of the
chapter held seven benefices worth a total of 9,200 pounds. It was said
that these chapter members made what they could, and that was a

good deal, and did as little as possible in return, which was almost nothing at all!

On 16 May 1848, Edward Horsman told the House of Commons—

> *"I could show you cathedral libraries containing rare and magnificent books, which anywhere else it would be a privilege to look into, but of which the last catalogue had been made in the last century. There are instances of persons waiting to visit these storehouses of knowledge, when no one of the Chapter knew who has the key, and when the lock was so rusty, that when found, the key would not turn and the door could not be opened; and in one case, the party who had charge of the library complained of the great annoyance that would be caused by clergymen coming to consult books."*

It was not difficult for the common man to conclude that the cathedral had little to do with religion. Frederick Temple, who later became Archbishop, attended St. Paul's one Sunday morning while still a young man, with the intention of remaining for the service of Communion.

When the earlier part of the service had concluded the verger came up and said, *"I hope you are not intending to remain for the Sacrament, as that will give the Minor Canon the trouble of celebrating, which otherwise he will not do."*

Having mentioned the problem of keys to cathedral libraries above, keys also became a problem at the local church level—keys to pews! In 1828, John Bird Sumner became the Bishop of Chester. On one occasion he found many of the congregation standing in the aisles next to empty pews whose doors were locked. He stopped the service and asked why these pews were not occupied while on the other hand a good number of people were standing. The answer came back, "The pews are private property and the owners have shut them up." He replied, "There can be no such thing in the House of God. Send for a blacksmith to take off the locks. We will sing a hymn while he does it." Unfortunately for the church, not all Bishops were of this sort.

L. E. Elliott-Binns wrote, *"The Church had lost its own heat and light, and possessed only 'such mimic flame as neither lights nor harms.'"*

A minor canon once said to Robert Gregory, referring to the Church: *"...this is an Augean stable that nobody on earth can sweep, therefore let things take their course, and do not trouble about them."* (From *The Autobiography of Robert Gregory*)

Confirmation was administered to large numbers of candidates at a time, who for the most part were quite unprepared. Sparke, then Bishop of Chester, informed Blomfield during the period 1810 to 1812, that at his last Visitation he had confirmed 8,000 children at Manchester in one day!

Men were ordained to the ministry without proper preparation with the exception of those who came under the influence of Charles Simeon at Cambridge. When Blomfield went to Chester he discovered that intoxication was common among the clergy.

> *"One was so drunk while waiting for the funeral that he fell into the grave; another was conveyed away from a visitation dinner in a helpless state by the bishop's own servants. A third, when rebuked for drunkenness, replied, 'But, my lord, I was never drunk on duty.'"*

Judging by numerous accounts written by credible witnesses in those days, the primary aim of the better class of clergy was respectability and decency, rather than holiness of life. The result was the adoption of a standard of life and service which could be characterized by two words—decent mediocrity.

The people began to despise the clergy and their main targets of criticism were the bishops because of their ill-gained wealth. The Bishop of Durham said in 1831 that the Church of England had never had such a large number of avowed enemies. A mob burned down the palace of the Bishop of Bristol. The Bishop of London cancelled an engagement for fear of violence. The Archbishop of Canterbury was mobbed in his cathedral city. Another mob scaled the wall of the Bishop of Bath and Wells' property in the night, and broke every pane of glass in his greenhouse, and killed one of his deer. The Bishop of Peterborough asserted, *"There never was a time when the clergy were assailed with so much calumny and so much violence as they are at present."*

Even as late as 1868, when Robert Gregory came as Canon to St. Paul's Cathedral, he reported:

> *"The choir men read letters and talked during the service, and it was never known for more than one member of the Chapter to be present at a service, except on very special occasions; the Minor Canons attended more regularly, because there was a fund divided amongst them according to the number of their attendances...I have several*

times gone to the Cathedral on Sunday mornings when there was not a single person present..."
(*The Oxford Movement and After* by The Rev. C. P. S. Clarke, M.A.)

Chapter Three

The Social Classes and the Labouring Poor

The Upper Classes

At the dawning of the 19h century, life was quieter, gentler, more local-ized in towns and villages, and urbanization had not yet set in. At one end of the social spectrum, nobility and the wealthier classes lived in substantial, and in some cases, palatial homes, surrounded by spacious grounds. The privileged classes included titled gentry, aristocratic landowners, large-scale businessmen, and country squires living in their ancestral properties. The prosperous tenant-farmer was regarded as "master" in his village.

On 28 October 1855, Catherine Booth wrote,

> *"This afternoon we walked through the park right up to the Duke of Devonshire's residence. It is one of the most splendid spots I was ever in. It is all hill and dale, beautifully wooded, and bestudded with deer in all directions. The residence itself is superior to many of the royal palaces, and the scenery around is most picturesque and sublime."*

Beatrice Webb, a socialist writer, referred to the aristocracy as *"a curiously tough substance"* which changed the least of all the classes in British life during the Victorian era. From this class came the officers in the military, members of Parliament in both parties, the upper posts in the Empire, and the people of power in local governments. Their homes and properties were serviced by a full range of workers who cleaned, cooked, did the laundry, raised the children, cared for the gardens and lawns, and cared for the horses and carriages. They enjoyed much leisure activity such as fishing, hunting, racing, shooting, and gambling. Not unlike today, it was always important for the wealthy

19

and the powerful to enter their children into the most prestigious schools, from their earliest years on through to university.

The latter part of the 19th century witnessed the emergence of a middle class. Real wages doubled between 1860 and 1914, the birth rate decreased, some labourers began to enjoy leisure time, and people entered into marriage somewhat later. Industrial progress was interrupted in every decade by setbacks, particularly in the 1880's, and the consequences were borne primarily by the labourers rather than the factory owners. This is when the term "unemployment" was given its modern meaning. Sons of manufacturers often opted to go into the field of commerce and these "handlers of money" constituted a good segment of the new middle class.

The Darker Side of Britain: The Destitute and the Labouring Poor

General William Booth, founder of the Salvation Army, published his famous book, *In Darkest England and the Way Out, in 1890*. He drew an analogy between the description given of the darkest jungles of Africa confronted by Livingstone and Stanley in their renowned exploits, and the dark and wretched conditions that were at the very doorstep of Britain among the poor and the slum dwellers. In the Providence of God, men and women of extraordinary courage, tenacity and energy were raised up to tackle the ills in society which the House of Lords would have preferred to ignore—judging by the way they fought all remedial undertakings which were brought before it, inch by inch! Leading lights who did battle for social change and improvement included such notables as William and Catherine Booth, Antony Ashley Cooper—better known as Lord Shaftesbury—and Dr. Thomas John Barnardo.

The prevailing opinion of the aristocracy was that the lot of the working poor was quite irreparable and were one to attempt to improve their condition, such efforts would endanger capitalism. Once capital was driven away then manufacturing would be thrown into chaos and the workers would be even worse off than before! The industrial world was viewed as a very delicate mechanism and to interfere with it would bring it into peril. It was almost a given, that every proposed Act of Parliament to relieve the plight of the working classes or the destitute, would be vigourously opposed, clause by clause, amendment by amendment, in the House of Lords. In the end, even if those Acts were passed, they were often either watered down considerably to the point where there was only a very marginal improvement of conditions for the poor, or, their stipulations and requirements were ignored throughout society.

Frederick De L. Booth-Tucker in his biography of *Catherine Booth* wrote that—

> *"The lowest classes are absorbed in the scramble for the crumbs which fall from the rich man's table. One Lazarus is bad and sad enough; but here are hundreds of thousands lying at Dive's door, whose destitution is even more miserable than that of their Eastern counterpart…And then there are the labouring classes, who live upon the borders of this human pandemonium, this earthly purgatory, this out-Hadesed Hades, and who are perpetually supplying the fuel for its flames. The conditions of society have made their burdens so grievous, their hours of toil so long, their means of subsistence so scanty, that they have but little time and opportunity to provide for the interests of their soul, so absorbed are they in caring for their bodies."*

Prior to the autumn of 1880 the Salvation Army had opened successful operations amongst the poor in Carlisle with many of the worst characters in the city being converted. At this same time the Bishop preached a sermon in the Cathedral strongly condemning the Salvation Army! In a reply to his criticism, Mrs. Booth gave an address in an old but crowded theatre in town. In this address she said:

> *"I have been in sixty-two towns in eleven months. In these towns I have seen hundreds of thousands gathered together in halls. Ah, there is nothing like seeing to realize. All the accounts I have ever heard or read had failed to convey to my mind anything like a true conception of the state of positive heathenism and ruffianism in which these masses live. Hundreds of these very men I should be afraid to meet at night—short-cropped, bullet-headed, gaol-bird looking men, of the bull-dog type—the terrible traces of debauchery and crime deep marked upon their faces, and dressed in such habiliments as showed where their money went on a Saturday night. Hundreds of these men are earning fairly respectable wages, and their wretched condition arises from their vicious habits."*

Mrs. Booth lamented the fact that there were those who professed to care for the poor in Jesus' name but who turned their efforts to oppose the work of the Salvation army. It is a remarkable record indeed to read of the persecution and imprisonment which officers of the Army endured in the course of their work among the down-and-outers.

"One of the first to be imprisoned was the General's son, Mr. Ballington Booth," wrote Booth-Tucker. "He had been sent to Manchester, and placed in charge of a large hall, capable of holding some 1,200 people. As usual, it was crowded, and many of the worst characters were saved. Writing with reference to his prosecution and imprisonment, he says:

> '*Since my last report I have spent 24 hours in Belle Vue jail, for upholding my Master's name to the perishing multitudes in the streets of Manchester. I was placed with the common felons, lived on a few ounces of bread and a little skilly, scrubbed my cell, and slept on a plank. But in all my life I never felt more blessed and encouraged than whilst there! The prison a "palace proved," and while Jesus dwelt with me I could feel, and sing, and realize—*
> *"Anywhere with Jesus,*
> *I'll follow anywhere."'*

Sanitary Conditions and Cholera

In 1838 the Poor Law Commissioners presented a report on the great burden being borne by the poor due to sickness and epidemics, due primarily to poor sanitation. They deemed it wiser to attack the matter of sanitation by providing positive improvements rather than continuously relieving poverty. Edwin Chadwick drafted a powerful document in 1842, describing the slums, overcrowding, the neglect of arrangements for running water or drains, the revolting conditions of burial, that were the cause of degradation and disease in English towns. Earlier, Dr. Southwood Smith, the pioneer of sanitary reform, had given evidence to a select committee of the House of Commons, and said:

> "*All this suffering might be averted. These poor people are victims that are sacrificed. The effect is the same as if twenty or thirty thousand of them were annually taken out of their homes and put to death. The only difference being that they are left in them to die.*"

Dr. Smith enlisted the support of Charles Dickens, Lord Shaftesbury and Lord Normanby. In a supporting speech Lord Normanby gave statistics of the death rate in Glasgow:

In 1811 the death rate was 1 in 39

In 1831 the death rate was 1 in 30

In 1835 the death rate was 1 in 29

In 1840 the death rate was 1 in 25

On September 1841, Lord Normanby wrote:

> *"What a preambulation have I taken today in company with Dr. Southwood Smith! What scenes of filth, discomfort, and disease!...No pen, nor paint-brush could describe the thing as it is. One whiff of Cowyard, Blue Anchor or Bakers Court, outweighs ten pages of letterpress. And yet the remedial Bills for ventilation, drainage, and future construction of the houses of the poor, brought in carefully and anxiously by the late Government, are not to be adopted by this: so I was informed this evening, and I bless God that I formed no part of it."*

Unstead reported that—

> *"sewers emptied into the nearest river, so that by 1858 the stench from the Thames was so bad that the windows of Parliament had to be closed during debates and there was talk of Parliament leaving Westminster. Yet private companies still sold piped water from the river! In the '40's when good-class housing was put up to the north of Hyde Park, the drains naturally were made to flow into the Serpentine, which stank to Heaven."*

Describing life in England at the early part of Queen Victoria's reign, the German socialist, Engels, wrote:

> *"A horde of ragged women and children swarm about, as filthy as the swine that thrive on the garbage heap and in the puddles...The race that lives in these ruinous cottages behind broken windows mended with oilskin...or in dark wet cellars in measureless stench and filth...must really have reached the lowest stage of humanity."*

He found these conditions in Manchester where 350,000 workers lived *"in wretched, damp, filthy cottages."* In Bristol, out of 3,000 houses, 1,300 had no water supply. In Leeds there were only 68 streets out of 568 that were paved, and 500 cellars were used as homes. Leeds could boast of 451 public houses but only 2 churches and 39 chapels. In Liverpool, one family in five lived in a cellar; in Manchester, one in ten, and only from 35 to 40 babies out of every hundred lived to reach the age of five. At Bradford, the average age at which a worker would die was 20 as compared to the rural county of Rutlandshire where it was 38 years. The gentry could expect to live until 52, on average.

In London some of the worst slums were located in close proximity to the homes of the rich. In one West end court 2,850 people lived in 95 houses. Slum areas of this sort enjoyed no indoor water source nor plumbing. One single tap within the court area was turned on for one hour a day. Common latrines or privies stood between the houses. With few paved roads in London the streets were often ankle deep in mud and manure. There was no regular system of garbage collection, water-supply, or sewerage. The cholera epidemic of 1831-33 led to the establishment of a Board of Health but still progress was slow. It is curious to note that in Nottingham, a Cholera Burial Ground was set aside where the poorest of the city were buried. Finally in 1870 The Metropolitan Board of Works provided six million pounds to put into place an effective sewage system. In a printed leaflet distributed by one of the Commissions examining the sanitation situation of London the following statement was made:

> *"Rome provided about twenty times as much water for her citizens as modern London."*

Norman Wymer's biography of Dr. Barnardo, *Father of Nobody's Children*, described the slum dwellers:

> *"Many were obliged to sleep on the hard floor in their ragged and smelly everyday clothes, companioned by rats, mice and myriad inhabitants of the insect world. Few had water or any form of lighting, and while some had a backyard 'privy', most had to rely for their sanitation upon pails and buckets, which, as often as not, they emptied unhesitatingly out of the windows...Since the law knew*

little leniency and many of the landlords no mercy, those unable to pay their rent were sent to prison without more ado—only to find, upon regaining their freedom, that their few modest possessions had been seized and sold in order to pay their arrears, and that they were homeless."

Those who found themselves no longer with a roof over their heads were faced with the choice of three alternatives: (1) seeking admittance to a workhouse; (2) sleeping in the streets at the risk of being arrested under the Vagrancy Acts and returned to prison; or (3) obtaining shelter in a common lodging house. The latter seemed to be the most popular choice even though these houses were generally run by prostitutes or the criminal element which used the houses as centres for fencing stolen property. Persons of all ages and both sexes would retire to dormitory-like rooms to spend the nights being overrun with vermin and surrounded by the filth of years.

At one stage, Dr. Barnardo was determined to gain personal experience of what the destitute boys of London endured in these common lodging houses. He grew a beard and dressed up as a vagabond. He and a colleague reached one of these houses just after midnight. A sign on the door read, "Beds for Single men 4d." Nearly all the occupants were boys ages ten to seventeen. The smell of the sleeping room was abominable and crowded with 34 boys who tucked their clothes underneath their heads at night to prevent them being stolen. The sheets were yellow and covered with the evidence of these waifs having done battle with insects in the past. Barnardo finally managed to go to sleep but awoke within an hour out of a dreadful dream that he had been exposed as a spy and for punishment was enduring pins being pricked into all parts of his body including his face. When fully awake he realized that he was being devoured by a swarming army of insects which not only covered his body and sheet but also the walls. It took a full week for his swollen face to return to the point where people could recognize him once again.

In its short life of 6 years, the Board of Health reported that in the cholera epidemics of 1849 and 1853, 58,000 people had lost their lives, and argued that if it had not been for their efforts, the death toll would have reached that of the continent, being, 600,000.

The onset of winter was ever a portent of suffering for the homeless, but the coming of summer gave little relief from misery. General Booth wrote that the return of summer was dreaded by the homeless because it meant the unloosing of myriads of vermin which rendered the nights unbearable!

Chapter Four

Working Conditions and Child Labour

Factory Workers

A reliable barometer in any society whereby its health and progress may be gauged is the condition of its children. The report of the Sadler Select Committee tabled in 1831-32 was a stunning expose of working conditions in factories, especially describing the plight of children. In all the manufacturing centres such as Manchester, Glasgow, Huddersfield, Dundee, Bradford, Leeds and London, young people working in the factories were old by the time they reached twenty years of age. The report included an account given by Joseph Hebergam, a worsted spinner of Huddersfield, then aged 17, describing his day's work at the age of seven.

> *"His hours were from five in the morning to eight at night, with one solitary break of thirty minutes at noon. All other meals had to be taken in snatches, without any interruption of work."*

When asked if he did not become drowsy and feel fatigued by the end of the day, his reply to the Committee was,

> *"Yes, that began at about three o'clock; and grew worse and worse, and it came to be very bad towards six and seven." "What means were taken to keep you at your work so long?" "There were three overlookers; there was one a head overlooker, and there was one man kept to grease the machines, and there was one kept on purpose to strap."*

Joseph's brother, who worked in the same mill, died at sixteen of spinal "affection" due to his work, and he himself began to grow deformed after six months of it. Joseph lived one mile from the mill and he found it very difficult to walk. His brother and sister therefore supported him under each arm to run him to the mill while his legs dragged on the ground! In due course the pain was such that he could not walk at all.

Another witness, an overseer in a flax spinning mill at Dundee, reported that there were nine workers in the room where he was in charge, all of whom had begun work before they were nine. Six of them were "splay-footed" and the other three were deformed in other ways. Samuel Coulson, a tailor in Stanningley, who had three daughters, described the life of the household when the mill was busy.

> *"In the ordinary time the hours were from six in the morning to half-past eight at night; in the brisk time, for six weeks in the year, these girls, the youngest of them 'going eight' worked from three in the morning to ten or half-past ten at night."*

The question was asked, "What was the length of time they could be in bed during those long hours?" Reply:

> *"It was near eleven o'clock before we could get them into bed after getting a little victuals, and then at morning my mistress used to stop up all night, for fear that we would not get them ready for the time; sometimes we have gone to bed and one of us awoke."*
>
> Question: *"Were the children excessively fatigued by this labour?"*
>
> Answer: *"Many times; we have cried often when we have given them the little victualing we had to give them; we had to shake them, and they have fallen to sleep with the victuals in their mouths many a time."*

In Bradford, John Hall, an overlooker in a mill, described the type of work children did in the mill which commonly resulted in deformities. Part of his testimony to the Select Committee included the following statement:

> *"I have the names and addresses, I think, of two hundred families that I have visited myself, that have all deformed children, and I have taken particular care not to put one single individual down to*

whom it had happened by accident, but all whom I judge to have been thrown crooked by the practice of piecening, and of throwing up the left shoulder and bending the right knee." (He was describing how the children had to throw the fly at the top of the spindle in such a way that it eventually resulted in a deformity in one shoulder and the opposite knee.)

A prevailing philosophy in those days was that *"human happiness was best secured by giving capital absolute control over the lives and liberties of men and women."* (J. L. Hammond and Barbara Hammond, in their biography, *Lord Shaftesbury)*

Children in the Mines

Children who worked in the mines of Britain had little to look forward to in life: their function was to eat, drink, sleep, labour long hours, and die prematurely. In May of 1842 a Commission brought a report before Parliament which took Britain by storm. The Hammonds, biographers of Lord Shaftesbury wrote:

> *"In every district except North Staffordshire, where the younger children were needed in the Potteries, the employment of children of seven was common, in many pits children were employed at six, in some at five, and in one case a child of three was found to be employed. Even babies were sometimes taken down into the pits to keep the rats from their father's food. The youngest children were employed as trappers; that is, they were in charge of the doors in the galleries, on the opening and closing of which the safety of the mine depended. For the ventilation of the mine was contrived on a simple principle; there were two shafts, one the downcast, the other the upcast. A fire was lighted at the foot of the upcast to drive the air up the shaft, and air was sucked down through the downcast to fill the vacuum. This air was conducted by means of a series of doors through all the workings of the mine on its passage to the upcast, and these doors were in the charge of a little boy or girl, who sat in a small hole, with a string in his or her hand, in darkness and solitude for twelve hours or longer at a time."*

The Commission reported,

"Although this employment scarcely deserves the name of labour, yet as the children engaged in it are commonly excluded from light, and are always without companions, it would, were it not for the passing and repassing of the coal carriages, amount to solitary confinement of the worst order."

The Hammonds continued their description:

"Children were also employed to push the small carriages filled with coals along the passages, and as the passages were often very low and narrow, it was necessary to use very small children for this purpose." Quoting the report, *"In many mines which are at present worked, the main gates are only from 24 to 30 inches high, and in some parts of these mines the passages do not exceed 18 inches in height. In this case not only is the employment of very young children absolutely indispensable to the working of the mine, but even the youngest children must necessarily work in a bent position of the body."* As a rule the carriages were pushed along small iron railways, but sometimes they were drawn by children and women, 'harnessed like dogs in a go-cart,' and moving, like dogs, on all fours. Another children's task was that of pumping water in the under-bottom of pits, a task that kept children standing ankle-deep in water for 12 hours...Accidents were, of course, frequent,—on one occasion three lives were lost because a child engineman of nine turned away to look at a mouse at a critical moment."*

The children who were brought from workhouses to work in the mines were made to work in certain conditions in which the miners themselves would not allow their own children to labour. If these unhappy boys refused to work in these assignments they were brought before magistrates and sent to prison! In some cases children were known to work double shifts, labouring in total darkness for up to 36 hours.

Some men actually wept when they heard the report of the Commission in the House of Commons, but by the time legislation to correct or modify these working conditions came before the House of

Lords emotions had subsided and the Lords were set to obstruct change.

Agricultural Workers

In rural areas farmhands lived in small cottages on the properties of the wealthy landowners. Lord Shaftesbury reported that the cottages were *"filthy, close, indecent, unwholesome."* He wrote that the workers were *"stuffed like figs in a drum."*

In 1851 Lord Shaftesbury visited some cottages on the estates of other landowners, and reported:

> *"Visited some cottages—thank God, not mine! What griping, grasping, avaricious cruelty. These petty proprietors exact a five-fold rent for a thing in five-fold inferior condition! It is always so with these small holders. Everything—even the misery of their fellows—must be turned to profit."*

In 1865 Shaftesbury proposed legislation designed to break up the system of gang labour in the agricultural industry. Gang masters would assemble workers from a wide radius and supply them in gangs to farmers. These gangs were predominately made up of children. In one parish eight such gangs were at work, each gang containing about forty children *"five of them mixed gangs, two of them composed only of boys, and one only of girls."* Two years later the Commission reported to Parliament and included an account of Hannah and Sarah Adams, aged eleven and thirteen, who worked for six weeks at Peterborough.

> *"Their home was eight miles away, so that they walked 16 miles a day. Their hours of work were from 8 a.m. to 5 or 5.30 p.m. They left home at 5 a.m. and returned at 9 p.m. A younger sister, Susan, aged 6, had worked with them at one time, but her strength had given out."*

When the Commission investigated the rural situation in Dorset they found that boys were employed at a very early age, six or under, and more of them were employed than in any other county.

In general, the farmers opposed education for the children because their experience taught them that educated labourers would refuse to work for the low wages they offered. Efforts to introduce trade unions into agriculture to improve conditions was defeated.

Chimney Sweeps—"Climbing Boys"

Charles Dickens' "*Oliver Twist*" in 1837 and Charles Kingsley's "*Water Babies*" published in 1863, made famous the hardships endured by chimney sweeps, or, climbing boys, as they were called. In 1873 Lord Shaftesbury drew to the attention of the House of Lords an inquest being conducted on a climbing boy, aged seven and a half years, who had been suffocated in a flue in the county of Durham. Year after year young children were subjected to this type of labour which often ended in their contracting a certain, revolting form of cancer directly due to their occupation. Even when legislation was passed in Parliament to outlaw the employment of climbing boy apprentices under the age of 8, the laws were ignored, and home owners, who were otherwise decent people, continued to employ young children to clean their chimneys. It had been reported to the House of Commons in 1840 that boys as young as 4 ½ and 6 were thus employed.

> "*Thus the mischief went on 'till public opinion was shocked by a terrible case at Manchester, in 1847, in which a master sweep, John Gordon, was tried for the death of a boy of seven, named Thomas Price. (See The Times, August 14th, 1847) The child was forced to go, for the second time, into a hot flue at Messrs. Tennant's chemical works; he screamed and sobbed, but in vain, for the master declared 'the young devil is foxing.' Finally, he was taken out half asphyxiated, thrown on straw, and cruelly beaten in the hope that he might be beaten back to consciousness. Soon after he died in convulsions.*"
> In the end John Gordon was sentenced to ten years transportation for the crime. (J. L. Hammond and Barbara Hammond, *Lord Shaftesbury*)

Chapter Five
The Plight of Lunatics

The higher ranks of society were opposed to any type of inspection of asylums or special houses where the mentally ill were kept for fear of family scandals resulting from publicity. Those who cared for "lunatics", as they were called, steadfastly maintained that there were no evils to be corrected. Many were prejudiced against lunatics due to a long-held belief that they were demon-possessed. A Committee of Inquiry of the House of Commons published a horrifying report in 1815-16. They drew attention to abuses of the York Asylum and of Bethlehem Hospital, Moorfields. It was revealed that 13 wretched lunatic women had been confined by day in a cell 12 feet by 7 feet 10 inches, without ventilation, and by night in four small secret cells, kept in so filthy and disgusting a state that their very existence was concealed from visitors, and that when they submitted their annual reports, 144 out of 365 deaths had been suppressed!

One of the worst cases was related by the Hammonds in Lord Shaftesbury's biography:

> "Of the scandals at Bethlehem, perhaps the most horrible case was that of William Norris, an educated man of fifty-five, who for more than twelve years had passed his life in a trough against a wall. He was bound by iron bars round his neck, waist, arms and shoulders. These bars were all connected by short chains with a sliding ring on an iron post behind, fixed in such a way that whilst able to raise himself in his trough and stand against the wall, he was unable to move away from it, and was unable to lie upon his side. For many years he had been under the charge of a keeper who was a notorious drunkard, and Norris's efforts to resist ill-treatment had only resulted in increasing the number of the bars that bound him."

The record continued. Back in 1827 the question of the treatment of lunatics again was brought before Parliament:

"At one establishment in Bethnal Green, 400 of these wretched beings were confined with no attempt to cure them beyond a visit from a medical man for an hour or two every other day. The so-called infirmary for the sick was in so disgusting a state that the keepers were unwilling to show it. There was no attempt at classification, except that the more violent were treated as 'crib-room cases,' that is, each of them was placed in a box, 6 feet long, covered with straw and chained by the arms and the legs. Fifteen of the 'crib-room cases' spent the night in a room 26 feet long, and it was the custom to leave them in their cribs for the weekend, without attention, till Monday morning, when they were taken out into the yard and plunged into cold water, even when ice was floating on the pails, to rid them of the filth in which they had been lying."

The following evidence was brought before the House of Commons by a Select Committee on Lunatics in 1859:

"When we began our visitations, one of the first rooms that we went into contained nearly a hundred and fifty patients, in every form of madness, a large proportion of them chained to the wall, some melancholy, some furious, but the noise and din and roar were such that we positively could not hear each other; every form of disease and every form of madness was there. I never beheld anything so horrible and so miserable. Turning from that room we went into a court, appropriated to the women. In that court there were from fifteen to twenty women, whose sole dress was a piece of red cloth, tied round the waist with a rope; many of them with long beards, covered with filth; they were crawling on their knees, and it was the only place where they could be. I do not think that I ever witnessed brute beasts in such a condition, and this had subsisted for years, and no remedy could be applied to it. It was known to one or two physicians at the Royal College, who visited the place once a year; but they said fairly enough that, although they saw these things, they could not amend them."

The accounts are as endless as they are desperate. And yet, as was too often the case, in the House of Lords, on June 24th, 1819, Lord Eldon recommended that a *"cool and dispassionate view"* be taken of such conditions, and went on to say, *"there could not be a more false humanity than an over humanity with regard to persons afflicted with insanity."*

* * * * * * * * * * * * * * * * * *

In summary, we have looked into the 19th century, from the Monarchy to the madhouses, from the Church to the chimney sweeps, from the houses of the aristocracy to the cottages of the poor agricultural workers. Urbanization was draining the towns and villages and filling London and other manufacturing centres. The gentry remained quite aloof and stable while a genuine middle-class was coming into existence. Low wages, deplorable sanitation, overcrowding, drunkenness, vice, and disease were the ugly companions of this dislocation of humanity. Internationally, Great Britain was extending its territorial conquests and making its might felt in such far flung locations as China, India, Burma, and South Africa. Back home, the Church of England's influence was being challenged by a rising tide of non-conformity which was led by pulpiteers, the like of whom they had not seen before, nor have they seen since to the same extent. The "Golden Age of Preaching" was ushered in, led by "Men who Moved the Masses."

For the purpose of narrowing our research we have selected nine of the pulpit giants of the Victorian era in order to explore their lives, preaching, and influence. We could have chosen more…men like Thomas Binney, F. W. Robertson, Hugh Price Hughes and others. We are introducing the selected nine men in the chronological order of their birth dates, not in any order that would suggest their measure of importance.

When spiritual conditions were at such a low ebb within the established Church, these men of God could not remain silent. With social conditions as deplorable as we have described above, these men could not remain idle spectators. Their prophetic voices were lifted up as a trumpet and their caring hearts compelled them to reach out to the masses in their misery. May their examples of character and ministry lure us all to higher heights of preaching power and deeper depths of compassion for the lost and the suffering about us.

PART II

Biographies of the Men Who Moved the Masses

Chapter Six

Alexander McLaren of Manchester

11 February 1826–5 May 1910

Godly Heritage

Alexander McLaren shrank from the very idea of a life biography being written about him. He contended that one of the preacher's first duties was to efface himself. John C. Carlile noted,

> *"Little men advertise themselves, but genius is generally clothed in modesty."*

McLaren, is how he signed his name, even though MacLaren is the spelling that usually appears on his published works.

Beecher used to say that the first thing a man should do is to *"choose a good father and mother to be born of."* Alexander's father, David McLaren, was born in Perth in 1785 and in his adult years became a city merchant. He was well known as a helper of good workers and as a gifted preacher in his own right. The *"Freeman"* described him as *"a Christian of considerable powers of mind, great force of character, and held in reputation among the brethren."*

Alexander's mother was described as Christ-like, of refined intelligence, and sweetness of disposition. David's parents nourished the ambition that, as the eldest son, he would enter the ministry of the Church of Scotland. But along the way, David became convinced of evangelical truths and could not be persuaded to go through with his parents' aspirations for him.

When quite young David attended Glasgow College, as it was then known, which later became Glasgow University. He became one of the pastors of the Brown Street Scotch Baptist Church. Following a common pattern among the eldership of churches in those days David was both a city merchant and shared the responsibility of preaching at the local church. The ministry of the church was conducted by a self-supporting, plural eldership. He held to the conviction that the obligations and privileges of clergymen and laymen alike, were equal.

It has been said that *"the father lives again in the son"* and this was apparently true in the lives of David and his son, Alexander. Alexander inherited some rare gifts of mental and physical qualities from his parents. David was described as a minister who *"excelled in exposition; his sermons were characterized by exact knowledge, careful thought, and a lucid style; these qualities reappear in his son."*

Alexander McLaren was born in Glasgow on 11 February 1826, the youngest, by five or six years, of a family of six children. The eldest son died early. The second, John Wingate, lived until 1874, and was a partner in a London firm with Australian connections. There were three daughters. Both Elizabeth (Mrs. Renshaw) and Jane lived past age 90. Christina (Mrs. Morrison) died at age 54, leaving a large family of sons and daughters.

Alexander spent his early childhood in Glasgow, becoming a scholar at the Glasgow High School where he learned the habit of patient plodding. Later he attended the University of Glasgow. His early years were linked with literary culture and strict religiousness. His teachers inspired him to make acquaintance with men of learning of bygone years. The man who most influenced him in those early years was Rev. David Russell, the Congregational minister of Glasgow, who later became McLaren's brother-in-law.

Through changes that transpired in his business, David left Glasgow in 1836 for Adelaide, South Australia, where he acted as the first manager for the South Australia Company. He remained there for four years. During that time he contributed much to the young colony's institutions and to the Free Churches. In Adelaide, there is a McLaren Wharf and a McLaren Vale, named after him. David's family remained back in Glasgow throughout this entire period. They attended the Hope Street Baptist Chapel under the ministry of Dr. James Paterson who continued in that pulpit for 46 years.

There is a confusion of two years in various accounts of Alexander's baptism and of the year of his father's return to England from Australia. The *Freeman* puts Alexander's *"conscious consecration to the Saviour"* at age eleven, which would be 1837, and then states that his father left for Australia sometime after that. This conflicts with the recorded 1836 departure date in other records. Carlile puts his baptism at 17 May 1838, and stated that *"he had no great tale of conversion to relate"* having been raised in a Christian home. The 1875 edition of the *Freeman* dated his baptism at 17 May 1840, and records that he joined the church one week later. The *Freeman* also records clearly that Alexander applied for church membership when he was 14 years old, which would confirm the 1840 date of his baptism. It stated that the boy, at age 14, like the man he later became, was *"remarkable for intelligence and frankness—a bold thinker."*

Alexander's father rejoined his family in London upon his return from Australia. An article in the *Freeman* noted that the family moved to London in 1842 which seems to be in conflict with Elizabeth T. McLaren's account, who put her father's return at four years after his departure for Adelaide in 1836, which would make his return date to be 1840. Subsequently, David died in 1850.

Stepney College and Entrance into the Baptist Ministry

The story is told that David took his son, Alexander, to the Rev. Charles Stovel, a great man among Baptists, to ask him if he thought Alexander would make a good minister. The old man gave a brief, noncommittal response, *"Well, well, perhaps he might."*

In 1842, Alexander appeared before the Examination Committee of Stepney College and was accepted as a student for ministry with the Baptists. Stepney College was housed in a quaint, castle-like structure which gave the impression more of a prison than of an academy! At that time its neighbourhood environment was much more pleasant than what that squalid, over-crowded section of London later became. Eventually, Stepney College was moved to Oxford where it is known today as Regent's Park College, incorporated in 1957 as a Permanent Private Hall of the University of Oxford.

Several ministers at that time thought that McLaren looked too much of a boy! When the Rev. Samuel Green returned home that day after Alexander's appearance before the committee, he told his son, *"the Committee has passed a Scotch lad named McLaren, who would cut all the others out!"* He described Alexander as *"tall, shy, and silent, very young-looking and not feeling at home in the new surroundings."* After a while his boyish smile and playful speech conquered all hearts and he made friends.

As a new student he was obliged to preach a trial sermon to members of the College Committee in the Library of the old Mission House. He sat at one end of a long table and the six old gentlemen sat comfortably at the other end. At the conclusion they decided that *"he would do"* but they would not permit him to go out to preach because he looked too young!

His first public service was conducted on a dull Sunday afternoon when he was still a freshman, in the old chapel at the side of the College. Only seven people showed up, who were *"about as impressible as the College Committee"* said McLaren afterwards.

He was graduated B.A. from London University before his term ended.

As to his gifts, character and disposition, he was a very hard worker with an honourable school record. He had the Scottish gift of persistent plodding, combined with the rarer gift of quick apprehension and shrewd insight into the meaning of things. He learned the habit of digging down to the roots of Hebrew words and exploring the intricacies of Greek verbs which largely contributed to his preaching power. He was greatly influenced by Principal, Dr. Benjamin Davies, who insisted on accuracy of Biblical exegesis and exposition, and ascertaining first-hand the grammatical meaning of the text through the use of the original languages. McLaren became very proficient in Hebrew.

In disposition, McLaren was of a retiring personality, a bit of a recluse—as John C. Carlile put it—*"by inclination a student, by temperament a recluse."* But once engaged in conversation, he was very lively and amused people with his stories about Scottish life.

As for those who influenced him most outside of College life, there were two: Rev. Thomas Binney of Weigh House Chapel on Fish Street Hill, and Edward Miall, Editor of the *Nonconformist*. McLaren claimed that Binney had taught him how to preach. At the end of his college experience, he expressed personally to Binney his gratitude for all he had learned from him, to which Binney replied, *"Do not speak about it, it is all such a poor thing."*

From Miall, who had an immense influence upon all young ministerial students in those days, he learned those principles of religious freedom which he always held dear thereafter, and his Liberalism in politics. McLaren believed in a Free Church in a Free State, and advocated the disestablishment of the State Church. Miall became an MP and helped to get legislation through Parliament which influenced public opinion toward the Free Churches.

Commencement of Ministry: Portland Chapel, Southampton

In 1846, at the age of 20, Alexander McLaren went forth from Stepney College to minister. His first settlement was at Portland Chapel, Southampton, where Rev. John Pulsford had preached for some years. Pulsford was followed briefly by a Rev. J. Ford. Portland Chapel was a Union church that embraced many variations of Christian belief and practice, which in due course led to internal conflict and strife. In 1844 the church voted to dissolve and the property was sold to the Baptists for 1,350 pounds. The building was constructed to seat 300.

Alexander McLaren first came as a student supply on 16 November 1845. After this first encounter the church asked him to stay on in a probationary capacity for another three months. After this period the church decided to issue him a call even though he had yet to complete one more year of study. During this initial year he preached on the first Sunday of each month right up until he was formally ordained. It was 1846 when he took up the full-time responsibility of the Portland Chapel pulpit and continued there until 1858. His stipend was set at 60-70 pounds a year.

In this more obscure setting, McLaren exercised a great deal of freedom in his exposition of the Scriptures. He often startled his hearers with his imaginative treatment of the texts and was regarded as sometimes novel, and always original. A fellow pastor in the same town, Rev. Thomas Adkins, along with several denominational leaders, were not at all sure of McLaren's orthodoxy in those early years. Was the temptation to be novel so great that he was willing to sacrifice sound doctrine? While he believed and preached strongly on punishment for sin he lacked conviction concerning the eternal state of the lost and of eternal punishment. He also entertained some thoughts about the actual communion between the living and the dead.

His lack of ministerial propriety, as they viewed it, did not sit well with the older pastors and leaders in the denomination. McLaren was not willing to wear the traditional ministerial dress in the pulpit and he refused to wear the traditional white tie. He also appeared to be quite careless about the colour of his clothes.

There were times after he had preached for 15 to 20 minutes when he would abruptly say, *"I have no more to say!"* He would then immediately sit down to the dismay of his people. Sometimes, in search of a precise word, he would stop for extremely long pauses. His people would become so uncomfortable that they felt he had broken down completely. One old Scottish lady in his congregation said that she wished to be in the pulpit with him so she could whisper the word for which he was groping into "the lad's lug."

McLaren once said of this pastorate:

> *"I thank God that I was stuck down in a quiet little obscure place to begin my ministry, for that is what spoils half of you young fellows, you get pitchforked into prominent positions at once, and then fritter yourselves away in all manner of little engagements that you call duties, going to this tea meeting, and that anniversary, and other breakfast celebration, instead of stopping at home and reading your Bibles and getting near to God. I thank God for the early days of struggle and obscurity."*

On balance, the reader should keep in mind that the above statement was made by a man who by disposition would gladly have become a recluse. Nevertheless, his point was still valid. Being a man of God and of the Scriptures, was not to be attained by becoming a social butterfly!

During his time in Southampton, the Chapel gradually began to fill up. Leading members of the Society of Friends attended his services in the evenings. On 20 June 1858 he preached his farewell sermon at Portland Chapel and moved on to take up the pastoral ministry at Union Church, Manchester, where he would serve for 45 years. As he prepared to depart, the Portland Chapel people acknowledged how *"painful the upward path"* had been for McLaren, especially in his early years at the beginning of this charge.

Marriage

While serving in Southampton he married his cousin, Miss Marian McLaren, of Edinburgh, on 27 March 1856. She was a woman of considerable education, fine literary taste, and had strong sympathy with Christian social movements. She became a force in mission and temperance work. Mrs. McLaren was a gifted conversationalist and a strong evangelical.

In the first year of marriage Alexander read aloud to his wife the fifth volume of *Modern Painters*, and later on, when they had children, whenever he had a free evening he would read to the entire family. He also competed with his children in the creation of fairy tales. In this manner, the father who was possessed with a vivid imagination, fostered the same attribute in his children.

The McLarens had five children in all. When Mrs. McLaren died on 21 December 1884, only two daughters and one son, Alister, remained. Alister was very active in Christian and social work. McLaren felt the loss of his wife very keenly and withdrew from any contact with even his closest friends for two weeks. Many felt that he might never preach again.

In a letter dated 1 September 1905, he made reference to the high value he placed upon the contribution his wife had made to his life and ministry:

> *"Of all human formative influences on my character and life, hers is the strongest and the best. To write of me and not to name her, is to present a fragment."*

Some time after her death, McLaren wrote,

> *"There has never been a cloud between us, and she never did a thing or spoke a word that was not full of love and unselfishness."*

He said that her loss left him with *"a haunting loneliness."* Nevertheless, after a three-week absence from the pulpit he resumed his regular duties.

Stage Fright

His daughter, Elizabeth T. McLaren wrote,

> *"He never appeared in public, he never preached, even to his own congregation, without going through a time of extreme nervous perturbation, as if THIS time, he was stranded."*

Sometimes his stage fright was quite alarming. On one occasion, after preaching an important message he was most depressed, but soon put the depression behind him by saying, *"Well, I can't help it; I did my best, and there I leave it."*

In all fairness to McLaren it should be noted that he was not alone when it comes to the matter of stage fright. Thomas Binney used to become so nervous that there were times when he refused altogether to go on to the platform. On one such occasion, one of his deacons opened the door and said firmly, *"Now, this is the way."* Carlile recalls being in the vestry with another very popular preacher, one of England's greatest, with thousands out in the auditorium waiting to hear every word which would fall from his lips, and yet the preacher sat down in tears and sobbed with sheer nervousness. Within a half an hour he displayed the courage of a hero and the boldness of a lion!

It was said of another very renowned preacher on both sides of the Atlantic Ocean, that he once mounted the pulpit with an air of a composed and accomplished orator, and then proceeded to fail miserably. He descended from the pulpit clothed in despair and humiliation. An old deacon placed his hand on his shoulder and said,

> *"Had ye gone up as ye came down, ye might have come down as ye went up!"*

Forty-five Years at Union Chapel, Manchester: 1858–1903

People from every imaginable church background attended the services of Union Chapel, Manchester. The large chapel which they built for McLaren became too small. They had 1,000 Sunday School scholars and two branch churches in densely populated neighbourhoods. Many Christian workers representing a wide variety of agencies attended his church, and ministers would throng to hear him, some taking weekends just to come and listen to his preaching at Manchester. At one point a meeting was convened especially for the Christian workers within his congregation and upwards of 200 attended. Charles Spurgeon and Henry Ward Beecher held him in high honour. He was regarded as *"one of the foremost preachers of the age"* and *"the most popular of preachers of missionary sermons."*

McLaren believed in extension church planting. In 1862 they started a branch church in Clowes Street, Garton. Meanwhile the congregation at Union Chapel increased until the building was crowded out. Eventually the church decided to move some distance from the city to a new site facing Whitworth Park. They formally opened what some called *"the Baptist Cathedral of Lancashire"* on 16 November 1869, in a building which seated 1,400 comfortably and could accommodate up to 2,000 if necessary. They built an adjoining hall which seated 400-500 which they used on week nights. McLaren's Wednesday evening service was much like Dr. Joseph Parker's Thursday mid-day service at City Temple. Parker had come to Cavendish Chapel, Manchester, at about the same time McLaren took up his responsibilities at Union Chapel and they became close friends from that time forward.

In 1875 he was elected to the Presidency of the Baptist Union for the first time, and was elected a second time in 1901. Later still, in 1905, he presided at the First Congress of the Baptist World Alliance.

In 1877 the University of Edinburgh conferred upon him a Doctor of Divinity degree. Some claim that this was the first time in history that such an honour had been bestowed upon a Nonconformist and a non-Presbyterian, but his daughter, Elizabeth, denies that this is true.

In 1881 his health gave way and it was feared that he might not be able to carry on. However, after a year's rest, he returned to his duties.

In 1883 Regent's Park College called him to take up the Professorship of Hebrew with the added stipulation that on Sunday mornings he was to preach in Bloomsbury Chapel. Calls to come to other pastoral charges could fill pages of the record, but in the end he declined all offers, even though he was sorely tempted to accept the invitation of the College. It proved very difficult to persuade McLaren to preach on special occasions. He never took popular subjects of the day into the pulpit. He ploughed a narrow furrow and generally it was within the Baptist denomination. He was reluctant to preach outside of it and yet, at the same time, he loved to minister in small village chapels. W. Robertson Nicoll claimed that he refused almost everything. *"He was always saying no."* Having chosen such a narrow path he was prevented from cultivating intimate friendships with a wide circle of influential and educated men of his generation.

Visit to Australia

During 1883 Alexander McLaren paid a visit to Australia on the occasion of the Centenary of the New South Wales Colony and the Jubilee of Victoria. The Baptists there wanted to have a prominent English preacher come to give them a boost in raising 50,000 pounds for church extension. Some wanted him to stay on in Australia following the precedent set by his father who had lived in Adelaide for several years.

McLaren departed for this trip with two of his daughters on 21 September 1883 on the P. & O. liner *BRITANNIA*. One press report referred to the daughters as "Miss McLaren and Miss Florence McLaren." The ship anchored at Large Bay, Adelaide, on 28 October and a large party came on board to greet them.

It is interesting to note that his daughter, Elizabeth, reported that her father counted his never having gone to the United States of America as one of his life's greatest mistakes!

As Others Saw Him

Although many said the same thing about himself, Dr. Joseph Parker maintained that *"there is no greater preacher than Alexander McLaren in the English-speaking pulpit."* Yet others have said this of Charles Spurgeon.

Dr. W. Robertson Nicoll paid tribute to McLaren in an article printed in the *British Weekly* in the next issue after McLaren's death. Among the exceptional qualities he attributed to McLaren were these:

> *"His natural gifts were extraordinary. He was out of sight the most brilliant man all round we ever knew. From his youth he looked like a Highland chieftain born to command...Before you knew he was a prophet you were sure he was a king...There was a kind of regal effulgence about him in his great moments. He might have been anything—soldier, politician, man of letters, man of science, and in any profession he would have taken the head. He was gifted with a swift and clear-cutting intellect. He had also a true vein of poetry and genius. He could master any subject...If ever anyone was apprehended of Christ Jesus in early years, it was Alexander McLaren. The religious training of his youth, which he loved to describe, seized him, held him, ruled him through all his many years. Never was any one more profoundly loyal to the lessons of the morning. He desired no other and no better thing than that the end of life should circle round the beginning, only with a deeper conviction and a stronger love at last...Those who observed him recognized that he*

drank from fountains older than the world, and for him they were always running fresh...He could not have been slovenly if he had tried to be...To him preaching was the exposition of the eternal divine thought. Anything less was not preaching...Dr. McLaren conceived it his duty to preach certainties, and only certainties... His sermons were...timeless—statistics, organization, machinery, crowds, elaborate music, display in advertising—these things were not his taste...He was clearly a man of genius, and men of genius are very rare...he did his work not merely for the time but for the time to come."

"He commanded words as an emperor and as a magician," Nicoll continued. *"In his loftiest flights one hardly knew whether he spake or sang. It was 'spirit half asleep or song half awake!'"*

Dr. Ward, Principal of Owen College, Manchester, himself a teacher of English language and literature of many years, said that he regarded *"Dr. McLaren's preaching as the chief literary influence...in the city of Manchester."*

He was a great master of style. His mastery of English in itself brought pleasure to the hearers in addition to the value of the sermon content. His style has been described as "severely logical." He linked points together in succession, each point dependent upon the previous one revealing a strict mental discipline. He was regarded as superior among preachers for his extremely accurate use of words. His diction was *"chaste...clear, and easy to follow."* Carlile said that McLaren had sympathy in his speech void of any judicial harshness. His voice bore a Scottish accent and had a rich musical quality which penetrated and filled all parts of any auditorium in London.

An anonymous description of his preaching was written in 1911:

"Dr. McLaren cannot be described. We may speak of the spare figure quivering with life and feeling; of the firm set mouth, the unmistakable sign of a tremendous will; of eyes that pierce and shine and seem to compass everybody and everything in their quick, lightning glance; or of the strangely magnetic voice—but in vain. We may describe his preaching as logic on fire or that his words thrill like electricity; that he speaks like one wholly possessed by his theme, or that the speaker's tout ensemble gives one the best idea possible of etherealized matter, of spirit overpowering matter; but it fails."

"Some heights, he gains at a bound and he bears his hearers upward, perhaps only for a few moments, but he has shown us the glory of the outlook from a mountain peak...A few bold sentences clear-cut, and the commonplace truth we had known for years was seen in a new perspective and beauty."

"The conservation of energy upon one purpose has contributed largely to his success; he could say of preaching, 'this one thing I do.' Alexander McLaren was called to be a preacher and to that end has been surrendered...he was a lover of his work."

John C. Carlile wrote:

"Fifty years ago (in the 1850's) the standard of preaching was not very bright. There were great preachers, of course, but generally the style of pulpit discourse was pompous and prosaic; dismal dullness was the rule. The men who have revolutionized pulpit methods had not appeared in the churches or were young, and had little influence upon their fellow ministers. C. H. Spurgeon had not come to London, with his splendid simplicity and brightness, to give the last blow to the sleepy style that had brought rest to so many congregations. Men were not declaring the message of God to their generation except so far as it could be given in accord with the social uniformity which had by long continuance become an unwritten law asserting more authority over the pulpit than even the Thirty-Nine Articles, insisting upon the submission of the preacher to the dictates of society which did not like to be disturbed, hated to be alarmed, and asked nothing more from the ministers than a confirmation of its prejudices."

But then along came pulpit giants like Spurgeon, Parker and McLaren. Hugh Price Hughes said that McLaren was *"supreme as the highest modern exponent from the pulpit of the Spoken Word."* Carlile referred to him as *"a conspicuous figure among the foremost of the world's preachers."*

He went on to describe him from another angle:

"The professional interviewer makes little copy out of him; he is extremely difficult to draw. We do not see his views on public questions, social and political, in the morning paper. He keeps steadily to his vocation in the pulpit which has become his throne. He has not

courted fame or wooed popularity; being 'lionized' is not to his taste. Perhaps he knows the value of the cheap applause the multitude bestows upon its favourites too well to care much for its roar."

The publication *Freeman* gave as the secret to his success,

"(1) that he was an analyst of surpassing ability: he distinguished between things which differ...detects shades of meaning...the relation of part to part, and each to the whole of the paragraph he expounds; (2) he had the power of seeing spiritual verities in the clear light of the intellect...his thoughts transcend sentiment...No man has so frequently aided us in the intellectual apprehension of the spiritual verities of the Gospel and the Christian life...His sermons are characterized by nervous thought, thought instinct and tremulous with life."

The *Freeman* went on to say:

"Mr. McLaren is above all things else a preacher of the Gospel. His one aim is to win souls...He preaches the Gospel with a freshness and force which are perennial."

Sermon Preparation and Preaching

On Tuesday, 23 April 1901, Alexander McLaren delivered his Presidential Address to the Joint Assembly of the Baptist and Congregational Unions at City Temple, London, near the close of Joseph Parker's life and ministry there. His topic was, *"An Old Preacher on Preaching."* In this message he defined the threefold duty and function of preachers:

(1) *"First and foremost the preacher is an evangelist...he has to tell a fact which is full freighted with gladness for a sad world."* He said that we must preach with urgency, tenderness, with the personal element, and have elasticity in his methods.

(2) *The preacher must be a teacher. Teaching and evangelism must go together. "The evangelist who is not a teacher will build nothing that will last...He is to be both at once, and to be both always."*

(3) *The preacher must also be a prophet, which is the ethical aspect of his ministry. "The prophet's chief function is to be an incarnation of the national conscience…We need to keep clear of popular currents of thought and practice, suspecting always that truth does not dwell with majorities, and that what the multitude acclaim, God is likely to condemn."*

At the request of Rev. T. Harwood Pattison, professor of homiletics in the Rochester Theological Seminary, McLaren wrote a letter to the students at the institution in January 1900.

"*I sometimes think that a verse in one of the Psalms carries the whole pith of homiletics—*

> *'While I was musing, the fire burned,*
> *Then spake I with my tongue.'*

"*Patient meditation, resulting in kindled emotion and the flashing up of truth into warmth and light, and then—and not until then—the rush of speech 'moved by the Holy Ghost'—these are the processes which will make sermons live things with hands and feet, as Luther's words were said to be. 'Then spake I' not 'Then sate I down at my desk and wrote it all down to be majestically read out of a manuscript in a leather case.'*"

"*May I add another text, which contains as complete a description of the contents of preaching as the Psalm does of its genesis? 'Whom we preach'—there is the evangelistic element, which is foundation of all, and is proclamation with the loud voice, the curt force, the plain speech of a herald; and there is, too, the theme, namely, the Person, not a set of doctrines, but, on the other hand, a Person Whom we can know only by doctrines, and Whom, if we know, we shall surely have some doctrine concerning. 'Warning every man'— there is the ethical side of preaching; 'and teaching every man'— there is the educational aspect of the Christian ministry. These three must never be separated, and he is the best minister of Jesus Christ who keeps the proportion between them most clearly in his mind, and braids all the strands together in his ministry into a 'three-fold cord, not quickly broken.' May the Rochester students attain to that ideal!*

Alexander McLaren"

Some felt that his most outstanding gift was *"almost perfect, spoken composition."* It was said that *"he created literature in the very act of delivery."*

In an 1875 publication of the *Freeman* appeared the following remark about McLaren's preparation for preaching:

> *"To the preparation of his sermons he brought the resources of a thoroughly trained intellect, a vivid imagination, and a taste not very far from faultless as regards literary expression."*

He also resolved early in his career that if he could not look his hearers in the face when he preached then he would give up altogether. He determined not to be tied to a manuscript. He was accustomed to writing out fully the first two or three sentences, calling this his method of *"pushing off from the shore and launching into deep water."* After that his notes were scant. He only clothed illustrations with words on the spot while he was in the act of preaching.

It was a complete mystery to McLaren how anyone could prepare sermons weeks in advance of preaching them. *"I must give it red hot!"* he said. He had been criticized that his preaching was too much characterized by high pressure but he retorted that if he could not preach *"red hot"* then he could not preach at all. It may seem strange to some that with all this heat in his preaching, privately, his shyness kept him from social contact and from visiting his people.

Carlile commented,

> *"The person who could sleep under his preaching should not be rebuked, for he would be very infirm in body and in mind."*

Though this suggests rather lively, animated preaching, it is reported that in the pulpit he was sparing of action and used few gestures.

The following story is told by John Carlile to illustrate the kind of preaching that invokes sleep rather than rapt attention:

> *"It is related of old Lord Landerdale that when he was suffering from insomnia and his doctor said that if he did not sleep he would die, a juvenile member of the family said, 'Why don't they send for the Rector—Grandpa always goes to sleep when he begins to preach.' The clergyman came and sat by his bedside, and sure enough, the*

patient slept, while the good man talked. Many preachers accomplish the same object without the beneficial results to health."

Dr. Clandish made the following remark regarding a sermon he had recently endured:

"It consists of an introduction, which might have been spared; a second part, which does not deal with the text; and a conclusion that concludes nothing!"

At the Jubilee Celebration of the Assembly of the Free Church of Scotland in 1893, conducted in the world-known Free Assembly Hall, Edinburgh, McLaren startled many hearers by his vehemence of tone and look, as he said, *"BURN YOUR MANUSCRIPTS!"* He had intended to direct his comments to the Students' Gallery, but it went out to the whole house. After, he thought it must have sounded *"awful audacity,"* but on second thought, he voiced the hope that it *"might be blessed to some younger ministers."*

In Manchester, his brother-in-law, Marian's brother, also named Alexander McLaren, came to live with them and the association was a happy one. One day the brother-in-law asked Marian if her husband was aware that he generally fed his congregation with *"a three-pronged fork."* McLaren quickly turned around to face his brother-in-law with a look of intense amusement, and replied, *"No, but now that you are kind enough to mention it I feel that it is true, and the three-pronged fork seems to me a thoroughly useful instrument."* Not only did most of his sermons have three main points, very often the sub-points under the main headings fell into groups of three.

Few men could get in touch with an audience as quickly as McLaren. His absolute self-command was the envy of many an orator. In a conversation with Rev. J. H. Shakespeare the subject came up about his simplicity of style. McLaren responded by asking Rev. Shakespeare if he knew a certain man in McLaren's congregation, a man who was not terribly brilliant and seemingly devoid of talent. McLaren said,

"Well now, often when I am preparing my sermons I keep that man before me, and say, 'What I have to do is to get this thought behind his skull."

McLaren's favourite authors included Thomas Carlyle, Emerson, Owen, Howe, Goodwin, and John Ruskin. He loved books but he was first and foremost a student of THE BOOK. Sir Walter Scott, on his deathbed, when asked which book he would like to have read to him to beguile the hours, replied, *"There is only one Book."* McLaren cared nothing for reading the sermons of others nor of biographies. He read widely and knew the best novels. He enjoyed reading books about travel. As for publishing his own sermons they had to be practically dragged out of him!

McLaren believed that the success of a ministry lay in the preacher's ability to cultivate the habit of meditation. He was very self-disciplined and claimed that if he could, he would outlaw newspapers and periodicals from the minister's study! He was also a keen observer of human nature.

McLaren's method of recording the sermons which he had preached over his lifetime looked something like this:

No.	Where	Text	When
1.	College Chapel	I John II.15	Oct. 29th, 1843

His first entry was recorded at age 18 and the last, No. 6,860, was entered on Nov. 21st, 1904, when he was 78 years old.

F. B. Meyer likened Dr. McLaren's sermons to a great cathedral:

> *"so exquisitely constructed were they, and so entirely complete in proportions." "When Dr. McLaren published his first sermons he taught all preachers that there was a way of dividing the subject into distinct parts; and when you read his volumes, you find in the first sentences of every sermon the lines on which he is going to treat the theme. That method has influenced most modern preachers, and so has Dr. McLaren's style of illustrating his subject by analogies drawn from nature and life. No more perfect selection of illustrations could be compiled, I believe, than from Dr. McLaren's sermons...To preachers he has been a model and an example which we have all tried to study."*

Oddly enough, Rev. J. H. Shakespeare reported that McLaren had a particular trait of being profoundly dissatisfied with anything he had preached or done. Even after preaching a great sermon he would be heard to say, *"A dead failure, I can never speak again!"* He went on to summarize comparisons between the styles of Spurgeon, Parker and McLaren, saying that Parker was noted for *"ornate rhetoric"*; Spurgeon's preaching was *"pregnant with humour"*; and that McLaren was equal to both Spurgeon and Parker in *"penetration,"* but that he *"surpassed both of them in beauty of style and richness of suggestion."*

Perhaps one of the greatest tributes ever paid to Dr. McLaren's preaching was when Thomas Binney came to hear him preach in 1870 at the Old Surrey Chapel. McLaren preached on *"The Secret of Power."* You will recall that McLaren had claimed that it was Binney who had taught him how to preach. On this occasion, Binney came under such powerful conviction through McLaren's preaching, that he left the building. When three days later someone remarked to Binney that this sermon preached by McLaren was just the kind of sermon, that he, Binney, would admire. To this, Binney replied,

> *"I did indeed admire it, though all the time I listened to it, the conviction came home to me that I had never really preached."*

An amusing incident occurred as a result of a British Weekly publishing an article concerning the more every-day perspective of Dr. McLaren's life. It was McLaren's regular habit to walk to the library with a bundle of books under his arm every Monday morning. For ten years his little dog followed him on this brief journey. The newspaper portrayed the dog as *"a magnificent collie"* which amused McLaren no end. He replied,

> *"that it was not the first mongrel which had been raised to the position of a thoroughbred by a newspaper's words!"*

Approaching Sunset

In later life McLaren withdrew from lecturing and from taking on various ministries outside of his immediate charge and insisted upon sticking to his own, immediate, pastoral responsibilities at Union Chapel. The formal end of his ministry at the Chapel is dated 1903. He spent the winters of 1904 and 1905 in Mentone, Southern France, in order to escape the British weather. This is also where Charles Spurgeon used to retreat and where he eventually died on 31 January 1892.

In the last meeting in which McLaren was prevailed upon to speak, and in his very last address to a large audience, he said the following:

> *"All our pleasant intercourse and our profitable reception of truth will be less than nothing unless we, in the depth of our soul and in the solitude of His Presence, live the life of consecration and self-conquest, and put it all into one primary thing—the life of Christ which is life indeed. That is, if I may say so, my last message which I desire to take into my own life, and to be in the spirit of all who have attended this wonderful Congress."*
> (Spoken in the last meeting of the 1905 Baptist World Congress held in London in McLaren's 80th year.)

Earlier in this same Congress, at which he had been elected President, he preached a short message on *"Two Crystal Phrases: 'In the Name of Christ'* and *'By the Power of the Spirit'"* in which he said:

> *"We are crying out for a revival. Dear Friends, the revival must begin with each of us by ourselves. Power for service is second. Power for holiness and character is first, and only the man who has let the Spirit of God work His will upon him, and do what He will, has a right to expect that he will be filled with the Holy Ghost and with power. Do not get on the wrong track. Your revival, Christian ministers, must begin in your study and on your knees. Your revival must be for yourselves with no thought of service. But, if once we have learned where our strength is, we shall never be so foolish as to go forth in our own strength, or we shall be beaten as we deserve to be."*

We conclude our review of Alexander McLaren's life and work with a small taste of one of his sermons, entitled, *"The Holy Spirit: the Earnest of the Inheritance"*, preached at Union Chapel, Manchester, in 1859. The text was Ephesians 1:13 & 14: "Ye are sealed with that Holy Spirit of promise, which is the earnest of our inheritance."

> *"Heaven is the perfecting of the life of the Spirit begun here, and the loftiest attainments of that life here are but the beginnings and infantile movements of immature beings…From the existing experience we argue the future blessedness; and then, catching a gleam of*

the future blessedness, we turn round and look at the present experi-
ence, and discern at the same moment how great that must be which
transcends it, and how small that is, which is going to greaten into
heaven! Dear Friends, what we know, and love, and believe, and
rejoice in, here on earth, is the manna in the wilderness; and we are
waiting for the better and settled food of the permanent home. We
get here the prelibation—the first taste and draught; but the full cup
is kept for us above; we wet our lips, in the midst of the hot struggle
on earth, with the sacred joys, hastily quaffed, of still communion
and thankful devotion; but the full draught, the best wine, is kept till
we get yonder, when the perfecting of the Spirit comes. Here, we
drink of the brook by the way, in the heat of the battle and the
pursuit; there, we shall lift up the head, and drink of 'the river of the
water of life that proceedeth out of the Throne of God and of the
Lamb.' The best of earth is the shadow of heaven; the shadow is like
the substance; but oh! The substance—'eye hath not seen, nor ear
heard, neither hath it entered into the heart of man to conceive, the
things that God hath prepared for them that love Him."

In Edinburgh, on 5 May 1910, at age 84, Alexander McLaren passed from the land of shadow, manna and of the brook along the way, into the realm of the full cup, substance and the best wine! He had lived and laboured for almost 25 years without the support and companionship of his beloved wife, Marian, who had predeceased him. He was cremated and his ashes buried in the Brooklands Cemetery alongside his wife and one daughter.

At a memorial service in Union Chapel, Rev. J. E. Roberts preached, and in tribute to Dr. McLaren and his preaching, said:

"Dr. McLaren's devotion to preaching was so complete that a fitting
motto for his life would be, 'This one thing I do.'"

Chapter Seven

Robert William Dale of Birmingham

1 December 1829–13 March 1895

The Dead Still Speak

Hebrews 11:4 declares of Abel, *"And by faith he still speaks, even though he is dead."* This is the verse that comes to the author's mind whenever he recalls the life and preaching of Dr. R. W. Dale of Birmingham. While enjoying reader's privileges at Dr. William's Library, Gordon Square, London, I studied Dr. Dale's Nine Lectures on Preaching which he delivered at Yale University in 1877. One hundred and ten years later, as I studied those lectures, I became totally convinced of the superiority of extemporaneous preaching over the use of a full manuscript in the pulpit. For over 35 years of ministry I had always carried a carefully prepared manuscript into the pulpit, but from the day I encountered those lectures in Dr. William's Library, I radically changed my preaching style and have never looked back since. It was unquestionably one of the most defining junctures in my ministry life. The handful of times I have used a manuscript in the past 13 years has been when preaching in the Vietnamese language, or, when speaking through an interpreter. In the latter case, having a manuscript in front of me helps me to maintain my focus and prevents me from being distracted when the interpreter and I are switching back and forth over a 30 to 40 minute period. But apart from those exceptional instances I have entirely departed from a habit of 35 years, to enter into the freedom of extemporaneous preaching. Thanks to Dr. R. W. Dale, who having departed this life long ago, still speaks.

Birth and Parentage

Robert William Dale was born in London, England, on 1 December 1829 possessing no remarkable heritage. His father, Robert, at age 22, married Elizabeth Young, the daughter of a tradesman. The couple were already related through marriages of relatives and neither had the privilege of much education. Mr. Dale senior was a man of average height with no noteworthy features. He was reserved and retiring in nature and consequently shunned society. He was not noted for enterprise or vigour.

Elizabeth was small and dark, and had an amazing fund of energy and enthusiasm which enabled her to inspire and motivate others. Undoubtedly, her son, R.W., inherited this characteristic of boundless energy from his mother. Elizabeth bore six children in all, but only two survived, Robert and Thomas. Robert was the only child in the home for the first ten years. This being the case, Elizabeth concentrated her affection on her "Bobby" and her enduring ambition for him was that he should become a minister of the Gospel. Rev. James Key said,

> *"For this she seemed to live, for this she prayed incessantly; for this she laboured; for this she would make any sacrifice."*

The family was poor and did not mix much with their more prosperous neighbours, but the Dales' steady, consistent lives commanded respect in the community. Robert and Elizabeth both belonged to the Tabernacle Church, Moorsfields, established by George Whitefield, and therefore sometimes referred to as the Whitefield Tabernacle, Moorsfields. The pastor was Dr. John Campbell at that time. It was under this pastor's guidance, and at this very church, where Charles Spurgeon got his start in the ministry.

Early Spiritual Experience and First Efforts at Preaching

Information concerning the boyhood of Dale is scarcely to be found anywhere. It is reported that he was always punctual about returning home at times fixed by his mother. He studied at several schools—one in Worship Square under Mr. Wilby who followed the "Pestalozzian" system, another at Rayleigh when he was ten, which proved to be an unsuccessful experience, and then transferred to yet another school when he was eleven. Dale's boyhood education came to an end in 1843 when he was only 13 ½ years of age.

He had two friends who happened to be brothers, George and John Offord. Their father, Mr. Offord, was a saddler and harness-maker. He used to talk with the boys while he worked, drawing them out on various subjects and then sending them off to write essays on assigned topics.

Looking back at those experiences of youth, Dale commented,

> *"I should find it hard to say for how much of my own preaching he was responsible; his conversations with me about his two great preachers, Mr. Binney and Alfred Morris, made impressions on me which must have done a great deal to shape my whole way of thinking about the preacher's work."*

At about age thirteen, the Rev. James Sherman preached a message which made a deep impression on young Robert. He left the chapel that day as in a dream, aware that something had happened which affected his life at its very centre. It was not until he was about fourteen and a half years old that he finally settled the question of his soul's relationship with God. The year was 1844.

That year he joined the Congregational Church in East Street, Andover. At that time he wrote:

> *"I ceased thinking of myself and my faith, and thought only of Christ, and then I wondered that I should have been perplexed for even a single hour."*

He would occasionally pray in public services and he gave short addresses in the Sunday School. At age fifteen and a half he preached his first sermon in April or May of 1845, in a room at Providence Cottage, Lower Clatford, then occupied by a basket weaver named Rolf. His text was Ezekiel 18:29 *"O house of Israel, are not my ways equal?"* His sermon was in defense of Calvinism coupled with an assertion of universal redemption! He preached a second time in a little chapel at Abbott's Ann. His preaching began to attract a great deal of attention. He was never timid about attacking great subjects. He also engaged in writing articles for papers, mainly the *Young Men's Magazine*.

Dr. John Campbell's Refusal to Endorse Dale's Application to Enter Ministerial Studies

In due course Robert returned to his parents' home intending to prepare to enter the ministry. He and his parents were shocked when they approached Dr. John Campbell to secure his supporting endorsement of Dale's ministerial training. Dr. Campbell refused with such definiteness that it gave every appearance of finality. He was a very autocratic personality, and yet, it must be said in all fairness, from the perspective of this highly respected man of God, Robert Dale must have appeared terribly immature being still under the age of sixteen. Dr. Campbell made no attempt to qualify his decision which made it all the more difficult for the family and others in the congregation to appreciate his handling of the matter.

Dale now had to make other plans for his life in the midst of this crushing disappointment. In August of 1845 he had to return to teaching, assisting Mr. Jardine at Brixton Hill. This did not prove to be a success, for Dale's mind was preoccupied with his desire to enter the ministry.

In 1846 he settled at Leamington, assistant to Mr. Muller. He joined the Spencer Street Congregational Church pastored by Rev. A. Pope and from time to time, he preached in surrounding villages. He returned to trying his hand at writing and produced a book entitled *The Talents*. During his sojourn at Leamington, Pastor Pope encouraged him to pursue his dream of entering the ministry.

Entrance to Ministerial Studies at Spring Hill College, Birmingham

In 1846 R. W. Dale applied to enter Spring Hill College, Birmingham. A Mrs. Cash and others at Leamington gathered some funds together (20 pounds per annum) to sponsor the young man. Sometimes during college vacation periods he would spend much time in her home with her children. It was Mrs. Cash who really opened the door into the ministry for Dale.

He was accepted into the College in the Autumn of 1847 when he was still only 17 ½ years of age. When he was being examined he felt insulted when John Angell James asked him to distinguish between justification and sanctification! The College had only been in existence for nine years. Dale recalls Thomas Binney preaching an "oration" on the mission of the Congregationalists to their times. Binney was said to have been the one who helped more than any other man to modify the traditional method and style of preaching among Nonconformists. He represented a movement—a departure from the limits of conventional orthodoxy—against formulas and phrases in which Evangelical doctrines were generally stated.

Dale was repelled by the preaching of John Angell James at Carr's Lane. He felt that James was not precise in his theology and far from original in his presentations. To Dale, originality *"was a pearl of great price: we were willing to sell all that we had to buy it."* The preaching of George Dawson in the city was regarded as so excellent that it had the reverse effect of causing Dale *"to shrink away from the ministry."*

John Angell James and Carr's Lane Chapel, Birmingham

By 1852 John Angell James had been pastor at Carr's Lane Chapel, Birmingham, for 47 years. He began in 1805 when he was just 20 years old. Carr's Lane had been founded in 1747 by devout members who withdrew from the "Old Meeting" which was drifting into Unitarianism and which eventually became the centre for that teaching in Birmingham. When James came on the scene, the church had about 150 members and had just survived three consecutive years without a pastor. There was first slow, and then rapid growth, which led to the construction of a new chapel in 1820. John Angell James became one of the most famous preachers of his time, in spite of Dale's early impressions of his preaching! He became quite a successful writer and was especially noted for the publication *The Anxious Enquirer*. He was an enthusiastic supporter of foreign missions, particularly the work connected with the London Missionary Society.

James frankly admitted that he lacked learning and originality. His intellect was unadventurous. He was a *"mere plodding, working husbandman, using old implements with some industry, and following old methods with a kind of dogged perseverance and considerable success."*

Soon after Dale's entry into College, James' attention was drawn toward him. James was an exemplary model of how an older brother can help develop a strong-minded younger brother. He was very kindly toward young Dale. A report once reached James that Dale was drifting into heresy or scepticism. James arranged a dinner meeting with Dale, one on one, which was not the normal pattern. Usually James would have three to four guests at one time. After the meal he invited Dale upstairs to his study, and after being seated, James came right to the point. He spoke very kindly but frankly, as a peer, rather than as one who regarded himself superior to his young friend. He was unable to correct Dale's error at that time, but the way he dealt with the young man won over Dale's heart and respect.

Eighteen months later, in 1849, Dale was summoned to preach at Carr's Lane in an emergency situation. One full year after that, James begged Dale to listen to *"no hint of solicitation about settling with a congregation without first consulting with him."* In 1851, James offered Dale financial help toward Dale's final year of study if Dale would agree to settle with him at the end of the year as his assistant. In the Autumn of 1852, Dale began preaching on the first Sunday of every month at the communion service when attendance would be at the highest level. Curiously, at age 23, this opportunity held no particular charm for Dale even though others would have gladly jumped at it. Dale much preferred to go to Germany to study. Also, he strongly doubted the stability of Carr's Lane, figuring that it *"would go to pieces as soon as James died."* He felt that James was the only factor which held the congregation together, and added, *"God bless his successor!"*

Apart from his desire to study in Germany, Dale would have preferred to establish a small church among the poor in a manufacturing section of the city, and thereby begin an evangelistic movement among that class of people.

A. W. W. Dale wrote:

> *"But Dale had already mastered the truth on which he laid such stress in later years—that a man who disregards duty to follow ideals of his own, however noble, who thinks first of his own preferences, or even of his own powers, and chooses his work instead of taking up the work to which he is called, is imperiling much more than mere success."*

Over the 1852 autumn months, up through to December, Dale had a growing ease and confidence about being at Carr's Lane, and his admiration for John Angell James deepened.

In 1853, Dale wrote to Mrs. Cash,

> *"Seasons of depression, heavy, terrible, overwhelming, come over me apparently without any very definite cause; stay in spite of means*

which seem most powerful to effect their removal; and then suddenly break off and depart at the bidding of a single word from a Christian friend; or a single train of commonplace reflections."

R. W. Dale's vision for the Carr's Lane congregation at this time, was to provide a church home out in the outskirts of the city for the wealthier people who were moving in that direction, so that Carr's Lane itself could evolve into a church for the impoverished multitudes which were more immediately at its doors.

His college training was now drawing to a close. Possibly, the person who had the greatest influence upon him at that time, was Henry Rogers, one of the professors. He was a philosopher, student of history, brilliant essayist, keen and subtle thinker, a wit, inspiring conversationalist, kindly, and a devout Christian gentleman. He was apprehensive of the narrow experience of seminary training and he strove to be more cosmopolitan in outlook and to compel his students toward original thought. As for Dale, he was never one whom any seminary could turn into a monk. He was *"built for the high seas."*

His college training ended in the summer of 1853 and in his London M.A. exams, Dale stood first in Philosophy winning the Gold Medal. This is especially interesting because his sermons reveal the mind of a philosopher more than that of any other trait.

Called and Confirmed as James' Assistant

In 1853 the church at Carr's Lane unanimously supported James' recommendation that Dale be called to come and be his Assistant Preacher. All throughout these years, James was a brilliant example of a godly mentor. He was supportive of Dale through thick and thin, even when Dale was wrong. Dale would have James' correction from time to time, but he always enjoyed James' unflagging support.

The first Sunday of August 1853 marked the formal beginning of Dale's duties as Assistant Preacher. During his early days there some felt he had heretical tendencies. James differed with him radically on several points of doctrine but he always staunchly defended his young charge.

In 1860, R. W. Dale was described as being still thin, 5 feet ten inches tall, clean shaven, with long black hair that hung over his cheeks and ears like a mane, somewhat careless in dress, but nevertheless conformed to the ministerial dress of the day. One description pictured him as having a swarthy appearance with lustrous eyes. Within two years he began to fill out and had his hair cut short and brushed back from his forehead. It was then that he refused to wear the traditional white tie and the ministerial costume, choosing rather to wear grey or lighter coloured clothes instead of black. During one winter he even wore leggings which the Volunteers had made fashionable. Many older folk were scandalized by all this and some even wrote in to the newspapers to voice their protests!

Dale did not believe in the distinction between clergy and laity. He eventually grew a beard and subsequently added a moustache—this in spite of well-meant objections that beards and moustaches *"invested the minister with an air of levity and worldliness."* He objected to the title "Rev." and in due course took up smoking a pipe some time after 1862, in his 33rd year, over the objections of older ministers. James begged him to give up the habit which was regarded with disgust and loathing by many in his congregation.

Appointed to be Co-Pastor, Ordination, and Marriage

On 6 August 1854 R. W. Dale preached for the first time in his new capacity as Co-Pastor. He was immediately put to the test. First of all, Elizabeth, his mother died, and then John Angell James became completely incapacitated by severe illness which greatly increased Dale's work-load.

In November 1854 Dale was ordained, 50 ministers being present! A few weeks after his ordination, on 21 February 1855, he married Elizabeth Dowling introducing a second important woman into his life by the name of Elizabeth. He lost the first Elizabeth, his mother, in 1854 and gained the second the following year. The wedding day was wintry and Dale had to ride through snow for several miles. Theirs was a good and enduring marriage. Elizabeth gave him faithful support, carried on much of the burden of family correspondence, and became involved in the work of the church.

The Death of John Angell James and the Call to the Carr's Lane Pulpit

When John Angell James died it only took a few days for the church to give unqualified support to call R. W. Dale to become their sole pastor. He had already spent six years there as Assistant Preacher and Co-Pastor.

Not only did Dale enjoy the support of the church membership, but also of the Board of Deacons. He described these old, conservative men as *"inconceivably grave men; men grave beyond the dreams of this generation."*

Dale was keen on expansion and outreach. A new chapel was erected at Edgbaston and other "colonies" were established at Moseley, Yardly and Acock's Green. Up to 200 members were taken from the mother church to establish these new centres, among them being some of the finest workers in the congregation. Dale was concerned for the children but he had no gift for preaching to them. His thoughts were not simple enough for them. Later, Dale discovered for himself that his thoughts were not easily understood by the majority of his adult members either! Someone had suggested that Carr's Lane congregation would never stand for doctrinal preaching, to which Dale responded, *"They will have to stand it!"*

At age thirty he experience a complete nervous collapse. From June to August he got completely away from Birmingham, traveling to the English Lakes at Rydal, Patterdale, and to the remote solitude of the Shetland Isles. By September he was recovered enough to return to his duties in Birmingham.

Dale set out to break down the prejudice *"that a minister existed for a limited number of Church members and pew-holders and not for the whole population of a city."* He began his work by taking a close, first-hand look at the business and industrial life in Birmingham. He studied factory, shop and office—all the facts pertaining to work and wages. Sometimes he knew more about a business than the proprietor himself! His interests then advanced to the wider issue of politics. He once said in lectures on preaching that he believed that the *"day would come when those who refused to vote would be subjected to church discipline as well as people who refused to pay their debts."* He believed that of all secular affairs, politics was the most godly because those who became involved do not seek their own personal benefit but the public good, the betterment of the community. Not all would agree with this lofty view of politicians today!

Charles Silvester Horne declared in an article he wrote on the life and career of R. W. Dale:

> *"England has never had a more perfect example of a man of whom it could be said that, every practical activity rooted itself in a spiritual principle."*

Storms, Battles, Causes, Struggles and Controversies

Dale was a man of massive and masculine intellect. Horne wrote that,

"It was never his way to evade discussion and controversy. He had a soldier's instinct for the storm-centre, and the happy warrior's joy in battle."

He never feared theology nor theological controversy.

"He had no sympathy with a tame and weak surrender where great truths were at stake, simply because, as is sometimes argued, good and pious people differ, and therefore it is best to leave the subject alone. He was drawn by sheer intellectual and spiritual interest to the discussion of the biggest and most momentous problems of life and religion, and believed that the Church of Christ in England would suffer irreparable loss if she did not face the problems of theology with as firm and inflexible an intellectual courage as the leaders of science or philosophy have dedicated to the problems on which they have spent their strength."

Along with the controversies and causes in which he became engaged, Dale continued to suffer periods of depression. In 1861, fears, depression, and haunting terror returned. He feared that he was losing his intellectual powers and his doctrines were becoming uncertain in his mind. All of this remained a private matter. Dale, like John Henry Jowett, kept no diary up until he was 60 years of age.

In the controversy over the publication of *Essays and Reviews*, Dale raised the fresh objection over this publication being sponsored by State revenue. This then led to a larger controversy in 1862 over the Bicentenary Celebration of the historical event when 2,000 ministers of the Church of England were driven from their churches and parishes. Dale became nationally recognized as a skillful and eloquent controversialist.

About this time, Thomas Binney visited Australia (in 1868-69) and strongly supported Dale coming there to pastor the Congregational Church in St. Kilda, Melbourne. That church issued a call for him to come to strengthen Congregationalism in Australia and in order for him to become involved in the Melbourne community. They also wanted him to become the President of a new college. Later in life, in 1887, at age 57, R. W. Dale did go to Australia for the Jubilee of Congregationalism in that land. At first Dale turned down the invitation, but in the end, at the insistence of a Mr. Richard Searle of Adelaide, he went. His sermons and lectures were well received and afterwards he returned to Birmingham the following year in 1888.

Like all tender-hearted pastors in similar situations, Dale struggled over his inability to adequately visit his people. He asked the church for an assistant who would be responsible only to him. He offered to provide 50 pounds per annum for this need but 100 pounds would have to be raised elsewhere, but these good intentions never came to fruition.

On 11 May 1864 he preached his great message, *"The Living God, Saviour of All Men"* to the Directors of the London Missionary Society at Surrey Chapel. He preached for two hours—far too long! They say that he followed the dangerous precedent set by John Angell James some years previously when James preached to the same group. James broke off from preaching after one hour from sheer exhaustion. He sat down to rest for a few minutes and while they sang a hymn people tossed oranges up onto the platform for James to eat and refresh himself. Afterwards he got up and *"thundered on for another hour."* (*Life of John Angell James*, pg. 144)

Dale sensed the solitariness of ministerial life and its injurious effect on spiritual health which inclined him to *"regard religion merely as a study and to deprive it of all liveliness."* His antidote was to propose an annual retreat for a limited number of ministers to get away for a week of spiritual refreshing following a set schedule. The plan never fully materialized although a modified scheme of having a day's meeting at regular intervals was instituted.

In 1865 Robert and Elizabeth's daughter, Alice, died of scarlet fever at age 6. Dale was 35 at that time. He grieved for Alice over many years but carried on his work. *"It is better to walk in the path of duty,"* he wrote, *"though with trembling steps, than to lie down on the earth and moan."*

In 1869 he was elected to the Chairmanship of the Congregational Union at age 39, making him possibly the youngest ever to occupy that office. Some claimed later that J. H. Jowett was the youngest.

When 1870 arrived R. W. Dale helped to lead the Nonconformist opposition to the Forster Education Bill. He came more widely known through this endeavour as a representative of a rising generation within the Free Church. Prominent politicians and party leaders recognized him. Dale fought hard for universal education and spoke against the Forster Act for its contempt of religious equality. Dale held to the principle,

> *"that in any system of national education secular instruction alone should be provided by the state and that the care of religious instruction should be remitted to parents and churches."*

He felt that in the 1870 Act, state recognition of denominationalism and essential Liberalism had been betrayed and the principle of religious equality dishonoured. In leading the revolt against Forster and Gladstone it did more than anything else to produce the reaction which brought Disraeli to power in 1874.

With respect to the question of a union being formed of the Roman, Greek and Anglican Churches, Dale felt it would be a calamity rather than a blessing. He wrote:

> *"…the irrepressible impulses of the Christian heart are not destined to be satisfied by the creation of a visible, spiritual empire whose power would be fatal to the freedom and energy of the intellectual and moral life of mankind."*

J. K. Mozley described the issue which finally brought to a close Dale's influence in the political arena.

> *"He was in favour of a measure of Home Rule for Ireland; But when Mr. Gladstone's policy took the form of excluding from Westminster the Irish members, Dale was unable to approve. Such a sentiment seemed to him to be 'hostile to constitutional freedom and perilous to the integrity of the Empire.' He took the side of Chamberlain and supported him at the general meeting in Birmingham, when in his speech to the Liberal 2,000, Chamberlain put his political fortunes to the severest test and came out triumphant. In a letter to The Times, which won the thanks of Mr. Gladstone, and in correspondence with Dr. Walsh, the Roman Catholic Bishop of Dublin, Dale strove for such a policy as might win general Liberal assent. But great as his influence was, the situation was too involved, the currents of opinion in political circles too perplexing and unstable, for anyone who*

was not himself in the House of Commons to rally opinion to one particular solution of the Irish question. So, after the hustled drama of the years 1885-86, with their two General Elections and the rending of the Liberal Party, Dale felt that his political activity had come to an end. He was a political exile, who could find his footing in no camp. Yet, if it had been a period of fruitless effort and disappointment, Dale might have found consolation, had he been the kind of man to seek it in himself, in the recognition that he had spoken words of permanent political value when he said, at a time when Mr. Gladstone's Irish policy was wrapt in obscurity, 'I hope the country will never give a blank cheque to any statesman.'"

"After one of the meetings of the Birmingham School Board, Canon O'Sullivan, the Roman Catholic Vicar General of the Diocese of Birmingham, with whom Dale was on terms of friendly acquaintance, remarked somewhat sharply to him, 'Dale, when do you mean to quit politics and look after your soul?' And this was the substance of Dale's answer: 'I have given my soul to Christ to look after; He can do it better than I can; my duty is to do His will, and to leave the rest with Him.'"

R. W. Dale loved the city of Birmingham. From 1870 to 1880 he was responsible with others for the great constructive work which covered Birmingham with Board Schools. He, along with Bright, made Birmingham the Mecca of the Liberation movement. From 1872 to 1878 Dale was the Editor of the *Congregationalist*.

Dwight L. Moody and Ira D. Sankey in the U.K.

In 1874 Dwight L. Moody and the singer, Ira D. Sankey, came to the U. K. and Dale was very slow to accept their methods. In 1875 the evangelists came to Birmingham and Dale was still very hesitant to endorse their ministry. To his credit, not only did he support their efforts, but to the surprise of many who thought they knew him well, after a few days, all his former hesitancy toward the Americans vanished. Dale was frankly amazed at what he witnessed. He told Moody that the work was obviously of God but he could see no relation between Moody and what he had done. To this Moody laughed and replied that he would be sorry if it were any other way!

Dale's impressions of the Moody and Sankey meetings were deep and lasting. He became convinced that the evangelists were agents of an invisible power mightier than themselves. One hundred and twenty converts were added to Carr's Lane alone as a result of the meetings. Dale publicly endorsed the American visitors. The one danger he saw was the insistence upon instant conversion whereas in England a gradual transition to faith was regarded as the norm. From this experience Dale himself was encouraged to take on evangelistic mission work, but after a few trials at Stratford-on-Avon, Manchester and Norwich, he concluded that he was not spiritually gifted for this type of work.

J. K. Mozley reported:

> *"He himself was no revivalist preacher; he recognized that his powers lay in building up the spiritual life of a congregation rather than converting the outsider. Nor were the methods which we are inclined to associate with revivals such as were naturally congenial to him; exuberant emotion expression was always foreign to his nature. But he had no doubt that the root of the matter was present in the preaching of the American evangelists, and he was far too generous and large-hearted not to bear witness to that fact. So, when the Archbishop of Canterbury, Dr. Tait, put out a statement unfavourable to Anglican cooperation in the mission, Dale took the field with a pamphlet of strong defence of the missioners on points where he believed them to have been misunderstood, if not misrepresented, and of more trenchant criticism than an Archbishop of Canterbury often has to endure."*

R. W. Dale's Reaction to the Deeper Life Movement

The 1875-76 movement for the deepening of the spiritual life did not receive Dale's support. He was not present in any of the meetings in Brighton, Oxford, or elsewhere. However, from written accounts of what was preached, he was repelled by what he regarded as unsound and uncritical use of the Scriptures, passion for allegory by which the plain sense of Scripture was distorted, and the incessant use of luscious and sensuous imagery derived from the language of human passion. He rejected outright the doctrine of 'sinless perfection' and the teaching on 'entire sanctification' he found to be not as objectionable but still unsatisfactory. However, he refused to join in an unqualified censure of the movement and its leaders. He felt that the movement had prophets but no teachers, and that they lacked an adequate conception of moral obedience and of the necessity of knowledge. He still felt, nevertheless, that these people did render the church a service by stressing sanctification through the power of the Spirit.

The Famous 1877 Yale Lecture Series on Preaching

In 1877 Dale was invited to Yale University in America to deliver the Lyman Beecher Lectures on preaching. Beginning in September he spent about one month visiting various Canadian and U.S. cities. He began his nine lecture series on October 11th and said that they were a pleasure for him to present rather than a task. These lectures were considered to be of permanent value as were the lectures delivered by Phillips Brook on one occasion, primarily because they were viewed as self-revealing.

Part of the self-revelation in this lecture series was the demonstration of R. W. Dale's humour, wisdom, and wit, both in what he said in terms of original expression and also in those quotations he passed along from others.

In his opening lecture he cautioned students to take their time in building up their theology in private and to not perplex their people with speculations.

> *"There is no need for being in a hurry. Do not be afraid that someone will get out a patent before you."*

He urged them to make sure they knew something before speaking publicly.

> *"We believe and therefore speak."* The problem today is that, *"We disbelieve and therefore speak!"*

Dale said that *"dullness was not necessary to the dignity of the pulpit"* and that it was very rare *"that a preacher need be afraid of being too brilliant."*

He said that Moody used the characters of the Bible as if he knew them personally and spoke of situations and places as though he had been there. He made the patriarchs as though *"they were born in Chicago."*

He advised that one must exercise great care when preaching in pulpits where people were used to humourless dullness.

"But if imagination, fancy, irony, and sarcasm make my brother to offend, I will become a fool for Christ's sake, and will be dull while the world standeth!"

Dale contended that either you read books with a purpose in view, with a problem to resolve, or else *"you end up like a racing of some little dog about the moor, snuffing everything and catching nothing!"*
"Work without prayer is atheism; and prayer without work is presumption," he counseled.

He quoted Rousseau, who said that when writing a love letter *"you should begin without knowing what you are going to say, and end without knowing what you have said."* He then added, *"but that is a bad way to write sermons."*

In a gentle jibe regarding married life, he cited the case of Joseph Alleine who died in Taunton Gaol. When he got married he received a letter of congratulations from an old college friend who wanted to follow Joseph's example, but he was wary. He asked Joseph regarding the *"inconveniences of a married life."* Joseph Alleine replied:

"Thou wouldst know the inconveniences of a wife and I will tell thee. First of all, whereas thou risest constantly at four in the morning, or before, she will keep thee till six; secondly, whereas thou usest to study fourteen hours in the day, she will bring thee to eight or nine; thirdly, whereas thou art wont to forbear one meal at least in the day for thy studies, she will bring thee to thy meat. If these are not mischief enough to affright thee, I know not what thou art."

Dale told the students to make sure that they said what they truly meant to say. *"Dr. Duncan—Rabbi Duncan—after listening to a sermon, declared that 'the idea of the preacher was in the sentence after the last.'"*

On the subject of mutual respect between the pastor and his people he said:

"There is a certain measure of respect due from the people to their pastor; you are most likely to receive it if you do not claim it; you

will never receive it at all if you forget that there is a certain measure of respect due from the pastor to the people."

Concerning the careful and labourious process of research and reading, classified as "professional studies" he said,

"You must be willing to accumulate a large amount of learning of which you can make no display in the pulpit and to carry on long and labourious processes of thought which will make no show in your sermons."

As to public prayers, he informed them that,

"Prayers are not works of art; they are great spiritual acts."

And regarding hymnology, he quoted an anonymous writer: *"Let me write the songs of a nation, and I do not care who makes the laws."* Dale added, *"Let me write the hymns and the music of the Church and I care very little who writes the theology."*

"Very much mischief might be averted if, in the selection of the organist and the choir master, Churches remembered that the spirit of the man who has charge of the music is at least as important as his musical skill. If your anxiety is to appoint a very fine player, the chances are that when you have appointed him his only anxiety will be to show you how finely he can play; and if in appointing a choir master you think of nothing except his musical taste and his skill in selecting and conducting a choir, you have no right to be surprised if he justifies your appointment by thinking of nothing but his choir and the artistic excellence of their singing."

Of note is the fact that the Chair which was established for this lectureship was in honour of Dr. Lyman Beecher, an eminent Congregationalist of a previous generation. Yale University asked R. W. Dale to help them find a successor to himself in this Chair. Unsuccessfully Dr. Dale urged both Alexander McLaren and Charles H. Spurgeon to accept it. Spurgeon replied in his typical style: *"I sit on my own gate, and whistle my own tunes, and am quite content."*

Unorthodox Views

As stated before, from Dale's earliest days of preaching and ministry, he was accused of heretical tendencies and his unorthodox views were not confined to only one or two points which might be charitably regarded as incidental or insignificant.

Dr. Guinness Rogers reported:

> *"As a student he went to the foundations of every subject he touched, and examined it on every side, and carefully as his opinions were formed, he would on the slightest provocation revise them again. Needless to say, he was an independent thinker, and on some points, reached conclusions in which he met but little sympathy from those most attached to him."*

Dale came to believe that man is not by nature immortal and consequently the souls of the impenitent were annihilated upon death, and only the souls of those who were in union with Christ were recipients of eternal life.

In his very first sermon preached in 1845 he asserted the doctrine of universal redemption for all mankind. When he delivered lectures on the Epistle to the Romans, he did conform to the usual Calvinist interpretation of St. Paul, causing some offense to certain of his congregation. He rejected the belief that Adam transmitted a morally evil nature, and went the next step of declaring that the death of Christ might atone for the sins of even those who had never known Him. One old fellow student friend remarked in a letter to Dale regarding Romans chapter five and of Dale's treatment of that text, *"I wish that Paul had never written that chapter, it has greatly disturbed your position at Carr's Lane."* Fortunately, this pessimistic evaluation of Dale's relationship to his congregation did not last long.

J. K. Mozley reported that in Dale's book that he authored in 1884, entitled, *A Manual of Congregational Principles,*

> *"Dale expounded a doctrine of the sacraments which led in some quarters to the complaint that he was teaching sacerdotalism and 'rank Romanism.' Dale's doctrine was certainly not that of the Roman Catholic Church or of Anglo-Catholic theology, and he appealed to the teaching of older Congregationalists in his defense.*

What is true is that Dale emphasized the importance of the sacramental side of Christianity in a way foreign to those Evangelicals whom Dale himself distinguished from the original Puritans. He taught that,

> *'the material elements are only symbols; but the rite itself is an act. And the act of Christ when He places these elements in our hands is a spiritual reality. It represents a real transfer of power.'*

So Dale, with his doctrine of an effective, not merely symbolic, act in the Sacrament, seems to anticipate in a remarkable way the teaching given by Canon Quick in his book The Christian Sacraments, which is far the most important modern American treatise devoted to the subject. The bread of the sacrament was for Dale, after consecration, the symbol of the Lord's broken body, but through the symbol there was the gift of eternal life. Thus the sacrament was not to be resolved into a mere memory of a past event stimulating pious feelings: there was in it all the reality of an objective, divine gift. In this emphasis Dale was at one with the attitude of High Churchmen, and here, as at other points in connection with the Church and the sacraments, his teaching sounds a note that was afterwards to be powerfully echoed, though in no such formal way as the word 'echo' suggests, by a great Congregationalist theologian whose outstanding ability, while still a young man, Dale was to recognize—Dr. P. T. Forsyth."

Begging to Differ with Fellow Evangelicals

Dale must be given full marks for his courage in challenging many beliefs and practices within evangelicalism which had flimsy foundations in Biblical truth, or none at all. He saw clearly the interaction between what was going on in the body with what was going on in the soul, for example. He failed to see why rising at an extremely early hour in the morning was a particularly superior spiritual practice.

"To make early rising, for its own sake, one of the cardinal virtues, has always seemed to me utterly preposterous. Why should we not wait, as Charles Lamb puts it, till the world is 'aired' before we venture out? If a man can do more work in the day when he lies till half past seven, than when he gets up at half past five, if he is better tempered at breakfast-time, if his mind is fresher and his heart kindlier,

for the rest of the day, it passes my comprehension why he should turn out at the earlier hour. Some people think he ought; and I have honestly tried to discover some intelligible explanation of what seems to me this singular article of faith, but I cannot."
(From his sermon, *The Discipline of the Body,* published in 1867)

Dale conceded that the interaction between the body and the soul was a mystery, but nevertheless a fact. He claimed that he would like to have the diaries of great saints who recorded their spiritual experiences and have them illustrated with notes by wise physicians who had known them intimately.

"Periods of spiritual desertion, when 'the light of God's countenance was hidden from them, apparently without any reason, might receive a very instructive explanation."

Dale did not ascribe all highs and lows of the spiritual life to physical causes but he went on to comment:

"It is, however, equally certain that body and soul, flesh and spirit, are so strangely blended, that the lights and shadows which chase each other across our interior life, do not all come from the upper heavens. By honouring the laws of our physical nature, some of us might come to live a more equable spiritual life."

The Tender-hearted Philosopher Deals Kindly with the Aged

Dale was as thoroughly practical as he was philosophical. While able to skip upon the mountains with brilliant insight into complex philosophical issues, he was at the same time able to reach down to the dark valleys of the frailties of man with tender expression and charitable understanding. Perhaps one of the most outstanding examples of this, was his sermon on *"The Kindly Treatment of Other Men's Imperfections"* published in 1867. He gives classic counsel regarding how to treat with kindliness and tolerance the aged among us. We are to excuse them as they sink into feebleness, even as their natures yield to selfishness, suspicion and meannesses. We must remember how the old man was, and forget how he is now.

"Treat him reverently, as you would the ruins of a cathedral. Here and there, though the walls are shattered and the arches broken, you may see the fragments of massive columns; and even the exquisite tracery (decorative patterns with branching and crossing lines, as in the upper parts of many church windows), *where it has been sheltered from wind and rain, has not altogether disappeared. You believe that although the temple is destroyed, Christ will 'raise it again' in more than its former stateliness and splendour. 'Walk by faith' and by memory, and 'not by sight.' Believe that the abounding and fruitful life you saw last summer and autumn will reappear when the spring returns, and in the 'winter' of his 'discontent' let the old man be still honoured and loved."*

What tender and sensitive musings!

A Fault Acknowledged: Better Late Than Never

We owe to R. W. Dale's son, A. W. W. Dale, the account of his father's self-evaluation of the effectiveness of his preaching after almost a lifetime in ministry. Even though as far back as 1860 correspondence reveals that Dale had some self-doubts, it was near the close of 1888 that Dale went to the little Welsh village of Llanbedr, about eight miles from Barmouth. There, Dale had established a second home off the beaten track—a little cottage which he had rented and furnished—where he could spend hours in quiet meditation and thought. On this occasion he reviewed both the spirit and the method of his own preaching and he concluded that for the future, preaching would become his chief, and perhaps, sole work. Dale was 58 at the time.

"His failure to reach men and to move them as he desired weighed upon him; and with unflinching self-scrutiny he set himself to discover how a fuller success might yet be won."

Some of the following record was penned over a period of months.

A man by the name of Mr. Mander was partially responsible for prodding Dale to examine the effectiveness of his own preaching. In one letter he pointed out what he felt to be defects in Dale's preaching:

"In my own estimation, he (Dale) always ranked higher as a teacher than as a preacher of the truth. If I read a sermon which I had previously heard him preach, it always proved superior to what was expected. The delivery had too little variety of tone, and as too impassioned, as a rule, and until his later years, was destitute of pathos."

Dale had an aptitude for *"massive intellectual and ethical arguments."* Horne records that Dale possessed—

"granite commonsense—the foundation of every fabric of philosophy or theology that we owe to him...he insisted on the proven facts, all the facts, so that scientific observation, analysis and coordination of actual experiences might lead up to sound theory and rational belief."

He served up strong meat at Carr's Lane and sometimes it was hard work to follow his preaching! As noted earlier, though he was concerned for children, he had no gift to preach to them because his thoughts were not simple enough. This inability to communicate with children should be a warning signal to any preacher who may also be having difficulty in communicating with adults but does not know it!

Now we return to the little cottage in the Welsh village of Llanbedr in 1888. In the midst of the "massiveness" of his intellectual exploration and analysis of great philosophical and theological issues—in the midst of the thoroughness of his argumentation and stateliness of his preaching style—somehow he was sacrificing making contact with his audience whom he intended to bless. In the plying of his craft he had lost sight of the people and of how best to reach them and effect change in their actual conduct. Though he had voiced these fears years before, this time at Llanbedr the reality of the situation caused him genuine grief which gave birth to a determination to change old patterns.

"I have been thinking much and with much concern about my preaching. It has a fatal defect. It is wanting in an element which is indispensable to real success. I do not think that I should state the exact truth if I said that I was not anxious for the conversion and perfection of individual men, and cared only for setting forth the

truth. But I fear that the truth occupies too large a place in my thought, and that I have been too much occupied with the instrument—the Divine instrument—for effecting the ends of the ministry, too little with the actual persons to be restored to God. This comes from a moral and spiritual condition which involves serious guilt. God forgive me! It is even now possible through the Divine grace for this sin to disappear. It lies deep. The particular result of it which I have marked is but one of its evil effects. I have again and again attempted to discover how to do my work more effectively—have honestly tried to make everything contribute to the usefulness of my preaching; but the central evil has remained: it is a want of conformity to the mind of Christ, a hardness of heart which must be subdued and melted by the grace and truth of God, if the few remaining years of my ministry—few at the most—are to have a different character from those which have gone before."

"To what extent have I failed for another reason—not recognizing in thought the discontent, the yearning for an unknown God, the reaching towards Christ, of many who are not decidedly Christians?"

"I felt rather strongly towards the close of last year that in one respect among others, my ministry—especially of late years—had been gravely defective. I have striven to press home upon men and to illustrate the very central contents of the Christian Gospel; but I have not recognized practically the obligation to use in preaching all those secondary powers which contribute to create and sustain intellectual and emotional interest in preaching. The more strenuous intellectual effort, in order to make truth clear and to put it strongly, has not been neglected; but there has not been the legitimate use, either in the choice of subjects or their treatment, of those elements which are of a rhetorical character, and which raise the audience into a condition which is perhaps friendly to the reception of Christian truth. I have a dread of aiming at the 'popular' method of treatment, arising from a dread of aiming at 'popularity'; but the two aims are wholly distinct, and it has been a fault not to aim at the first. I have set myself to remedy this during the present year, and hope, with God's help to succeed."

"I fear that I have not secured sufficient variety of subject for the various intellectual, ethical, and religious conditions of the congregation; and during my recent absence from home, I drew up a tentative scheme of topics which I will try to work. It covers a month.

(1) *Morning: Spiritual, Experimental, Higher truth*
    Evening: Ethical
(2) *Morning: Ethical, Elementary Evangelistic*
    Evening: Elementary Experimental
(3) *Morning: Expository, Historical, Ecclesiastical*
    Evening: Doctrinal, Evangelistic
(4) *Morning: Doctrinal*
    Evening: Evangelistic

"These conclusions are in part the result of meditation suggested by a conversation at the Church Fellowship conference just before I left home. Mr. Mander read a paper on what could be done to contribute to the strength and efficiency of our church life. He began with the pulpit, and the conversation was very much arrested at the fist part of his paper. It was urged by several that my preaching moved at a height—intellectual and spiritual—far above that of the congregation generally. The prayers, too, were also too far removed from the actual experience of the people. Hardly any of those present are able to be present at the evening service, and the criticism—which was as kindly as it was frank—was truer of the morning than of the evening services. There was specially a request for more ethical preaching, and a curious, half-suppressed antagonism to Paul. It was a very interesting talk. Notwithstanding the kindness of the dominant element of criticism—that sermons have an intellectual, literary, and spiritual quality which commands the sympathy and gratitude of the best and most cultivated, an opinion which it would not be easy to justify to the extent to which it was urged—it pained me a great deal at the time, and kept me awake for many hours. But I ought not to have felt the pain, and I hope to profit from the criticism. The conclusion I reached while away from home was that it was more accurate in its appreciation of defects than it seemed to me at the time, though the positive suggestions for improvement seemed, and still seem to me, wanting in discernment."

"Is it too early to record the hope that God has given to me a new element of power in my preaching? The word which has been often used to denote what critics regarded as the excellence of my preaching and speaking really suggested the qualities in which both have been defective, and the preaching more than the speaking—'stateliness.' That is not the characteristic of effective preaching; and it suggests a

whole set of intellectual, ethical, and spiritual elements which account for failure. I think that in the sermons of the last two Sundays, the 'stateliness' has disappeared, and that there has been more of brotherly access—intellectual, and, if I may put it, rhetorical access—to the people. The intellectual quality has not, I think, been inferior to what I have usually reached, but on the whole, higher; but the 'stateliness' has gone. In preparation I aimed at more freedom, and in preaching, God gave it me. But I trust that there was something far more central than a mere rhetorical change. Yesterday was the first Sunday after the issue of the scheme for prayer in the letter prefixed to the Church Manual. I believe that throughout the services there was a new presence of the power of God. May it continue!"

It may seem strange to the reader that in his famous Yale lecture series on preaching eleven years earlier in 1877, Dale stated, *"I have tried to hit hardest at the evils which have lessened the power of my own ministry."* In 1888, he was still struggling with those 'evils' in a little rented cottage in Llanbedr, Wales!

Preparation for Preaching

Dale believed, that *"since we have to preach, we ought to learn how to preach well."* Dale's 1877 Yale lecture series reveals much about his own method of sermon preparation and the general focus of his subject matter. In this section we shall take excerpts from Dr. Dale's lectures which reveal his own convictions and practices in the preparation of sermons.

Quoting Nathaniel Culverwel, he said that he always reverenced *"a grey-headed truth."* He did not seek to be novel but rather to travel *"a well-beaten track."*

Regarding the study of subjects which by nature he did not like or value, he advised, *"A study which repels you is invaluable."*

He tried to resolve theological issues in private to his own satisfaction so as not to attempt to use preaching as a means of clearing his own head. He first made sure of his position and then preached the truth as he best understood it.

Dale quoted Alexander Vinet: *"Preaching is an action"* which was meant to *do* something. It is meant to make truth clearer, to challenge to action, to persuade men toward moral behaviour and not merely to expound upon some text the preacher fancies.

Dale held that some men who had been brilliant in university failed as preachers through sheer indolence. If a preacher desired to be permanently effective he must form and maintain habits of regular and strenuous intellectual activity.

He had a reputation for detail and thoroughness.

> *"Every subject on which we intend to speak should be in our complete possession as a whole and not merely in its various parts...get hold of all the points of a truth at once, at one time, so we become familiar with the relationship between the successive points." Preaching must be logical...test the strength of every link in your reasoning."*

Before attempting to devise the plan of the sermon, Dale insisted that all the research on the subject matter be completed first. He argued against arranging the material until one actually had all the material in hand to arrange. The alternative was to draw up a plan before one's research was done, and then afterwards, when fresh material was discovered, it had to be forced into the introduction, which would make for a very lengthy introduction, or it simply could not be fitted into any place else! Dale maintained that a great part of the preparation must be completed before anything is put down on paper.

He gave much attention to reading and he always read with a pencil in his hand. He read in various languages—Hebrew, Greek, German, French and English—and tried to read books written by authors of all religious denominations on the subject of preaching—*no matter how dull!* He said that every one will *"remind you of some fault that you are committing habitually or of some element of power which you have failed to use."*

He studied the sermons of successful preachers. He said that an artist will not be satisfied to read scientific treatises on his subject but rather he must go to the galleries of Florence and Rome to see how the great masters produced their work. Whereupon Dale recommended a long list of preachers whose sermons should be studied:

> *"Bossuet, Bourdaloue, Massillon, Lacordaire, Ravignan, Monod, Bersier, Latimer, Jeremy Taylor, Barrow, South, Tillotson, Howe, Owen, Watts, Chalmers, Edward Irving, Guthrie, Robert Hall, Dr. McLaren of Manchester, Charles Spurgeon, Thomas Binney, James*

Parsons, John Henry Newman, Dr. Pusey, Archdeacon Manning,
Frederick Robertson, Cannon Liddon, Theodore Parker."

Dale also studied the speeches of great secular orators, such as,
Lord Erskine, Charles James Fox, Plunket, Grattan, Lord Brougham,
Mr. Bright.

"Close familiarity with a few great books will do more than anything
else to enrich and discipline your mind."

He believed that one half hour of reading could yield the substance
of three to four sermons. In later years Dale went through books much
more rapidly picking up main points and summarizing the whole,
making plain the gist—rather than ploughing through phrase by
phrase, word by word.

A knowledge of history was important to the preacher and his work.
Dale once saw a title, *A Knowledge of His Own Times Important to a*
Christian Minister. Dale mused,

"A knowledge of other times than his own, important to a Christian
minister. We would be more hopeful now in our task if we knew of
the battles and victories of other times—we need not be 'out of heart'
in our day."

Dale read his Bible regularly with such helps at hand as lexicons,
dictionaries, and a commentary, and recorded *"raw material ideas"* in a
notebook. He also noted down those *"shafts of illuminating ideas"* which
shone forth when he read general and theological books.

As for the subject matter, he urged students to choose those subjects
which touched their people most personally and deeply. *"Choose those*
subjects which touch the great duties, great hopes and fears and sorrows of
human life." And these truths must grip the preacher's heart before
they will grip the hearts of his hearers.

"What poets feel not, when they make
A pleasure in creating,
The world in its turn will not take
Pleasure in contemplating."

To add what Dr. Brooks would call "symmetry" to his preaching, Dale advised choosing about twenty topics to preach on for the year ahead.

In choosing texts,

> *"don't try to display your wonderful ingenuity by drawing things out of texts which were never there in the first instance...like a magician who rubs a coin and produces a canary...We admire conjurers and preachers...but keep them separate!"*

He urged the students to ask, *"What is the sermon to do?"* The answer to that question will determine the whole method of preparation. He must see in the distance the object toward which we are aiming, otherwise we waste time. Archbishop Whately once criticized a preacher's effort by saying, *"He aimed at nothing, and hit it!"*

> *"The preparation burden will be greatly lightened if we know what the object is we want to gain—that, in itself, will suggest what we are to say. For example, if the object in view is to prove a Christian doctrine, then we must line up the arguments. If it is to explain a truth which is not commonly clear, then we ought to ponder on some of our own people in the congregation who are least likely to understand that truth and figure out what must be said to explain it to* <u>them</u> *as if in private. Or, if some practical end is in view, we must first instruct their conscience regarding duty or giving up sin and then proceed to warn and challenge them. In short, once we know the object toward which the sermon aims, then we must ask ourselves, 'How can we project this truth into the very depths of the thought and life of the congregation so they will never lose it...how can we constrain them to discharge the duty.'"*

He counseled that we must not be afraid of being too simple and that we should speak as though the people knew nothing of the subject. A judge of the Supreme Court once told Finney, *"Ministers do not exercise good sense in addressing the people. They are afraid of repetition."* We would preach "more effectively if instead of taxing our intellectual resources to say a great many things in the same sermon, we tried to say a very few things in a great many ways."

In the earlier part of Dale's ministry he was taken up with theology and theological speculation, but later he became more aware of the needs and perils of his people and consequently, *"Christian morality began to assert its claim to an equal place."* Dale saw that it was necessary to emphasize Christian conduct as well as Christian Truth. We stress again—Dale had to learn to care more about men than about learning and literature.

In his sermon entitled *The Work of the Christian Ministry in a Period of Theological Decay and Reconstruction,* preached on 23 June 1880, to students of Airedale College, Yorkshire, he said:

> *"...the condition of the people who listen to us should help shape our own conception of our work...the large majority of our listeners should affect us most. Don't preach sermons on Buddhism to people of North Yorkshire. We must preach to the people who are present to hear us."*

Dale contended that the preacher must keep his *"fancy fresh"* and his *"imagination active."* He does not rely upon sermon illustrations to serve as *"windows"* to illuminate the truth he expounds.

> *"The very way in which the preacher expresses his thoughts casts light upon the topic. This freshness of expression requires vivid imagination."*
>
> *"If your imagination is vigorous, you will so use these words as to restore to the worn coin the sharpness of the original impression, and to the canvas, the brilliance and the richness of the original colouring. The difference between vivid and languid speaking depends very largely upon the extent to which the imagination contributes in this way to the expression of thought."*

Dale felt that imagination was much more akin to emotion than to logical understanding. We need to move men toward the grasp of truth which they presently know only by the intellect. In order to nurture originality Dale counseled students to *"look at God, Heaven and Hell— through your own eyes."*

Near the close of the sermon preparation process, Dale would test the strength of his ripening sermon with several questions:

Does it contain an adequate amount of positive Christian truth?

Is it likely to secure the ends for which it is prepared?

Is it likely to be monotonous?

Is it interesting?

Does it say what I meant it to say?

Dale argued for freedom, variety and flexibility in the form in which the sermon was preached. He felt it was not always necessary to announce the premise in advance nor the outline one intended to follow. He thought that in some cases this practice actually aroused antagonism toward the sermon and unnecessarily erected intellectual and emotional hurdles which might be difficult to surmount.

Dale cited Joseph Parker's practice which was to delay the design of the introduction to a sermon until he had decided how the sermon will end. Quoting Pacal, Parker said,

> *"The last thing a man finds out when he is writing a book is how to begin."* He went on, *"The style and size of the porch ought to bear some proportion to the style and size of the house."*

An introduction should be as brief as possible—best to spend more time in the application of the text—and that the preacher ought *"to get to work as soon as possible!"* *"On occasion when the text is announced first, the introduction should spring quite directly and naturally from it."*

Dale pointed out that the application of the truth was extremely important to Parker. It is *"a great and fatal mistake to leave the sermon to apply itself to the hearts of men."* The flip side to that coin is that it is also a mistake to turn the entire sermon into one prolonged application following the oft-repeated practice of Finney. Henry Ward Beecher described Jonathan Edwards' preaching in this way:

> *"In the elaborate doctrinal part...he was only getting his guns into position, but in the application, he opened fire on the enemy!"*

Dale added that *"many take so much time getting into position, they never fire off a shot!"*

Manner of Delivery

As previously noted, Dale's preaching was not marked by dramatic emotion. Dale had a disdain for sensational preaching which was always straining for excitement. He referred to it as *"melodramatic and hysterical"* preaching. He refrained from the use of dramatic powers and impassioned rhetoric. He claimed that it may produce an effect upon the emotions which may be mistaken for penitence, adoration or faith.

> *"But if the effect which we produce is not produced by the clearness and energy and earnestness with which we illustrate the very truth of God, we shall save neither ourselves nor them that hear us...Most generally the men who are tempted to preach in this style are mere charlatans."*

Having said all of that it is only fair and honest to note that when he evaluated his own preaching in retrospect in Wales in 1888 he did express regret that he had not used a more popular manner of preaching so as to move his audiences to ethical behaviour and action.

On 27 July 1879, Dale preached to the Methodist Conference conducted in Carr's Lane. It was his great sermon on *"The Evangelical Revival"* in which he appears to have some second thoughts about emotional expression:

> *"We independents—we ministers, I mean—are still a quiet people, not easily excited. We are reserved. We shrink from eccentricities. We are rather ashamed when we are mastered by emotion. We want to serve God 'with the spirit' but we are especially anxious to serve Him 'with the understanding also.' Our people are the same. They come to church to be taught, not thrilled—not to be excited or soothed or charmed by the eloquence of the preacher."*

Though Dale did not strive to be dramatic, he did try to be interesting. Quoting Emerson, he said,

> *"Eloquence must be attractive...It is the virtue of books to be readable and of orators to be interesting."*

In fact, Dale contended that the preacher should be so interesting that it would take effort on the part of the hearer to think of anything else!

George Dawson once said to Dale,

"When I speak, I make up my mind that the people shall listen to me; if they don't listen, it doesn't matter what you say."

Dale cited the example of the rare power of rhetoric and exposition in the presentation of the budget by Gladstone. He explained the budget for three straight hours and the audience hung on every word! Dale claimed that the root of this power lay in *"honest intellectual habits."*

Regarding the debate as to the virtues, or otherwise, of extemporaneous speech vs. reading a complete manuscript, Dale's general practice was to preach from a carefully prepared outline; the opening passages were most complete; they then diminished in completeness...sentences would represent paragraphs and words would represent sentences, the conclusion being the latter. If it were a very special occasion then he would write a complete manuscript and read it, *"shifting the little sheets from left to right as he proceeded,"* noted Dr. Guinness Rogers.

Quoting M. Coquerel, extemporaneous preaching was defined in this way: the preacher—

"...knows what he is going to say, but does not know how he will say it."

Hooker warned that the disadvantage of extemporaneous sermons is that they *"spend their life in their birth, and may have public audience but once."* *"Manuscripts, on the other hand, may be repeated even to the same congregation seven to eight years later because of the great changes that take place in the composition, age and maturity of the people."*

John Angell James, Dale's predecessor at Carr's Lane, said,

"If I preach without reading (the manuscript) I shall be miserable for three weeks—miserable until I am in the pulpit; if I read, I shall be quite happy till I begin to preach, though I shall be miserable till I finish!"

Dr. Guinness Rogers reported that sometimes Dale would break away from a carefully prepared manuscript into unpremeditated speech, which was a dangerous habit, *"for sometimes he swamped the effect of his careful meditation with a sudden torrent of eloquence, the rushing splendour of which was remembered long after the rest of the discourse had been forgotten."*

Perhaps the jury is still out regarding Dr. Guinness' judgment of Dale's *"dangerous habit"* if the unpremeditated portion of the sermon was the part that stuck in the hearts of his hearers!

Later Years: Achievements and Accolades

So great was Dale's influence in Birmingham that when Mr. Chamberlain was first returned as the parliamentary representative of the borough, a London newspaper proclaimed that the new member had been returned as *"the representative of Mr. Dale."* When Chamberlain got wind of this he graciously responded, *"If that be so, there is not a member of the House of Commons who will have a better, wiser or nobler constituency."* (From J. H. Jowett, M.A., D.D.: *A Character Study by Frank Morison*)

"An unworldly man of the world," was Dr. Rogers' description of Dr. R. W. Dale. He knew and understood the world and its tendencies, but *"I never met a man more free from the taint of its spirit."* There was in Dale a rare and unique *"union of the saintly temperament with the practical judgment."* A marked characteristic of the man was his thoroughness.

> *"This gave immense power to his oratory whether in the pulpit or on the platform...He gave, and rightly gave, an impression of whole-hearted sincerity."*
>
> *"He was incapable of intrigue or of playing with great principles, and what he did, he did with both hands earnestly."*

J. K. Mozley wrote:

> *"He had many of the gifts which bring success in secular pursuits: readiness of speech, practical sagacity, a definiteness of outlook and purpose which did not fall away into the cantankerousness of mere self-will. His temper was that of the statesman who tries for the best possible, not of the extremist who will have nothing but the best (as he sees it) whether it be possible or not. Dale, indeed, was one of those who shows how great and noble a thing the Christian character can*

be in all human pursuits, how a man who is really a Christian is thereby made more of a man, not less."

Dale was referred to as *"the noblest Roman of them all."* Charles Silvester Horne contended that Dale was the *"one who did more than any other teacher and leader of my generation to shape the ideals and determine the life work of the younger ministers."*

At age 39 R. W. Dale refused an invitation to succeed Thomas Binney at Weigh House Chapel, London. Binney resigned in 1869 after forty years of ministry in that pulpit. In 1869 Dale was elected Chairman of the Congregational Union and in 1871 he preached the Congregational Sermon.

R. W. Dale's considerable giftedness and involvement in the life of the city and of the nation led to his being recognized by the University of Glasgow when it conferred on him the Degree of Doctor of Laws in 1883. It was reported that the Americans were offended because Dale would not use the D.D. degree bestowed on him by Yale University.

In 1884 his youngest daughter, Claire, died of lung disease at the age of 18. He himself was severely ill at that period and for some time afterwards.

In 1885 he was made a member of the Royal Commission on the working of the Elementary Education Acts. In 1877 he ministered in Australia and upon his return to England he declined the invitation to take the Chair of Theology at New College, London, in a letter to the Rev. Dr. Kennedy written on 24 March 1888. His observations and impressions gained while visiting both the United States in 1877 and Australia in 1887 were published in 1878 and 1889 respectively under the titles *Impressions of America* and *Impressions of Australia*, and give rare insights into the society and culture of those two countries in the latter half of the 19th century. Both publications make for fascinating reading.

In 1889 they moved Spring Hill College from Birmingham to Oxford, reconstituting it as Mansfield College. Though Mozley reported that Dale had at first been unconvinced of the wisdom of this venture, in the end he accepted the post of Chairman of the Council and was invited to preach the first sermon in the College Chapel. In 1891 he was nominated President of the International Council of Congregational Churches.

Homegoing

> *"In the early months of 1895,"* wrote J. K. Mozley, *"the weakness of the heart from which he was suffering increased, and on the 13th of March the earthly end came. On his study table was found a sheet of an unfinished sermon. What was written was characteristic of his mind and teaching. Unworldliness, he was saying, was not a rigid observance of external rules, but a spirit and temper revealing a settled purpose to do God's will always, a spirit created, among other things, by the power of the great hope, the full assurance of the richer life to come. It was the spirit in which he passed into that higher world where his heart had long been at home."*

It is somewhat amazing, compared with today's standards, that John Angell James and Robert William Dale occupied the Carr's Lane pulpit for a combined total of almost ninety years! James began in May of 1806 and Dale died in March of 1895. It is staggering to think that one church had only two pastors throughout most of the 19th century.

When John Henry Jowett succeeded Dale at Carr's Lane, he testified that the experience of following Dale in the pulpit saved him from becoming merely a "pretty preacher." The sheer pressure of the high tone and standard of Dale's ministry was one of the primary motivating forces which propelled Jowett to attain the high standard of preaching power which he so ably demonstrated at Carr's Lane and elsewhere.

Chapter Eight

Henry Parry Liddon

20 August 1829–9 September 1890

Sir Edward Parry's Godchild

Henry Parry Liddon's father, Matthew, had been an officer in the Royal Navy and had the distinction of serving under the command of Sir Edward Parry at the time they were attempting to discover the Northwest Passage. Upon his retirement from the navy, Matthew married Ann Bilke who subsequently gave birth to their eldest son, Henry, at North Stoneham, near Bishopstoke, on 20 August 1829. Henry was baptized the following month on the 26th of September, and one of his godfathers, the above mentioned Sir Edward Parry, bestowed his name upon the child.

Young Henry enjoyed a thorough-going evangelical upbringing. In 1832, when Henry was but three years old, the family moved to Cloyton. He was sent off to boarding school at Lyme Regis in 1839. During those years at school he played no games, engaged in no sports except swimming, but collected coins, read military history, wrote dramas and acted them out, and wrote sermons which he sent home to his maiden aunt.

In 1844, Henry entered King's College, London, boarding with Assistant Masters. He was of a consistent, serious disposition even from his early teenage years. He was described as *"sweet, grave, thoughtful and complete."* Frederic Harrison described him at age 17 as being *"entirely a Priest among boys."* Who would ever expect that this tender lad would develop into the courageous apologist for the Christian faith that he became?

Christ Church College, Oxford

Matthew Liddon showed some of his son's youthful sermon manuscripts to Dr. Barnes, the Canon of Christ Church, and Henry was
thereupon offered a Studentship at Christ Church in October of 1846.
Henry was still only 17 which made him at least one year younger than
his peers. This Studentship status was to stay intact for the remaining
44 years of his life which made it possible for him to spend time at
Christ Church on an annual basis.

At Christ Church he played no sports but cultivated a taste for good
music. His one and only athletic triumph was the rescue of Historian
H. N. Oxenham from drowning during a "Reading Party" in Wales!

A Frail Vessel

Even at this early stage in life Liddon's biographers describe how
fragile his health was. Throughout his youth his physical frame was
described as *"spare"*, but on balance, his appearance overall was somewhat striking. He had a face of almost faultless beauty, olive-toned
skin, straight jet-black hair, and piercing eyes. Some surmised that he
was either half-French or half-Italian because of his swarthy complexion. Later in life he became rather portly, his hair turned white but his
eyebrows remained black. George W. E. Russell said that his physical
attractiveness ended with his face when he became an adult. He had
neither figure nor carriage. *"His height was not proportioned to his width."*
His bearing was not impressive.

Liddon suffered from disabling, violent headaches and rheumatism.
The pain in his head would become so sharp and intense that it made
him quite deaf. The act of preaching exhausted him. Pusey rebuked
him for his long-winded preaching when he wrote,

> *"You preach sermons an hour long at St. Paul's and nobody hears*
> *you, and you are knocked up for a fortnight afterwards. You have*
> *done nothing."*

After preaching at St. Paul's Cathedral in the morning he could do
little else for the rest of the day, except read the Lessons at the great
evening service. Preaching, for Liddon, has been described by one
observer, as an act of self-sacrifice.

On 16 June 1881, when Liddon was not quite 52 years of age, he wrote,

> "...you give me credit for unlimited resources both of mind and body, whereas I am in reality a poor creature who has soon got to the end of his tether and ought to make way for younger men who have not lost their energy and freshness."

In spite of his constant ill health, he had an excellent appetite and ate heartily, which of course contributed to his portly figure in later years. He also enjoyed a glass of wine. His work routine started in the very early portion of the day.

As he entered upon his later years he suffered much from insomnia and would go for walks late at night. Many believe that Liddon died prematurely at age 61 because of a great mistake in judgment when he took upon himself the mammoth, all-consuming task of writing up the biography of Dr. Pusey. Principal Johnston said,

> "...beyond any other cause it led to his early death." Russell's judgment was that "the assumption of this gigantic labour was Liddon's great mistake."

Liddon's Private Life and Personality

Liddon remained a bachelor all his days. His sister, Mrs. Ambrose, lived with him at # 3 Amen Court for the entire time he was Canon at St. Paul's Cathedral. He loved children and animals, especially cats, but never got on to familiar terms with horses! His niece said that as soon as he arrived on a visit to her home, he would send for the parrot to sit in his room to keep him company. He would also attempt to bribe the dog to do the same.

Though frail in health he still possessed a vivacious personality. He was sensitive, alert, and appeared "surcharged with moral electricity, which tingled and flashed and sometimes scorched." (G. W. E. Russell.)

It is said that cheerfulness was a part of Liddon's religion. He enjoyed social occasions and was always in good trim feeling quite at home in the presence of company. His humour, described as "effervescing and not always restrained," would often spark uproarious laughter. In fact, some found his jokes a "sore trial." One who knew him well said that his two main enjoyments in life were conversation and landscape. He was distinctly musical and poked fun at those for whom music was only *"a scientific form of noise."* He approved of the use of classical music in the services of the Church and especially favoured Bach's Passion music.

Liddon loved architecture, painting, poetry, and did considerable reading in German literature and in Eastern religions, particularly Buddhism. He had several personal friends among German scholars which led him to travel to their homeland often. While he always kept himself abreast of the latest developments in scientific thought, at the same time he was familiar with Greek and Latin classics.

He was possessed of a strong personality and vehemently attached to his own personal views. How he was perceived in this regard was evidenced when the See of London became vacant with the death of Bishop Jackson. Many urged the Right Honourable W. E. Gladstone to appoint Liddon to this Bishopric. On 9 January 1885 Gladstone wrote to the Archbishop of Canterbury concerning Liddon:

> *"He has been nearly the first to associate a great thinking force with the masteries of a first-rate preacher…May he not perhaps be called the first champion of belief?"*

But the Archbishop replied, saying that he feared lest some day Liddon would—

> *"find some uncompromising protest dearer than the love of unity."*

And the Archbishop was not far off in his assessment, whether or not we agree with his seeming concern for unity over against the value of defending the truth. When Bishop Tait promoted the abandonment of the Athanasian Creed, Liddon regarded this as an attempt to remove the landmarks of the faith and threatened to withdraw altogether from the Church of England if any changes were made in the Creed. Liddon spoke out strongly to defend the Creed in a sermon dated 20 October 1872. The battle raged on for several months and in the end Liddon triumphed!

Liddon's strong character was again manifested when at Easter of 1859 he was eased out of being Vice Principal of Cuddesdon Diocesan Training College for the Clergy. His views on the subjects of the

Eucharist and the Confession were at variance with his Bishop, plus Episcopalians and Puritans alike put pressure on the Bishop to oust him.

With the dissolving of Parliament in 1868 and the resultant departure from office of Disraeli, Gladstone came in and made what Liddon regarded as some disastrous appointments. He appointed Dr. Tait, Bishop of London, to the Primacy, and Dr. Jackson, Bishop of Lincoln, to the See of London. Liddon could not restrain himself from speaking out against these appointments.

After Liddon's Bampton Lectures in 1866, he traveled for two months in Russia. Later in life, when he resigned his professorship in 1882 in order to write Dr. Pusey's biography, he again traveled to Russia as well as to Palestine and Egypt.

Appointments and Ordination

Vehement attempts were made to convert Liddon to Roman Catholicism when he was granted an audience with Pope Pius IX in Rome in September of 1852. After all, Liddon was a staunch disciple of Anglo-Catholic sacramental theology and practice. But on 19 December of that same year he was ordained Deacon in the Cathedral Church of Christ, Oxford, by the hands of Bishop Samuel Wilberforce.

Soon after, in January of 1853, Liddon became Curate to Rev. W. J. Butler at Wantage. Even at this early stage he preached, *"very long, very eloquent, very impassioned sermons."* Dr. Pusey strongly urged him to abandon his manuscript in favour of extemporaneous oratory.

His Vicar wrote:

> *"Nothing could exceed the beauty of his language, or the majesty of his thought. Strange, however, to say, his preaching was not popular among the Wantage folks. He had formed his style at that time much on the French or foreign model, and he used action and manner which our old-fashioned Berkshire parishioners could not appreciate."*

Liddon's lack of robust health began to bother him at Wantage.

On 18 December 1853 he was ordained a Priest by the Bishop of Oxford. In October of 1854 he became Vice-Principal of Cuddeston Diocesan Training College for Clergy, but as reported above, he was eased out of that position by Easter of 1859 because of the conflict between him and his Bishop over the subjects of the Eucharist and Confession. Liddon wrote of this setback: *"It was the only great disappointment of my life."*

The first sermon ever published by Liddon was preached at St. Giles Church, Oxford, on the occasion of Lent 1858. It was entitled, *The Repentance of Ahab.*

In 1859 he was appointed Vice-Principal of St. Edmund Hall, Oxford, but due to ill health he was obliged to resign this post in 1862. However, Dr. Pusey advised him to stay on at Oxford at Christ Church College, to defend the faith against the attacks mounted against sound doctrine through the publication of *"Essays and Reviews"* and by the *"aberrations of Dr. Colenso."*

In 1863 Liddon was appointed Examining Chaplain to Dr. Hamilton, Bishop of Salisbury. Dr. Hamilton then appointed him to a "Prebendal stall" at Salisbury. In effect, this prebend, or, small regular payment for ministerial services, provided Liddon with a modest income.

Bampton Lecturer and New Champion of the Oxford Movement

In 1866 Henry Parry Liddon delivered his famous Bampton Lectures on the subject of *The Divinity of our Lord and Saviour Jesus Christ.* It was a lecture series of eight magnificent sermons preached before the University of Oxford. In the last will and testament of the Rev. John Bampton, Canon of Salisbury, Bampton bequeathed not only lands and estates to the university but also made provision for eight lectures to be presented annually *"at St. Mary's in Oxford, between the commencement of the last month in Lent Term, and the end of the third week in Act Term."* (Quoting from Brampton's will) The purpose of Liddon's lectures was to take note of those assaults upon the doctrine of the divinity of Christ and to present the Biblical argument in defense of the doctrine. Liddon had already gained a great reputation as a preacher in both London and Oxford.

The Rev. Aug. B. Donaldson wrote,

> *"The Oxford Movement at this time seemed specially to demand a great orator who should proclaim the long-forgotten truths of the Catholic faith, with a persuasive eloquence that was the fruit of clear conviction and the outcome of a character trained in deep spirituality."*

The Oxford Movement had fallen on hard times before Liddon had come upon the scene. Officially this movement had begun on 14 July 1833, when Mr. John Keble, the most distinguished Fellow of Oriel College, preached a sermon before His Majesty's Judges of Assize at St. Mary's, the Oxford University Church. The sermon was later published under the title, *"National Apostasy."* It was a ringing call to churchmen to realize the immediate danger in which the English Church stood, and to rally to her aid. King William IV was in the middle of his reign. Liddon was just about to turn four years old the following month after the preaching of this sermon!

The dangers to the Church were many. They were first of all, political in character. The Church had long been associated with the Tory Party, but now the people were turning away from the Tories in droves because the Tories were opposed to change. The popular support shifted to the Whigs who had allied themselves with Dissenters and the emancipated Roman Catholics. The Church of England was never more unpopular and there were even acts of violence against her Bishops. The most immediate and direct cause for the birth of the Oxford Movement was the cutting by half of the Irish Sees. To many, the Oxford Movement appeared to be an attempt to bolster up the waning power of the Tories and to support the continuation of the vital link between the Church and State.

Then, there was the revival of Erastianism inspired by the 17th Century writings of Englishmen Selden and Hobbs who contended that neither the Church nor the Bible was the final authority in religious belief, but the State.

The influence of theological and philosophical liberals from Germany and France crossed the Channel convincing the English that rational intelligence, education and civilization would cure all the evils and sorrows in society. It called for more education, enlightenment and reason and tended to destroy the basis of Biblically revealed religion.

But the gravest danger to the Church was from within. There was basic ignorance of the principles for which the Church stood. Clergymen had gradually forgotten their calling. Their chief employment was to win an appropriate life, and Bishops were lax in their examination of ordinands. An earlier indication of the low ebb to which the Church had sunk at the beginning of the 19th Century, was that on Easter Sunday of the year 1800, only six persons attended St. Paul's Cathedral for Communion.

The Oxford Movement attempted to prevent a swing back to Roman Catholicism. It was a reaction to the teachings of *"Broad Churchmen"* who had held sway at Oriel College from 1800—such men as Archbishop Whately, Dr. Arnold and Bishop Hampden. Arnold had proposed to solve all church problems by linking the Church of England with all forms of dissent and forming a policy of undenominationalism which would be a break from historic Christianity as the Oxford Movement leaders would view it. The Oxford Movement took an opposite tact:

> *"...to put before men the old idea of the Catholic Church with its divine origin and its ministry reaching back through the Apostles to the Lord and to make men see in it no mere State Establishment, but a visible Society, founded by the Lord Himself, with tremendous powers and supernatural claims."*

They began to preach again the forgotten doctrine of the Holy Catholic Church.

Ten days after Keble's sermon was preached, four men met at Hadleigh in Suffolk, from July 25th to 29th, to lay down the outline of a practical scheme to promote their cause. They represented all the old universities: Dublin, Oxford and Cambridge. They eventually designed an Address to the Archbishop, signed by 7,000 clergymen and a Lay Address from 230,000 heads of families in 1834.

These four men were:

Rev. Hugh James Rose, Rector of Hadleigh (a Cambridge man). He had preached on the Movement's principles for seven years at Cambridge before the Movement was born.

Rev. William Palmer, a Dublin graduate, who had settled at Oxford.

Rev. the Honourable Arthur Philip Perceval, Rector of East Horsley, Surrey, and a Royal Chaplain; an Oriel man who had been a Fellow of All Souls.

Rev. Richard Hurrell Froude, Fellow of Oriel, the only Oxford leader.

They published the famous Oxford Tracts and those who followed their teachings became known as Tractarians. The tracts began to be published in 1833 and were sold for one pence each. They promoted Apostolic Succession for Bishops. Dr. Pusey joined in publishing tracts by writing Tract # 18 on the subject of *"Fastings"* in 1834. His involvement added a new level of respectability to the Movement. Later, in 1835, he published three more tracts, numbers 67, 68 and 69. The Movement became associated with his name. Followers of the Oxford Movement then became known as *"Puseyites."* By that same year of 1835 the Movement became a power abroad through the spiritual power of the preaching of Newman, vicar of St. Mary's, the University Church at Oxford. In 1836 Evangelicals allied themselves with the Tractarians to protest the appointment of Dr. Hampden to the Regis Professorship of Divinity. Hampden had thrown doubts on the Creeds and their authority. (Interesting side note: Evangelicals were also known as *"the Peculiars"* in that era!)

Dean Church had described the leaders of the Oxford Movement as *"the salt of their generation."*

However, by the time that Liddon arrived upon the Oxford scene, the salt had begun to lose its savour. The Movement had suffered great setbacks with the loss of some of its leaders. It seemed to many that Henry Parry Liddon was destined to *"carry the Movement forward into the forefront and centre of English life."* Liddon was indeed inspired by the holy, earnest lives of the Tractarian leaders and was especially an admirer of Dr. Pusey.

In his renowned sermon on *The Bones of Elisha,* he likened the bones to the sacred past including the teachings and personalities of the Apostolic age and subsequent faithful spiritual leaders throughout Church history. He said:

> *"If a Church is stricken with the languor of death, it must be quick-ened in the old ways—by contact, new and earnest contact, under the guidance of the Spirit, with the sacred past...The real sense of Scripture, the majesty and pathos of the Apostolic Age, the great teachers later on, who ruled the thought of the undivided Church—Augustine, Jerome, Chrysostom, Athanasius—those who tower so high above the diminished stature of any in our impoverished and divided Christendom—these were for such a Church, the bones of Elisha!"*

The Bampton Lectures of 1866 trumpeted the entrance of a new champion upon the field of battle. Donaldson wrote:

> *"It was felt throughout England that these lectures, delivered with so much force and fire, had translated into splendid oratory the literature of the Tractarian Movement, which aimed first and foremost at presenting once more before men the true living Christ...There was a holy vigour and sanguine enthusiasm pulsating through all the lectures, and men felt that a great and gifted champion of the Catholic faith had been given by God to His Church."*

A surprising and interesting footnote to this story is that Liddon had to take on this lectureship on short notice on account of the illness of the Rev. A. W. Haddan.

During this era, students at Oxford, ordinarily impatient with sermons, thronged to hear Liddon preach at St. Mary's, many being content to find only standing room for upwards of an hour. Liddon was generally depressed by the changes that had taken place at Oxford over the years. He was unhappy with the abolition of religious tests and the consequent admission of non-churchmen to Fellowships and Tutorships. Oxford had become a *"chaos of disintegrated convictions."* It had changed into *"a place of purely secular instruction,"* Liddon said, *"which might have been founded last week by a company of shareholders."*

Liddon's subsequent appointment to the Canonry of St. Paul's was regarded as a great step forward for the Tractarians, as their cause would be supported *"by an orator who was a professor and a theologian of the highest calibre, with rare gifts of nature, trained with conscientious industry, and consecrated to the service of God."*

Canon of St. Paul's Cathedral

On 27 April 1870, Liddon was installed Canon of St. Paul's Cathedral in London, and on May 1st he preached his first sermon there. He was elected to the Dean Ireland Professorship of Exegesis at Oxford on June 11th. On June 22nd he received the honourary degree, D.C.L., and in November of that same year, 1870, he was honoured with a D.D.

The acoustics of the Cathedral were such that Liddon found it difficult to control his voice to suit the strange environment, and to concentrate his mind upon the content and order of his sermons in extemporaneous preaching at the same time. This led him to revert back to using a manuscript throughout the rest of his ministry. His manuscripts were comprised of small sheets strung together at the top corner. George Russell commented that he had never seen a preacher handle a manuscript so well.

People flocked to hear Liddon preach at the Cathedral. Many would arrange their summer vacation in August to come to London to sit under his ministry.

Twenty years prior to Liddon's arrival at St. Paul's, Charles Kingsley described conditions at the Cathedral—conditions which persisted up until 1870.

> *"The afternoon service was proceeding. The organ droned sadly in its iron cage to a few musical amateurs. Some nursery maids and foreign sailors stared about within the spiked felon's dock which shut off the body of the Cathedral, and tried in vain to hear what was going on inside the choir. The scanty Service rattled within the vast building, like a dried kernel too small for its shell. The place breathed imbecility and unreality, and sleepy life-in-death, while the whole 19th century went roaring on its way outside. And as Lancelot thought of old St. Paul's, the morning star and focal beacon of England through centuries and dynasties, from Augustine and Mellitus, up to those Paul's Cross sermons whose thunders shook thrones, and to Wren's noble masterpiece of art, he asked, 'Whither all this?' Coleridge's dictum that a cathedral is a petrified religion, may be taken in more meanings than one. When will life return to this Cathedral system?"*

The installation of Liddon in St. Paul's pulpit marked a turn-around in the life of the Cathedral. In spite of the fact that he ministered in London contemporaneously with both Parker and Spurgeon throughout his entire twenty years tenure at the Cathedral, some regarded Liddon as *"the greatest English preacher in his day."*

Lord Acton wrote on 14 January 1885,

> *"Assuredly, Liddon is the greatest power in the conflict with sin and in turning the souls of men to God, that the nation now possesses. He is also among all the clergy the man best known to numbers of Londoners."*

The Dean of St. Paul's on 8 January 1885, referred to Liddon as the Church of England's *"greatest preacher,"* her *"most learned theologian"* and *"one of the most brilliant intellects and most attractive characters among her clergy."* Within the confines of the Church of England, and not taking into account the great nonconformist preachers of that day, this judgment was probably quite accurate.

Liddon's Preaching

Liddon was regarded as a *"born preacher."* The excellencies of his preaching are legion, and, studied point-by-point, form a worthwhile refresher course on homiletics. He had a magnificent voice and his usual *"sweet"* tone could change to a sterner and even scathing sound. Often he would begin a statement with an almost imperious note, *"Depend upon it, my brethren..."*

On the subject of his voice, Paget wrote,

> *"...that matchless voice which to those who listened seemed like an intrinsic part of his witness to the beauty, the glory, the supremacy of the truth that came by Jesus Christ."*

Perhaps, on balance, we should mention the main defect of his discourses by admitting that he generally preached too long, even though his audiences were reportedly riveted in their seats throughout his sermons in spite of their length. He preached for one hour and forty minutes on occasion and usually never less than an hour and a quarter. However, George W. E. Russell once testified:

> *"...the large audience has preserved such silence, and displayed such fixity of attention, as to recall the triumphs of the opera rather than of the pulpit...Whereas an ordinary preacher finds it difficult to gain a hearing even for a quarter of an hour, Mr. Liddon has riveted the attention of his audience for more than an hour and a half."*

He once preached an hour and forty minutes on the subject of prayer and Russell remarked,

> *"...he set forth the result of such reading and thought as would equip an ordinary preacher for a year of pulpit eloquence."*

Rev. August B. Donaldson reported that when Liddon preached his lengthy discourses his audience scarcely knew where the time went they were so attentive.

> *"The Dean's verger kept a record, and has stated that the longest was an hour and twenty minutes, the shortest, three quarters of an hour. And yet there were many like Dean Stanley, who once said, 'Liddon took us straight up to heaven, and kept us there an hour.'"*

On Good Friday of the year 1868, Thomas Binney, pastor of The King's Weigh-House Chapel, London, listened to Liddon preach for one hour and twenty minutes, but commented that he *"listened to him with unabated interest."*

Another feature of Liddon's preaching, which some might regard as a defect, was his repeated reference to his sacramentalist views in sermon after sermon. He was always and forever an Anglo-Catholic.

Russell thought that another possible defect of Liddon's sermons was that they were *"better fitted for the eye than for the ear."* What he meant by this was that one never got the full weight and power of Liddon's sermons until one read them in print after they were preached. The sermons were packed with carefully researched content and development of argument, the genius of which one might miss upon a first hearing of them.

A Summary of the Strengths of Liddon's Preaching

(1) Met the real needs of people

Liddon ever addressed the practical, plain duties of life. Practice, conduct and character were never out of sight when he preached.

In a Preface to a book of Liddon's sermons published in 1907, entitled *Sermons at St. Paul's and Elsewhere*, Dr. Francis Paget, Bishop of Oxford, wrote the following story:

> *"In these few pages I will only try to tell what seems to me to have been a very deep and fruitful element in the power of his preaching. He himself told it unconsciously, I think, in some words which he spoke to me about thirty years ago. He had appointed me to preach on a Sunday evening in St. Paul's, and across the door of the cab as*

*I was coming away after the service, he made his only comment on
the sermon. 'Goodnight,' he said, in the quiet, penetrating voice
which his friends can never forget, 'Goodnight. I dare say you will
come in time to know what people really need.'"*

Paget went on to write that Liddon's eagerness to meet the real
needs of people—

*"kept him unexcited by his own eloquence and unharmed by other's
admiration...His vast learning, his strong logic, his sense of lucid
order, his sustained grasp of a conception, his brilliant faculty of
expression, all went straight and worked hard to advance his single
intention of giving 'what people really needed'...His mind and heart
were always pastoral."*

(2) Charged with Enthusiastic Vitality

A writer in the *Saturday Review*, 24 August 1889 edition, reported that
Liddon's whole argument was steeped in emotion. He summed it up
very well with the short statement, *"The light is never dry."*

Russell described him on one occasion: *"He was alive all through
vivid, vivacious, sensitive, alert."* Another writer said his preaching was
marked by an *"almost fierce intensity of feeling"* and with *"strength and
vitality of character."*

It is little wonder that Liddon was so exhausted and drained of emotion after he preached, especially when such intensity of emotion was
maintained at a high pitch for over an hour on each occasion.

(3) Development of Irrefutable Argument

Dr. Benson, who later became Archbishop of Canterbury, wrote of
Liddon's preaching in 26 July 1876:

*"I have been hearing Liddon at St. Paul's. Very beautiful and very
eloquent, yet the art part of it does not seem so unattainable. But he
unites many charms. His beautiful look and penetrating voice are
powerful over one, and then his reasoning is very persuasive. He
does not make leaps, and dismiss one with allusions, or assume that
one knows anything. He tells it all from beginning to end and seems*

to assume nothing. But all his physical and intellectual structure is quite swallowed up in spiritual earnestness, and he is different to other preachers, in that one feels that his preaching in itself is a self-sacrifice to him—not a vanity nor a gain..."

Another referred to his *"lucidity"* saying that Liddon saw things accurately and clearly and that if the hearer would attend to what Liddon was saying, he too would see accurately and clearly. He was methodical and logical in his reasoning, step-by-step. He had the power to lead a large audience carefully through the course of a careful argument, and hold their attention throughout. After hearing Liddon preach one always felt that he had been carefully taught. To his credit his oratory never rose to vague, non-sensical rhetoric. It was clear and inclusive. Russell commented that his *"vigourous flow of rhetoric had been disturbed by no bursts of vague eloquence."*

Russell answers his own question:

"And what is the secret of the preacher's success? In the first place, he has something to say. Instead of clap-trap sentiment, or vague declamation, he gives the results of long study and careful thought...each sermon sums up the reading and the thought of years...Liddon is a reasoner as well as a scholar...He knows not only what to say but how to say it. In the power of clear, vivid and strong statement, he has no rival among English preachers."

George W. E. Russell summed it up this way:

"It was Liddon's special strength that in an age which deifies Nebulosity, and mistakes vagueness for depth, he based all that he taught and all that he practiced on the dogmatic foundation of the Atoning Sacrifice, offered once for all by Incarnate God."

(4) Genuine Humility

There is practically no reference to himself in any of his sermons, not even any personal testimonies. The closest he seems to come to such is when he gave the story of a little boy being sent off to boarding school for the first time, in a sermon entitled *"The First Five Minutes After Death"* preached at St. Paul's. Undoubtedly he drew upon his own childhood experience and memories to describe the feelings of the boy in the story.

Dr. Francis Paget, Bishop of London, said,

> *"I doubt that any great and popular preacher of recent times has talked or thought less about himself."*

(5) Relating Scripture to Modern Times

In a notebook stored in the Library of Keble College, Dr. Bright wrote:

> *"One of the signal excellences of Liddon's preaching was his power of vitalizing Scripture events, and bringing them into close relation with the present."*
>
> *"There surely never was a preacher who, in dealing with the past, had his eye more thoroughly and practically open to the present, who felt more intensely the 'solidarity' between human nature in modern England and human nature in the days before the Incarnation. What made Liddon so vitalizing a preacher? What but his supreme devotion to a Christ alive for evermore."*

(6) Respect for his Audience

In a lengthy article printed in the *Guardian* on 24 July 1889, listing several of the points of excellence in Liddon's preaching, the journalist wrote,

> *"It is not often that one whose gifts are so rare and brilliant…can refrain so steadily from any sign of conscious superiority in their exercise."*

The article stated that Liddon had a sincere and unfailing respect for those to whom he preached.

(7) Scholarly Without Being Boring

This same *Guardian* article commented, that in the preaching of Liddon, there was *"the wielding of learning without pedantry."*

Along a similar vein, Dr. Paget wrote:

"Whatever he might say about modern Oxford, he was deeply and unalterably an Oxford man, in culture, in affection, in habit of mind; yet the most loyal Londoner under the dome of St. Paul's never doubted that he and the preacher understood one another. Since tastes differ, 'academic' may be a term either of praise or of blame; but in neither direction would any one have used it to describe Dr. Liddon's preaching."

Liddon was ever a theologian and a scholar and all his sermons bear these trademarks, but his preaching would never be perceived nor described as being pedantic, boring, or academic.

(8) Preached With a Definite Aim

In most of his sermons there was a *"hook"*—either he sought to convert the unconverted or to reel in the nominal Christian to a place of correct practical, moral action or behaviour.

Dr. Paget quoted Bishop Dupanloup on this point:

"Bishop Dupanloup, in speaking of those who preach without any definite aim or expectation, compares them to a man whom he had watched fishing, in the most unpromising part of the river, and who met the advice that he should try elsewhere with the answer that he was only fishing to amuse himself."

Liddon never preached merely to amuse himself, to fill in a pleasant hour on a Sunday morning! He preached with an aim in view, with a specific purpose. Often he would signal his application by saying, *"Now the lesson we learn from this is…"*

Rev. Darwell Stone summed up his opinion of Liddon's preaching in an attempt to explain why it was people literally lined up to hear Liddon preach: (1) his skill as an orator (2) his strong conviction and fierce intensity of feeling, and (3) he spoke of the unseen, the eternal.

An aside: Liddon always wore his clerical garb, even on holidays, perchance he met with an opportunity to minister.

Liddon's Influence Over Educated Young Men

In addition to his preaching, Liddon's second great work was his individual influence over educated young men. Rev. W. M. Whitley, M.A. said,

> *"His work was to staff the Church of England with men of spiritual life, earnest in the salvation of souls."*

He added, that Liddon was *"a great preacher, a stern defender of his faith, and a prophet to young men."*

Mission Work and Social Action

Liddon was very zealous in his support of mission work at home and abroad. He also favoured social action with the qualifying comment:

> *"These are not the Gospel, but they are, and may be, its handmaids."*

In later years he did not value preaching in various pulpits throughout the country to congregations of which he knew virtually nothing, as much as holding forth from one pulpit charge. Later still he refused to preach outside of St. Paul's due to the exhaustion which the act of preaching exacted upon his frail constitution.

Writing Pusey's Biography: *"Liddon's Great Mistake"*

In 1882 Liddon resigned from the Dean Ireland Professorship of Exegesis at Oxford and from preaching before the University, in order to give himself to the writing of Dr. Pusey's biography in four volumes. Many of his colleagues believe that this was a grave mistake which actually led to his premature death. It was also at this time that he undertook his travels to Russia, Palestine and Egypt.

John Octavius Johnston said that the task of writing Pusey's biography should have been given to someone else to do. Liddon was too exact and detailed in his approach and it turned the work into an overwhelming burden. The work kept him from more important labours for which he was especially gifted. In the end the sheer drudgery wore him down.

In 1886 he was made Chancellor of St. Paul's. The publication of *Lux Mundi* was a great grief to him and he spoke out against it in the form of delivering a series of lectures on the religion of the Incarnation. The article on the Atonement by Arthur Lyttleton rejected the substitutionary death of Christ.

Early Death

On Tuesday, 9 September 1890, Henry Parry Liddon passed into the Presence of his Lord at age 61. The Church lost one of her most brilliant and ardent champions of the faith. Liddon House on South Audley Street, London, was founded in his memory with the purpose of assisting the education of Anglican Churchmen.

Chapter Nine

Joseph Parker

9 April 1830–28 November 1902

Hailed as the greatest pulpit orator in his generation, the complexity of Joseph Parker's personality was as difficult to define as was the structure of his sermons. Those who have attempted to account for the paradoxical qualities of his character have been equally unsuccessful in explaining the genius of his preaching power.

Joseph was born in the ancient town of Hexham on the river Tyne in Northumbria on April 9th, 1830. His father, Teesdale Parker, was the illegitimate child of a wild, irresponsible, roving, Irish labourer, who ran off on Teesdale's mother, Ann, after she became pregnant and before they were to have been married. Ann was cast off by her respectable family and raised her son alone in abject poverty. Though shamed by moral failure, Ann was described as a deeply religious woman and did her best to raise her son in the faith of Christ. Teesdale became a skilled stone mason. In his earlier years it appeared that he was heading in the same direction as his careless father but in the Providence of God he was soundly converted to Christ in a Methodist meeting. He became a faithful pillar of the chapel and a man of influence in the community. In due course he left Methodism and cast his lot with the Independents which was a growing movement at the time.

Some who have attempted to interpret Joseph Parker's life and character report that he suffered from low self-esteem largely due to the shadow that was cast forward across the family by his father's illegitimate birth. This personality flaw manifested itself in various ways. He constantly needed the reassurance of his wife and the supporting encouragement of large audiences. The unanimous observation of his peers, that Joseph was possessed of a massive ego, may well have been accounted for as an over-compensation for feelings of inferiority. Dr.

Robertson Nicoll said of Parker, *"the occasional brusqueness and egotism of his manner was in reality a mask of shyness."* In personality he became fiercely independent and was somewhat aggressive. His voice was rich and powerful and yet it possessed *"a caressing and tender quality."*

Dr. Fosdick once wrote,

> *"The idea that we are made great by our superiorities and ruined by our inferiorities is a dangerous half-truth. Genius is commonly developed in men by some deficiency that stabs them wide awake and becomes as major incentive. Obstacles can be immensely rousing and kindling. Men have their inferiorities to thank for their eminences."*

The circumstances of Teesdale's birth aside, a factor over which neither father nor son had any control, Teesdale became a strong and noble person in Hexham...by Joseph's own reckoning, his father had *"the strength of two men and the will of ten."* His mother was of a softer nature—loving, mystical, spiritual, whose Bible was her daily counselor. Often lay preachers were entertained in their home which exposed young Joseph to many religious discussions.

Parker testified concerning his own spiritual sensitivity when only a child:

> *"From a child it has, if I may say so without being misunderstood, always been natural to pray. I felt after God. I expected Him. I tarried for Him as for One with Whom I had an appointment. I have never lost that feeling of expectancy and nearness."*

It was while on a walk during a summer's Sunday evening, with his father and a *"most intelligent Sunday School teacher,"* that Joseph was gently guided to pray to receive Christ into his heart and life. In his own words, Parker wrote of this life-transforming event:

> *"The whole scene is ever before me. The two men, father and teacher, explained to me what they knew of the power and grace of Christ, and by many loving words they tempted my tongue into its first audible expression of thought and feeling. It was a summer evening, according to the reckoning of the calendar, but according to a higher calendar it was in very deed a Sunday morning, through whose*

white light and emblematic dew and stir of awakening life I saw the
gates of the Kingdom and the face of the King."
(*Great Christians*, edited by R. S. Forman; London, 1934:
section on *Joseph Parker* by Angus Watson.)

In appearance Joseph was described as being short, with a rather
large head, crowned with a mound of dark brown hair. His school-
mates dubbed him *"the champion marble player."* In retrospect he
commented, *"No one could stand before me in the matter of marbles!"*

Through a series of schools and teachers young Parker studied
mathematics, Greek, Latin and his mother tongue. He took particular
delight in mastering the English language. In the study of Caesar,
Ovid, Lucian and Homer, his devoted teacher required his scholars to
paraphrase the writings of these authors, not only to translate them.
Parker excelled so much in his studies that he opened his own school
to teach grammar, algebra, Latin, Greek, and single and double-entry
book-keeping. He then expanded his knowledge by delving into such
subjects as architecture, astronomy, and natural history. Every week he
received expert tutoring in the Greek New Testament. Joseph taught
Sunday School and in his spare time kept his father's accounts. From
his early youth he formed habits of thoroughness and industry which
stuck with him for the rest of his life.

At the age of 14 his formal education was interrupted when his
father determined that young Joseph should succeed him in his trade
but it did not take long for it to become apparent that the lad was better
suited to a different pursuit in life. William Adamson gives an account
of the determining moment in Joseph's life when he renounced all
thoughts and plans for him to become a stone mason.

"One day, it is said, when he descended from the scaffold with an
empty hod, in which he had carried lime up to the builders, he threw
it to the ground with the exclamation, 'God Almighty never
intended Joseph Parker to spend his life in carrying lime and
building houses.'"

Within the year he headed back to school.

At age 18, on a beautiful spring day, Joseph attended an open-air
meeting at Wall, a few miles from Hexham. Suddenly he was *"overpow-*
eringly seized with the idea of preaching a sermon." He stood up on the

sawmill on the village green and preached from the text, *"It shall be more tolerable for Tyre and Sidon in the day of judgment than for you."* He hurled all the thunderbolts of an outraged heaven upon approximately 100 rustic farmers who were assembled there…a group of people whom Parker described *"as inoffensive a congregation as ever ploughed the land and reaped the crops!"* Angus Watson once heard Parker describe this event. Parker said,

> *"My first platform was not a pulpit, but a sawpit. Round me the fields were clothed in the splendor of Spring; the gentle cattle were lowing in the pastures; and all Nature was rejoicing…"*

But Parker added that he would never dare to preach that message now!

After his third sermon, which Parker described as *"an equinoctial gale,"* he had the definite conviction that God had called him to give his life to the Christian ministry.

When he was still in his youth he adopted the practice of tithing and planning his giving. Later on he was able to help other ministers who were in need. He memorized poetry, the sermons of Wesley and Whitefield as well as the election speeches of Fox. Parker joined a group of lay preachers who traveled throughout Tyneside ministering in village chapels and preaching in the open air which was quite in vogue during that period.

First Marriage and First Pastoral Charge

In 1851, while only 21, Joseph Parker met and married Ann Nesbitt of Horsley-on-Tyne, the daughter of a small Tyneside farmer. From all accounts the marriage was a happy one but destined to be shortened by Ann's premature death 12 years later.

On Joseph's 22nd birthday, 9 April 1852, he left Newcastle-upon-Tyne for London, where he joined Dr. John Campbell at the Moorfields Whitefield Tabernacle, a church originally founded by the great George Whitefield. His wife, Ann, was left behind. Dr. Campbell was regarded by Joseph's parents as *"a kind of denominational god."*

At this period of his life his physical appearance is described as,

"...a thick-set country youth, somewhat short in build, with a leonine head, thick brown hair, small, deep-set eyes, which kindled to flame when he was excited; a firm, strong mouth, and aggressive chin, and a voice which had in it the varying music of the winds."

Even then he was regarded as being unusual in his manner. He possessed a high level of maturity and poise beyond his years.

To Parker's pleasant surprise, Dr. Campbell was wanting just such an assistant and urged him to come at once for a trial period of three weeks for which he would be remunerated with three guineas per week. The three-week trial period turned into a nine-month period of ministry with Joseph preaching three times a week. During this period he was obliged to write out all his sermons which then were criticized by Dr. Campbell. Once past this hurdle Parker committed the sermons to memory and recited them in the pulpit.

A decision was taken for him to study philosophy, logic and Greek under Dr. Harcus at London University. Years later he was berated by some for failing to obtain a more formal collegiate training. Undoubtedly his own experience in these matters led him to believe that the standardization of education for Congregational ministers had the end effect of promoting mediocrity and destroying individuality.

Banbury Congregational Church

In 1853, less than a year after taking up his duties under the tutorage of Dr. Campbell in London, Parker received a call from the Banbury Congregational Church which was situated in an agricultural community similar to the one in which he was raised in his boyhood. In this same year Parker was formally ordained to the ministry. His stipend was set at 130 pounds per annum (one account put the figure at 120 pounds) and a house rental of only 6 shillings a week. When he arrived there were only 50 people in the congregation. In short order the building was packed out and another building was erected and opened by the Rev. Dr. R. W. Dale of Birmingham. This building, too, was soon overcrowded.

Watson records an amusing account which Parker wrote about his dress when he arrived in Banbury.

"My clothes did not require many wardrobes for their accommoda-tion. When I asked my draper-deacon how much he would want for a black suit, he said that if I did not object to a certain quality of cloth he could let me have a suit at a very moderate price; whereupon I answered, 'Now remaineth black, shiny, and cheap; but the greatest of these is cheap.' I got the suit—I wore it—I remember it."

Parker continued:

"I was, as may be recollected, twenty-two years of age, very thin, with a large head thickly covered with darkest brown hair, and wearing a collar as high as Mr. Gladstone's, and a white neckerchief that lacked nothing of amplitude nor display; put upon all this a tall, silk hat and you will see what a figure I cut in the early 'fifties.' At this time of life, and in this garb and fashion, I went upon my pastoral journey."

Over his five-year sojourn in Banbury, in addition to the magnetism of his preaching, the noteworthy growth of the church was due to the variety of strategies he employed. It was here in Banbury where he learned the power of the pen and the value of the press. He made extensive use of the local press by publishing one article after another in order to reach out to the wider community. He hazarded life and limb in the face of fierce opposition by preaching in the open air in the local cricket field. He invited preachers of note to come into his pulpit to enrich the spiritual life of his people. Such men included well-known Congregational ministers such as the great Thomas Binney, John Angell James, James Parsons and others.

He also entered into public debate with the then famous leader of the Secularist Party, Mr. George Jacob Holyoake who had been popular for years as a lecturer on atheism. Holyoake posed the question as to why God did not come to the rescue of His servant Stephen when he was being stoned. Parker's reply was memorable, claiming that God performed the greater miracle of giving Stephen a forgiving heart toward his murderers. Later, Jacob Holyoake called Joseph Parker *"the greatest orator of the pulpit in his time."*

Parker preached on Sunday and three times during each week. In those days before compulsory education, Parker took it upon himself to teach young people grammar, Latin and history.

Five years passed by. Shortly after having entered into a building program Parker received a call from another church, a call which he felt difficult to accept when it was first issued.

Cavendish Street Chapel, Manchester

The year was 1858 when the Cavendish Street Chapel approached Parker. It was the most wealthy and influential church in the denomination which posed somewhat of a test of Parker's character. His keen sense of responsibility toward his present charge compelled him to completely overlook the prestige of the congregation which was beckoning him to come. The Banbury church had incurred a debt of 700 pounds, and as Parker put it, *"While the debt remains, I remain."*

The Manchester deputation thereupon returned home and within a 17-day period managed to raise 900 pounds to pay the debt and then reissued a call to the Banbury pastor. Parker' reply was almost a plea for Cavendish Street to withdraw their invitation! At the very least he threw up enough possible obstacles which would have made it easy for Cavendish to have second thoughts.

> *"As a minister I claim the utmost freedom of action...I promise no deference to usages and precedent. What appears to me right I shall do and what appears to me wrong or insufficient I shall unequivocally...reject...I cannot visit for the sake of visiting. At all times I am ready to obey the calls of the sick and the dying, and to guide the truth-seeker; but in continuous rounds of so-called pastoral visitations I do not believe and such I cannot promise."*

Parker found the candidating process to be cold-blooded and annoying.

> *"To my great surprise, I was invited to preach a Sunday or two in Cavendish Street Chapel, Manchester. I never was more coldly received in my life. I was the guest of a millionaire provision-merchant, who never uttered a word of sympathy or appreciation regarding my services. One of the deacons, Mr. Kershaw, M.P., bluntly inquired how long I had been at Banbury, and there our intercourse ceased. Having preached two Sundays, I was told that the Rev. Samuel Martin of Westminster, was unable to preach on*

the following Sunday, as he had promised to do, and I was asked whether in the circumstances I would remain and preach the Sunday School anniversary sermons. I had been extremely annoyed by the want of recognition on the part of the deacons, and I am afraid I showed some sign of resentment, certainly I displayed no particular anxiety to continue a work which had been so completely ignored. Whether any better feeling supervened, I do not at this time remember, suffice it to say that I remained a third Sunday amongst the Congregational millionaires of Cavendish Street Chapel. It was a cold atmosphere. Every man seemed to be looking at me over the top of a money-bag. Some of the people seemed to be paralyzed or stupefied. Altogether the experience was unique and memorable."

In the end Parker accepted the call to Cavendish Street in spite of the inauspicious introduction. Soon the church filled to capacity. His annual stipend was 425 pounds. For eleven years, until 1869, he faithfully ministered the Word in Manchester and left a lasting impression upon the religious life of the British Midlands.

Angus Watson wrote,

"His work at Cavendish Street carried him to the highest pinnacle as a preacher; his reputation became national; his preaching, intensely dramatic, and with a breadth of outlook which was far ahead of his time, set a new standard in the ministry and created a new tradition."

More than one person has commented that Parker's voice was the most powerful and musical they had ever heard.

Within three months of Parker's acceptance of the call, in accordance with the custom of that period, 240 extra sittings were let. The membership increased rapidly. In 1860 alone, 134 new members were received and the membership roll continued to rise afterwards to exceed 1,000, with every seat in the building being let. The Sunday School alone had 1,400 scholars with 84 teachers. He became involved in a large number of humanitarian agencies and other activities which demanded vast resources of energy.

Parker made a comment which every pastor reading these lines will appreciate:

"Add to this voluminous correspondence—perpetual interruptions by persons who have something to say, and others who have nothing to say—...Never an evening at home, except Saturday, and even then people come, and assign as their reason for doing so that they felt sure the minister wouldn't be out. He who sees the minister in the pulpit only knows little or nothing about his work. It is the tear and wear of all kinds of engagements—preaching, classes, committees, and visitations without end—which exhaust every energy of mind and body."

Parker's humourous, courageous and somewhat outrageous personality had a special appeal to young students. Parker was firmly convinced that spiritual preparation for ministry was of superior value to mere intellectual training. In his autobiography, he commented:

"Non-conformity has never been able to dispense with the labours of untrained, irregularly trained, or inadequately trained preachers and pastors. Richard Baxter said, 'I can disgrace no university, for I am of none.'"

Second Marriage

Annie became seriously ill toward the end of 1863 and gradually her life ebbed away. Once she had departed to be with Christ, Parker felt desolate within his home. Adamson remarked that the lion in the pulpit was but a boy under his own rooftree, so very much dependent upon Annie's comfort and encouragement. It is interesting to note that many years later in 1899, after a very happy second marriage—and in the very year that his second wife died, when the Horsely Congregational Church was rebuilt, Parker put in a beautiful stained memorial window in honour of his first wife, which included the following inscription:

"In loving memory of Ann Nesbitt, for twelve years the devoted wife of Joseph Parker, minister of City Temple, London. This window is reverently and gratefully erected by the man whose life she did so much to mould."

While visiting Sunderland on a preaching mission, Joseph Parker was entertained in the home of Mr. Andrew Common, J.P. a staunch non-conformist, and a wealthy shipowner, well-known throughout the north of England. Emma, the oldest daughter, was passing into adulthood and completing her education. She was popular at school and within the community, intelligent, charming, musical and beautiful. After a short courtship Joseph Parker and Emma Common were married in the Grange Congregational Church, Sunderland. Six deacons of the Manchester church were in attendance. It proved to be a marriage made in Heaven! Joseph referred to Emma as *"my life's wisest and dearest counselor."* He was 34 years old and Emma was but 18.

Angus Watson wrote:

> *"...she gave to him a happiness and a comradeship which was the richest experience that was to come to him. He met her during his second pastorate at Manchester, at a time when his reputation as a preacher was at its zenith, and she shared some of the great days of the City Temple ministry. She was not only a strikingly beautiful woman, but her cultured mind harmonized perfectly with the mystical side of his deeply religious nature. Their comradeship was perfect, and when he suddenly lost her after thirty-five years of unbroken happiness, destiny struck him a blow from which he never recovered. He loved to tell a story of them which revealed his pride in her, an incident the humour of which is typically Northumbrian. Walking down the Strand one day with his wife, he heard a passerby remark, 'There goes beauty and the beast, making reference to the heavy features of the preacher in contrast with the striking beauty of his wife. Turning on the man Parker threw out the challenge, 'Who dares to call my wife a beast?'*
>
> *He never was blessed with children, and a woman less tender and understanding than his wife would have found the task of living with him a call on all her spiritual resources. But that she loved him deeply and admired him intensely is certain, and the brightest days in his somber life came to him while they shared the years together."*

Parker said of Emma, *"At school she was known as 'Fresh Breeze', in our home she was known as 'Sunshine.'"*

Poultry Chapel, London

In 1869, in his fortieth year, Parker was called to Poultry Chapel, London, to succeed Dr. James Spence. This was the oldest Congregational church in London dating back to the 17th century when Dr. Thomas Goodwin was Chaplain to Oliver Cromwell and was the church's first pastor.

Henry Parry Liddon came to St. Paul's Cathedral the following year, and thus, in the Providence of God, throughout the entire twenty year period of Liddon's ministry at St. Paul's Cathedral, there were Charles Spurgeon, Henry Liddon and Joseph Parker, all ministering in London at the same time. That era has been referred to as *"The Golden Age of Preaching."* Later, between the years 1897 to 1901, Joseph Parker, G. Campbell Morgan, and F. B. Meyer were in London at the same time during Morgan's first pastorate at New Court, Tollington Park. Charles Spurgeon had already preached for 15 years in London ever before Parker came upon the scene, and 16 years before Liddon.

Parker began to attract large crowds numbering one thousand both at Poultry Chapel and later at City Temple where the congregation moved five years later. He started a Thursday noonday service which proved to be an immediate success and continued these for more than thirty years. He became known as *"a preacher to preachers."* In many firms the employees drew lots to determine who would get to go and hear Parker at noon. Actors, authors, journalists, artists, politicians and clergymen from all denominations, were among the throngs who came to hear him. The proportion of men to women was 20 to 1.

From the outset it had been determined that a *"new Mecca of Nonconformity"* was to be built at Holborn Viaduct. City Temple, *"a stately mausoleum"* was to cost 50,000 pounds, which was an enormous sum in those days.

City Temple

Originally the church had intended to call Dr. Parker and commence his ministry in a new building. However, three years and eight months were to have elapsed before the congregation was able to lay the foundation stone for the new structure at Holborn Viaduct. In May of 1874 the congregation was finally able to move into their new home which they named City Temple. Though no one could have predicted it at the time, Joseph Parker was to spend the rest of his life ministering in this place. By the time he had finished his tenure in City Temple's pulpit and had stepped aside, it was generally acknowledged that City Temple had become *"the greatest and most powerful centre of nonconformist teaching that London or England possessed."* Parker was also hailed as a *"pulpit genius."* He ministered with unabated strength for approximately 33 years, preaching in the Temple itself as well as throughout England and the United States.

By Angus Watson's account,

> *"No other Church had ever been administered as this was. He was its minister, its treasurer, and its deacons. He took the collections from its stewards each Sunday, paid the costs of the church, published no accounts, and held few church meetings. The City Temple was not a church so much as a preaching station. When he died, there were only 70 members on the active church roll. He was the autocrat personified—no one questioned the wisdom of his rule, or dared to challenge his decisions. He was a Nonconformist autocrat at a time when Victorian Independency was one of the great influences in Christendom."*

Parker's sermons were published and 4,000 were sold on a weekly basis. So great were the demands upon his time (some of those demands being clearly of his own making as we have seen above) that he issued the following tongue-in-cheek statement:

> *"As an arrangement for self-protection, I am driven to announce the following as my charges for general public services; in all cases, traveling expenses must, of course, be paid:*
> *"Preaching on behalf of the salaries of poor ministers, nothing;*
> *Preaching for ministers whose salaries are less than 100 pounds per year, nothing;*
> *Preaching at the openings of chapels, 6 volumes of standard literature;*
> *Attending tea meetings, 50 pounds;*
> *Going to bazaars, 100 gns.*
> *Serving on committees, 2,000 pounds."*

To demonstrate how Parker could poke fun at one of his own well-heeled church members who served as a trustee, Margaret Bywater quotes Parker in her Heritage Biography published in 1961:

> *"One of the trustees unfortunately knew a few legal phrases without knowing any law and his influence upon the other trustees was likely at one time to be most disastrous. His legal phrases staggered some of his poor laymen; as, for example, when the trust deed was read to him, he said, 'It is void by generality.' Thereupon we all looked aghast and wondered how deep was the awful pit concealed under such an expression. When one of us humbly volunteered a suggestion, he promptly retorted, 'that is ultra vires' and we were snubbed and silent. Whatever can it be to be ULTRA VIRES? some of us inquired with the air of convicted criminals...It was in vain that our solicitor gave assurances...All went for nothing. Something was 'void by generality' and something was 'ultra vires' and therefore the opinion of the learned counsel had to be obtained. In my judgment, this simply meant that money and time was to be wasted...but what was the word of a minister to the word of a trustee who could say 'ultra vires?' The minister went to the wall and the trustees went to Sir Roundell Palmer."*

Joseph Parker: The Man

Parker was indeed an enigma—a personality difficult to understand, explain or account for. He possessed a mixture of qualities which ofttimes appeared to be in contradiction with each other. He was the tough autocrat in the City Temple, but as dependent as a child in relation to Emma within their home. He could be impatient and intolerant toward those who wasted his time—he could not easily tolerate fools—but he could be surprisingly gentle toward children and babies who disturbed the quietness of the sanctuary. While it was universally agreed that he was possessed of a massive ego, he could also engage in self-deprecating humour. He was a strange mixture of both positive and negative personality traits.

William Adamson reported that Parker was a child of impulse from the days of his youth. If you tried to predict what course of action he would take he was just as liable to take an opposite route. It was Adamson's opinion that it would be difficult to hold such a man in warm affection. While admittedly wonderfully successful in his public ministry, in private, he was never a truly happy individual throughout his lifetime. Only Emma seemed to rise above all his aggravating and contradictory features and provide for him a companionship and support beyond the ability of any of his other acquaintances. In fact, he had very few close friends.

Mrs. Burnett Smith, a novelist and an intimate friend of the Parkers, gave the following insight into their Hampstead home:

> "The pair were made for each other, and his wife understood the silent sensitive man perfectly. Their circle of friends was a narrow one, for his life was too thronged easily to keep his friendships in repair. A constant stream of visitors waited upon him, and these he did not always interview with patience if their purpose was trivial."
>
> "He was meticulously tidy in all his habits, and their beautiful home was the constant pride of them both. One reaction he inherited from the far-off days of poverty—he expected to be kept informed of the most trivial items of household expenditure. Very shortly after his marriage, Mrs. Parker, losing patience with him, brought him the household accounts and demanded that thenceforth he should keep them himself. This he did from that day onward, to his wife's great amusement."
>
> "Each morning, when his secretary had dealt with his pressing correspondence, he slipped out to his well-beloved Hampstead Heath, where in silent communion he prepared his work while he walked."

One evidence of his rather eccentric side, was his insistence upon having a bath installed in City Temple, so that he could bathe two times a week before preaching. *"After it, the exercise of preaching is delightful!"* said Parker. Another account relates that he bathed every morning plus once every Thursday before going into the pulpit before the noonday service.

Commenting on the connection between spiritual and physical health, Parker once said,

> "No man can have an evil purpose in his heart regarding his fellow man without his health suffering."

He advocated and practiced walking and advised young men, *"If you think you haven't time, get up an hour earlier."* He was always punctual and despatched correspondence replies upon receipt of letters. Professor W. F. Adeney said that—

"City Temple affords a good lesson for punctuality; you might set your watch by the time of Dr. Parker's entrance into the pulpit."

Stories of his over-sized ego are legendary. When invited to preach in a small insignificant village chapel, he could reply by writing on a postcard,

"Can an eagle sit on a sparrow's nest? Yours truly, Joseph Parker."

Once, when introducing the renowned Henry Ward Beecher to his audience, Parker simply issued the terse statement,

'In the presence of great men, lesser men keep silence: Henry Ward Beecher."

On balance, Parker himself spoke disparagingly of his own ability to dress properly:

"I wear a gown in the pulpit because I have the worst coat in the denomination. The gown saves a tailor's bill. I never could learn to dress myself."

The more tender, gentler side of Parker is revealed in the account of Albert Dawson as to how Parker dealt with crying babies in the church.

"Babies in church, however restive they may be, never disturb Dr. Parker. An infant, having made itself heard one Easter Sunday morning, the Doctor paused in his sermon and smiling, said, 'I love to hear that little voice.' A similar incident occurring at a Good Friday service, he said, 'I never turn a baby out of church. I don't know what the child was saying, but I know it was all true.' At a Sunday evening service, he said that he was distressed that a child

had been taken out the previous Sunday evening. 'This church was desecrated by that act. I think that child is here tonight, and I wish it to make any noise that is satisfactory to itself.' On another occasion, he said, 'It is a poor congregation and it is a poor preacher that can't have a little child going on just as it pleases for the time being. He took a little child, and set him in the midst of them.'"

Albert Dawson maintained that Parker had a natural tendency toward skepticism and that he had *"brain enough for half-a-dozen men."* He felt that the true secret to Parker's success was his life-long, unbroken record of self-mastery, self-discipline.

Angus Watson wrote:

"The loneliness of his early days followed him all his life. He had a host of admirers, but few close friends, and he died as he had lived, a man sufficient to himself. Self-centred and vain in part of his nature, he feared the power that had come to him, and dreaded that at last it might depart. Saving others from the perils of fear, himself he could not save. He was a giant with an Achilles heel, too conscious of the heart's deceitfulness ever to trust his own entirely. Generous to a fault, he sometimes appeared to love material gifts too much, and yet, those who needed his help always found in him an understanding and responsive heart."

"When the great burden of his responsibilities weighed too heavily upon him, he turned again to his home haunts in the North country (or, to the Swiss mountains, which he loved to visit) and became once again the lonely lad of his boyhood amid the heather-clad moorlands, listening to the voice of the wind on the heath, and seeking again the dreams of his youth..."

Published Writings and Sermons

It would appear that Joseph Parker was born to preach. In his autobiography, Parker wrote:

"It was a family anecdote that early one Sunday morning, when walking with my father, I was found standing at a gate with my index finger pointing to the sun, saying aloud, 'What are these arrayed in white, brighter than the noonday sun?"

From that moment his father was convinced that Joseph would become a preacher. In addition to memorizing much poetry, the boy bought copies of the speeches of great orators and pinned them to his bedroom wall paper, memorized them and *"declaimed them aloud in my solitude to excited, but invisible, juries."*

Albert Dawson was hired by Parker to be his literary assistant—his *"amanuensis."* He served in this capacity for 6 ½ years with a salary of 100 pounds per annum. Parker wrote:

> *"I want an amanuensis who can write easily to dictation, say, not less than 60 words a minute; a very clear, long-hand writer; his whole time will be required; on no account must he get it into his head that he can PREACH, for when that lunacy gets into a man's head, he is (unless a genius) much worse than he were dead and buried."*

Parker's most widely known publication is the 25 volume *The People's Bible*, a compilation of 1,000 sermons, preached through the entire Bible over the span of 7 years, 3 times a week. Albert Dawson continued:

> *"During the preparation of The People's Bible, I took down every syllable of every prayer and every sermon and sent direct to the printers my verbatim transcript of those required for periodical publication. I have never yet succeeded in getting Dr. Parker really to read the proof of any one of his sermons."*

Why Dr. Parker did not like to read his own sermons after he had preached them, we do not know. He used a few pencilled notes in the pulpit and preached extemporaneously. Parker's decision to completely waive the task of editing was in marked contrast to the practice of his contemporary, Charles H. Spurgeon. Spurgeon spent most of every Monday revising his stenographer's report of his Sunday morning sermons and he severely revised them before they went to the publishers.

It is interesting to note that Parker actually preached better when he was aware that his sermons were being recorded. The prospect of a vastly wider audience inspired him. Equally noteworthy was the fact that he rarely quoted others. In a thousand pages of *The People's Bible,* there is not more than a dozen direct quotations from other men, according to Dawson.

Parker published between 50 to 70 volumes over the course of his ministry. Among them were *Ad Clerum: Advices to a Young Preacher; Short Arguments on Religious Mysteries; The Working Church: An Argument for Liberality and Labour; The Testimony of an Enemy: A Sermon to the Young; Church Questions: Historical and Moral Reviews; Hidden Springs; The Chastening of Love: or, Words of Consolation for the Christian Mourner; John Stuart Mill on Liberty: A Critique; The Pulpit Analyst—a magazine edited by Joseph Parker; Ecce Deus: Essays on the Life and Doctrine of Jesus Christ with Controversial Notes on ECCE HOMO; The People's Family Prayer Book; The Pulpit Bible (Authorized Version with Marginal Notes); Henry Ward Beecher: a Eulogy; None Like It: A Plea For the Old Sword; The Inner Life of Christ As Revealed in the Gospel of Matthew; Tyne Folk: Masks, Faces, and Shadows; Christian Profiles in a Pagan Mirror; Regenerated London: A Plea for a Laymen's League; A Preacher's Life: An Autobiography and an Album...*and many others.

Parker's Method and Manner: Preparation and Preaching

Parker judged that the pulpit must be his primary and pre-eminent concern, for if he failed there, failure in all other departments of his ministry would be inevitable.

The ultimate end and aim of all preaching in Parker's view was expressed in *Ad Clerum:*

> *"The great object of our ministry is the salvation of souls...I know of no bitter irony, or more humiliating satire, than to be told that we have delivered splendid discourses, and yet to know that not one soul has ever been led to Jesus Christ by a ministry so flatteringly described."*

Parker's preaching was not the only drawing card in the City Temple's program. The church also had an able organist, a large choir, violinists, and an especially gifted cornet player. In this regard Parker's program stood in marked contrast with Spurgeon's use of music at the Tabernacle. Spurgeon's song leader was equipped only with a tuning fork—no choir and no organ were allowed!

As noted earlier, while still in his teens Joseph Parker became a member of a band of lay preachers who traveled throughout Tyneside preaching in village chapels and in the open air. His method of preaching could be characterized as extemporaneous, fiery messages calling men to repentance and faith.

While at Cavendish Street Chapel, Manchester, Parker delighted in long texts and consecutive expositions of parts of the Scriptures. As an expounder, Adamson claimed that he looked more to *"the whole than to parts, to the spirit than to the letter, to the essential than to the accidental."*

Once when speaking of a learned exegete whom he highly regarded, Parker wrote:

> *"He takes a microscope, and examines with great minuteness the meaning and value of every Greek particle, preposition, and verb; whereas I would like to catch the whole spirit of the revelation, making its amplitudes my own."*

Whereas the praise of his pulpit power was shouted from nearly every housetop in his day, seeking to analyze or even appreciate Parker's preaching from the written record of his sermons is an exercise in frustration and futility! After reviewing both the written record of his preaching alongside of the extravagant accolades which were showered upon him for his preaching prowess, this writer can only conclude that the written form concealed his greatness rather than revealed it! His sermons were lacking in any discernable structure and he either violated homiletical principles, abandoned them altogether, or, attempted to create a new form which was distinctly his own. What was alleged to be a textual or expository treatment of Scripture would end up as a topical discourse more often than not. A text of Scripture would often be but a launching pad for what he really wanted to say and back to which he never returned. Even his lofty rhetoric, for which he was renowned, soared to such heights at times that it had little meaning-content.

But having said all that, William Adamson listed Parker, along with Spurgeon and D. L. Moody, as the three *"most powerful spiritual forces at the end of the 19th century."*

Alexander Whyte of St. George's United Free Church, Edinburgh, visited London, and in one day heard *"…the three preachers in all London I was most anxious to hear."* In the forenoon he heard a Mr. Maurice; in the afternoon, Dean Stanley; and in the evening, Mr. Spurgeon. Then, on another Sunday, at a later period, he went to hear Dr. Parker preach on two occasions.

> *"...and I shall never forget the impression—the profit of that outstanding day—originality, individuality, freshness, richness, suggestiveness—what a mass of manhood and mind in our friend! He is by far the ablest man now standing in the English-speaking pulpit. He stands in the pulpit of Thomas Goodwin, the Atlas of Independency, the pulpit genius of all the Puritans, and a theologian to whom I owe more than I can ever acknowledge of spiritual light and life. And Dr. Parker is a true and worthy successor to this great Apostolic Puritan."*

The Rev. Dr. John Watson ('Ian McLaren') wrote of Parker:

> *"Dr. Parker...occupies a lonely place among the preachers of our day...There is no man, so it seems to me, who so distinctly suggests that quality of genius which cannot be traced and which cannot be acquired, which is the direct gift of God, and rises like a spring in the midst of flowers. His position among preachers is the same as that of a poet among ordinary men of letters."*
>
> *"Before this man's vision the magnificent common-places of the Gospel reappear in their pristine beauty and majesty, so that you seem to have heard them for the first time as they came from the lips of Jesus or the Apostles, and obscure and unpromising passages and incidents yield up their treasures like mines that have suddenly been opened."*
>
> *"The power of his preaching lies in the contact of a mind of perpetual and amazing originality with the sublime truths of the Gospel, and the faculty which Dr. Parker possesses with all men of intellectual genius of discovering the principles which lie behind what seems the poorest detail, and which resolve all things into a unity..."*

Margaret Bywater called Parker *"the most outstanding preacher of his time,"* this, in spite of the fact that he was a contemporary of Charles Spurgeon, Henry Ward Beecher, Henry Parry Liddon and F. W. Robertson. He had the essentials of simplicity, integral appeal, conviction and Biblical exposition. G. Holden Pike described Parker as *"as preacher of extraordinary power...like McLaren, a preacher's preacher."*

Like all outstanding orators, Parker was dramatic in his delivery as well as humourous. It was reported that young people were in the majority in his audiences, and 75%-80% were young men.

Many tried to account for his greatness. William Adamson, commenting upon the opinions of this one and that, wrote:

> *"His egotism, says one; his dramatic action and his humourous and pithy sayings, his general eccentricities and his surprises, say others. Those who seek the explanation of his greatness and power in these directions would measure the solar system with a yard wand. That he is an egotist, as all men are, cannot be denied, but it should be remembered that here is an egotism, which, if strong, acute, and full of distinctive character, is precious, and remains a possession of the race."*

Adamson went on to define the individual characteristics which made up the entire portrait of Parker's greatness:

> *"He had a strong, marked, and magnetic personality; his voice was wonderful in its fibre and compass, possessing tones rich and varied—sometimes like thunder, and then, as gentle and pathetic as a mother's pleading; his delivery was arresting, free from monotony in thought and utterance; and the substance of what he said is what held the minds of his hearers."*

Albert Dawson also remarked on Parker's vocal qualities, describing his voice as *"magnificent"* *"matchless"* and that it rang out *"resonantly."*

He added that at age 71 Parker was at his best!

T. Fisher Unwin reported that Parker had a habit of dropping his voice at the end of sentences. To this criticism Parker once replied that throughout 25 years of ministry he had taken note that those who were somewhat deaf sat as far away from the pulpit as possible!

Angus Watson gives this description of Parker "at work" in the pulpit:

> *"To those who never heard him preach, the power of his oratory is almost beyond description. To see him in the City Temple pulpit was an experience never to be forgotten. His massive figure and his*

leonine head at once fixed the attention, and his voice, rich as an organ, held his audience spellbound. It rose and fell in sonorous periods, as he poured out his perfectly phrased sentences. He was a superb actor, and he delivered his thoughts with a dramatic force that kindled each sentence. His sermons were an example of perfect English; every word the inevitable one for its purpose, each thought challenging and full of surprise—the whole constructed like a stately building, graceful in model and design. The gleaming eyes, the vigorous gesture, the constantly changing inflection of his voice, now soft as a whisper, then challenging as a trumpet; the whole effect was so memorable as to be almost overwhelming. No one had ever spoken like him; he created a new tradition, and established a vogue which others vainly strove to copy. It was no surprise that thousands who usually never entered a church, crowded to hear him, and that among his audiences were to be found the outstanding statesmen and public men of his time. Visitors from all over the world were to be found in his audiences, and what he had to say in his sermons was quoted freely in the press next day as a prominent item of news. He created a public opinion which helped to shape the history of his time; his pronouncements on the topics of the day were as eagerly read as those of a Cabinet Minister. Gladstone and other public men honoured him with their friendship and quoted him in their speeches."

He was not regarded as a poetical preacher but rather more intuitional and mystical. Adamson said that *"he presents his conceptions rather in the setting of the imagination than in the framework of the logical faculty."* This is an extremely important observation. He used the instrument of his imagination, conveying truth by painting pictures on the hearts and minds of his hearers rather than by explaining abstract theories to the intellect.

Angus Watson tried to describe this mystical and melancholy side of Parker. He said that in Parker there was a vein of mysticism *"haunting and unexpected, an undertone of music like the winds blowing softly over his Northern fells."*

Parker, himself, admits to this.

"The family eyes have never been externally large, but always large and keen in their inward relations and activities. I must in some

degree take after these women—for I, too, see the wind, and the things that fly in it; and I, too, hear its moan, its cry of pain, and its glad upbreaking of the winter, that a highway may be made for the green spring and the red-lipped summer. I thank God for this inner vision, for it often makes solitude a very festival of joy. It was this introvision that led Dr. John Pulsford, the mystic, to describe me as 'a pulpit clairvoyant or medium.'"

Watson completes his description:

"Here was the contradiction of his message—the sturdy mental challenge of a massive mind—the torrential eloquence which blazed out like volcanic lava, with a wistful background of melancholy, as of one who saw visions and dreamed dreams. Eloquence and poetry, invective and closely-reasoned arguments, thrilling periods of sheer oratory, all delivered with the turbulent force of a swift-running river, suddenly dying away to musical softness—here was preaching of a seer and a prophet. Vainly one tried to measure the man. He fitted no mold that lesser mortals could cast; he constantly was breaking new ground and enunciating new discoveries."

Parker's own summing-up statement on homiletics appeared in *Ad Clerum: Advices to a Young Preacher* published in 1870:

"Be earnest; be natural; be as unlike a book as possible—that is about all I have to say upon the science of homiletics..."

When describing earnest men he wrote,

"...there was going out of them a constant and heavy expenditure of life, and that all their powers were steadfastly set in one unchanging direction."

"On the other hand there have been fussy and effusive men who have acquired a great reputation for earnestness, when they should justly have had a name for making a great noise and a great dust. Such men have generally lost themselves in petty details; they have no clear plan, no broad and far-reaching lines of movement; their programme is made up of hop, skip and jump, whimsically varied

with jump, skip and hop; you will have no difficulty in identifying the men when you have to suffer from the noise and dust in which their shallow lives are wasted, but you may have a momentary difficulty in your way of their vexatious intrusion."

Thus for Parker, earnestness lay at the heart of the science of homiletics...and naturalness. In portraying the manner of those who are unnatural or mere imitators of others, he introduced a hypothetical *"Mr. Dexter."* This man was a miniature version of the great Thomas Binney. Mr. Dexter was very serious and pompous and uses an eyeglass set in a gold frame, giving the impression of much study, or as Parker put it, *"ministerial martyrdom."* The fictitious Mr. Dexter even copied the gestures, twitches and pointing habits of Mr. Binney. Parker continues:

"Such is the penalty of popularity! Dogs paint themselves tawney, and then set up for lions; dwarfs buy high-heeled boots, and give themselves out as giants. There are many who imitate Mr. Binney's mannerisms who knew nothing of his wonderful insight and spirituality; they think that when they have borrowed his hat they have also borrowed his brains."

Notable individuals testified to the impact Parker's preaching had upon their lives. Rev. Dr. Raleigh said that he never heard Parker preach except it stirred "the war horse in me, and made me more anxious to carry on the warfare against evil." Rev. George Gladstone said that he always felt "more determined after a sermon from this preacher, to be a faithful minister of the Word and that no grander work is possible to man than to unfold to his fellows the manifold grace of God."

As for the dramatic and stunning effect of his preaching upon a gathered assembly, Parker's stinging attack upon the Turks, after the Armenian massacres, and upon the ex-Kaiser for his declaration of friendship with the Sultan of Turkey, probably is unparalleled in its impact. He stunned the audience when with blazing eyes he thundered from the pulpit to a tense and approving assembly, "God damn the Sultan!"

Both Spurgeon and Parker preached through the Bible year after year, but there was a significant difference between the two. According to Adamson—

> *"Mr. Spurgeon's sermons were constructed on the old model, with heads, subdivisions, and applications; were popular and effective when delivered, and before being printed were carefully revised by the preacher. The City Temple sermons were without heads or formal divisions, and of a high style of literature, studded with gems of thought and chaste epigrams. When they were spoken the preacher had done his work, and the reporter and printer did the rest."*

One could not place Parker in any particular category of school when it came to his method of expositing the Scriptures. He stood alone.

As reported earlier, for many years Parker chose long passages of Scripture and expounded them in a manner more in keeping with proper homiletical form. Later on, he only chose a few suggestive words and treated them in a discursive way with analytical reasoning, informally passing from one thought to the next without any clear plan. Trying to discover structure in his printed messages is a waste of time! He would seek to enforce and illustrate the central thought of the brief text and make its application to everyday life. But often by the end of the message the idea was more prominent than the text, the text having been left in the dust somewhere near the entry-gate to his sermon! In the latter part of his life's ministry, he gave up expositing theological concepts and doctrines and presented Christian truths in solution rather than doctrinal form. Some feel that this was to his loss.

Dawson believed that the further Parker got away from his manuscript the better he preached.

> *"Usually he covers the ground outlined in his notes, but I have known him to devote practically the whole sermon to the first head. Sometimes he seems to be literally 'possessed;' his voice takes on a peculiar swing, there is a steady, even flow of words, the pauses are few, and he seems to be merely the medium through which a message is being delivered."*

Parker had little patience for those who sought their texts in any place other than the Scriptures. He rarely chose political or social themes upon which to preach although he maintained that in the course of preaching he touched on such issues. Parker once said,

"I have nothing to preach to my fellow-men if it be not the Gospel of Jesus Christ and the doctrine of the Cross."

Adamson, commenting on this statement wrote,

"Herein is found the secret of his confidence and the source of his power."

In the judgment of Albert Dawson, Parker was never at his best when he preached on special occasions—in fact, he was often at his worst! On such occasions Parker would prepare a complete manuscript and read it from the pulpit and the difference between such performances and his usual style of extemporaneous preaching was the difference between night and day. Dawson drove home his point by saying, *"...to hear him repeat a sermon or speech that he has first written, is to me like witnessing a procession of corpses."* But having said that, Dawson, Parker's amanuensis, went on to praise Parker's preaching as compared to the preaching of others in his day:

"At one time or another I have 'taken down' all the leading British, and not a few, American preachers, and several of our greatest public speakers, including W. E. Gladstone; but I have yet to hear the orator who in extemporaneous utterance equals Dr. Parker in richness of vocabulary, aptness of phrase, rhythm of sentence, perfect finish of style, faultlessness of elocution, and I may add, spontaneity of wit."

Dr. Joseph Parker was a strong advocate of extemporaneous preaching, or, *"free speech"* as he called it. In his book, *Ad Clerum: Advices to a Young Preacher*, he wrote:

"When I advise you to be as unlike a book as possible in the method of your delivery, you will understand that I wish to dissuade you from the unnatural and evil practice of reading your sermons in the

ordinary course of ministry. You will say that this is strong language; so it is, but it is the language of strong conviction. Having tried both methods, the method of free speech and the method of reading, I can give an opinion founded upon experience, and I now give it as entirely favourable to free speech. The pulpit will never take its proper place until the habit of reading sermons on ordinary occasions is entirely abandoned; it is official, and heartless, and ought to be put down. Let me try to win you to the side of free speech—in other words, to the side of earnestness, reality and power."

When some objected by pointing out that some preachers were quite effective preaching from full manuscripts, Parker replied,

"Call them effective readers of eloquent addresses, call them dignified or vehement repeaters of elaborate dissertations; but preachers in the apostolic sense of the term they certainly ought not to be called!"

In chapter IV of this same volume, *Ad Clerum*, Parker set forth the steps he recommended young preachers to take when preparing to preach extemporaneously. I shall quote Parker but will add numbers to his points for ease of consideration.

1. *"Take as your text a paragraph from the Apostolic writings."*
2. *"Read it carefully in the original language."*
3. *"Trace the various meanings which may be attached to its principal words in other parts of the New Testament."*
4. *"Having satisfied yourself as to the grammar and meaning of the passage, commit your decision to writing."*
5. *"Then take the opinion of two or three of the most critical expositors, and see how far your judgment accords with theirs."*
6. *"Having thus secured a firm standing-place (which is often quite unattainable without rigid criticism), you may write in regular order the principal thoughts which the passage suggests to your mind, and this memorandum will be the skeleton of your discourse."*

7. *"Now proceed to elaboration, writing upon wide lines so as to leave room for erasure and interlining."*

8. *"Having completed a full draft of all your divisions begin at the beginning, and strike out all the long words and all the superfine expressions; let them go, without murmuring! Particularly strike out all such words as 'methinks I see' 'cherubim and seraphim' 'the glinting stars' 'the stellar heavens' 'the circumambient air' 'the rustling wings' 'the pearly gates' 'the glistening dew' 'the meandering rills' and 'the crystal battlements of heaven.' I know how pretty they look to the young eye, and how sweetly they sound in the young ear; but let them go without a sigh; if you have spoken of God as the Deity, put your pen through the word 'Deity' and write 'God' in its stead; if you are tempted to tell your hearers that Jonah spent a portion of his life under the care of a 'submarine custodian' don't hesitate to say plainly that it was only a whale; if you should so far forget yourself as to write the word 'pandemonium' put it out and write the monosyllable over its ruins; and if in a moment of delirium you should write 'my beloved, come with me on the pinions of imagination,' pause, and consider soberly whether you had not on the whole better remain where you are."*

    In another paragraph Parker warned, "You may write the most faultless sentences and elaborate the most skillful paragraphs, and you may become absorbed in the idolatry of your own genius."

9. *"This process being completed, greatly to the disfigurement of your manuscript, rewrite the discourse with the most watchful care, determined that everybody who hears you shall not be left in doubt of your meaning.; write as if every line might save a life."*

10. *"And when you have made an end of writing, put the manuscript away, and go to your public work with the assurance that all faithful and loving service is accepted of the Father and will be crowned with His effectual blessing."*

    "Work thus diligently at the beginning of your ministry, say for the first five or seven years, and the advantage of the discipline will show itself down to your latest effort as a preacher."

Parker once asked Thomas Binney what he thought was the best method of preaching, and he replied, *"gather your materials, and set fire to them in the pulpit!"*

Parker acknowledged that in the heat of delivery and of being inspired by the crowd, fresh ideas will come to mind. He went on to give counsel regarding three aspects of this matter.

(1) Cultivate to the fullest extent the great gift of mental composition and this will save time and the drudgery of writing. One preacher of wide reputation told him that he could *"compose a sermon from beginning to end without ever writing a word!"* Parker said that the ability of composing one's address in one's mind *"...will almost double your life and will certainly impart to your speech a freshness and strength which are unattainable, except in very rare cases, by the monastic penman."*

(2) Beware of *"the awkward difficulty which is often occasioned by the brevity of one's memoranda."* In other words, when your manuscript is finally reduced to a brief memorandum, or outline, which you will carry into the pulpit, make sure that the recorded *"prompts"* are explicit enough to remember what fuller thought they represent. *"Let me advise you to be explicit in your notes so that your invention may not be hampered by a faithless memory,"* Parker advised. Sometimes the preacher is confounded when he glances at his brief outline and cannot for the life of him remember what a brief word or phrase means. An outline, or memorandum, should be brief and concise but not so brief as to be unintelligible!

(3) Be on guard against the possibility of violating good taste in the rapidity and heat of extemporaneous speech. More than one preacher, while caught up in the heat of passion delivering his sermon, has fallen prey to a desire to be humourous or clever, and as a result he blurts out some expression or story which may prove to be offensive or unsuitable. In spite of this danger Parker still urged young preachers to take the risk and to preach extemporaneously.

Question: in Parker's view and practice, was the use of a manuscript in the pulpit ever justified? The answer is, yes. He defined the circumstances which might call for its use.

(1) when the preacher might be addressing not only his equals but his superiors in culture and information.

(2) when there is a demand for high effort in criticism or controversy.

(3) when it is important to restrain all passion and to give a judicial statement of a difficult subject.

(4) when presenting an essay, or a series of essays, on doctrine which the people may be advanced enough to appreciate.

He warned against attempting to preach *"clever sermons"*—turning up strange texts as if to say, as you gaze down at your congregation, *"There! What could you, or what could any man but myself make of a text like that? Now let me show you how clever I am!"* He advised that all such sermons should be burned!

Parker passed along the advice of his first mentor, Dr. John Campbell, on this point:

> *"In choosing a text, don't be anxious to find anything very peculiar...Never disjoint the sentence, always have complete sense...take the whole idea...Having chosen a suitable text, confine yourself to it entirely—<u>make it speak</u>: there <u>is</u> music in it; pray that your fingers may touch the chords aright, so that melody may be evoked...You are not expected to preach a body of divinity in every discourse. Some pulpit ramblers range the whole field, <u>flying</u> everywhere, but <u>digging</u> nowhere."*

The Death of Emma

All students of biography and history will have noted that all truly great men and women of God have experienced at least one personal tragedy, some heart-wrenching experience of grave proportions in their lifetime. For Charles Spurgeon, it was the tragedy of the Surrey Music Hall on 19 October 1856. For Parker, it was the homegoing of his beloved Emma at 9:30 p.m., on Thursday, 26 January 1899. Emma endured 107 days of illness before the end came. As breath by breath her life slowly ebbed away, in spirit, Parker was also dying a slow death.

"Day by day the wilderness encroached upon my own withering life," he wrote.

She died in his arms, her last words being, *"Keep me—hold me."*

> *"Then the panting, succeeded by the long breathing—then the lessening respiration—then less—then Heaven!"*

In his own autobiography Dr. Parker continued:

> *"In that dark hour I became almost an atheist. How could I be otherwise—my chief joy taken from me—my only joy—the joy that gave*

gladness to everything else—the joy that made holy work a holy sacrament? O the Gethsemane bitterness! The Calvary solitude! I had secretly prayed God to pity me by sparing her, yet He set His foot upon my prayers, and treated my petitions with contempt. If I had seen a dog in such agony as mine I would have pitied and helped the dumb beast; yet God spat upon me and cast me out as an offence—out into the waste wilderness and the night, black and starless. 'My feet had well-nigh slipped.' Then a cruel voice said: 'Renounce Him! Defy Him! He forsook His own Son on the cross. Hate Him, and join us, whom He derides and torments as devils.' My soul was exceeding sorrowful even unto death. In that anguish I heard another voice, say, 'My dear, all is well; the mystery will be explained. Even at 68 your work has hardly begun.' I knew her tone. It sounded clearly in my soul's soul, by which sign I knew that this radiant daughter of God had seen the beauty of the King. From that hour I was enabled to take up my ministry and to do the divine bidding with a warmer zeal. God help me, and God help all stricken souls!"

"In many a sacred picture Emma revisits the memory of my desolated heart."

Parker had decided at her death (a) to take up his work at once, or (b) abandon it forever—abandon it and sink in despair! He chose the former alternative: he buried her on Monday and then preached on Thursday of the same week from the text, *"And none spake a word unto him, for they saw that his grief was very great."*

Parker continued: *"…when the richly-treasured casket reached the bottom of the grave there went forth from that saintly crowd a sob as of orphanage and as of life made desolate. In that heart-breaking moment I entered on my old age, and owned with bitterness that death had won a battle with as strong a love as ever fought the last enemy."*

"God has driven me into the dark path, and for the moment has handed me over to the cruel tormentor. My faith is undergoing the agony of crucifixion. To what end I know not. Not a gleam of relieving light can find its way into the secret cave of such lonely distress. Life seems now—perhaps only for a moment—not worth living. I have lost my other heart. My soul's treasure has been stolen. I am poor indeed…I am so lonesome, so desolate, so helpless."

The wreath he provided for Emma's funeral bore the following words:

"Heart of my heart, life of my life: she is not here, she is risen. Joseph Parker."

The End

In spite of his brave attempt to carry on, and although there were other noteworthy accomplishments to record, Joseph Parker never fully recovered from the emotional trauma of Emma's loss. Some say that he lost the will to live and in the end, died of a broken heart. Certainly, his latter years were lonely ones.

In 1901, as Chairman of the Congregational Union, he preached for one hour and forty minutes! In 1902, he was elected President of the National Free Church Council. At one point he had actually severed his connection with Congregationalism. The university of Chicago honoured him with a D.D. degree.

Finally, on 28 November 1902, not quite 3 years after Emma's death, Joseph Parker died in Hampstead (in London). According to Margaret Bywater, at his death, *"Joseph Parker was without a doubt the biggest figure in modern London."*

T. Fisher Unwin said that Parker's death—

"seems to have been the severest loss which the Church Militant on earth had suffered since the passing away of C. H. Spurgeon about ten years previously."

Near the close of his life, knowing that he had never been an easy person to understand, he wrote about his reception in Heaven.

"I hope to be welcomed by many a comrade who did not quite understand me down here in the cold grey clouds of time…
'We shall know each other better
When the mists have rolled away.'"

Chapter Ten

Charles Haddon Spurgeon

---

19 June 1834–31 January 1892

The First of Seventeen

It will soon become apparent to readers of this study that claims made by this one and that as to who was the *"greatest preacher"* in the Victorian era, are made on the basis of personal taste and subjective evaluation in addition to objective analysis.

Dr. D. Martyn Lloyd-Jones called Charles H. Spurgeon *"undoubtedly the greatest preacher of the 19ᵗʰ century."* Frederic C. Spurr wrote, *"It mattered little at what hour of the day he preached in any part of Britain, there would always assemble an enormous congregation."*

Spurgeon began his climb to the heights of pulpit ministry from a very low rung indeed. He was only three years old when Queen Victoria ascended to the British Throne. On 19 June 1834, ten days after the death of William Carey, *"The Father of Modern Missions,"* Charles was born in Kelvedon, Essex, into a lower-middle-class family which had been non-conformist for generations. His father, John Spurgeon, was 24 at the time of Charles' birth and his mother, Eliza Jarvis Spurgeon, was just 19. John did double duty, first as a coal yard clerk, and secondly as the honourary pastor of the Independent Congregational Church, Tollesbury, for a period of 16 years.

Charles was the firstborn son. Eliza gave birth to 17 children in all, nine of whom died in infancy. Only two boys and six girls survived.

Sent Away to be Raised By Relatives

Due to what was described as *"unfavourable circumstances,"* 10-month old baby Charles was sent off to live with his paternal grandparents, the Rev. and Mrs. James Spurgeon, at Stambourne, and this is where he was raised for the following six years. His maiden aunt, Ann Spurgeon, also helped to care for Charles and undertook to educate him. Ann was only 17 when Charles first arrived in their home. Rev. James Spurgeon ministered at Stambourne for 54 years until his death in 1864. It was not until Charles was 7 years old that he was returned to his parents in Colchester in August of 1841.

Early Years and Conversion in a Snow Storm

In 1844, when Charles had reached the age of 10, he vacationed at his grandfather's home in Stambourne. Rev. Richard Knill, minister of Queen Street Congregational Church, Chester, came on deputation on behalf of the London Missionary Society. This man of God put Charles on his knee and prophesied concerning the future of the lad:

> *"This child will one day preach the Gospel, and he will preach it to great multitudes. I am persuaded that he will preach in the chapel of Rowland Hill."*

At age 14 both Charles and his brother James studied at All Saints' Agricultural College, Maidstone, because their uncle was a tutor there. Young Charles was rather small for his age and of pale complexion. It is reported that as far as cricket and other such games, *"he had no taste, being not very muscular, and he was rather timid."*

In September of 1849, while still only 15 years of age, Charles made his first public address at a Missionary Meeting, four months before his conversion. He had an avid interest in missions and had at one stage considered that perhaps God would have him preach the Gospel in China.

Charles Spurgeon was converted to Christ on Sunday, 6 January, 1850, when he was still 15 years old. A snow storm caused him to turn aside into a Primitive Methodist Church in Artillery Street, Colchester. There were only 15 persons present at the service and the preacher who was appointed to minister that Sunday never showed up. Consequently, a poor local minister was obliged to step in at the last minute and chose as his text Isaiah 45:22:

"Look unto Me and be ye saved, all the ends of the earth."

That morning, Charles placed his faith in Christ for salvation and his sinful heart became whiter than the snow that was blanketing the area outside. There is now a tablet at this little church which reads,

"Near this spot C. H. Spurgeon looked and lived."

In a tract, written by himself, Spurgeon describes the life-changing event of his conversion. He said that a very *"stupid"* layman took the pulpit that morning. He had to stick to the text because he had nothing else to say! *"Look unto me, and be ye saved, all the ends of the earth."* The layman didn't even pronounce the words correctly!

> *"There was, I thought, a gleam of hope for me in the text. He began thus: 'Dear friends, this is a very simple text indeed. It says look. Now that does not take a deal of effort. It ain't lifting your foot or your finger, it is just look. Well, a man need not go to college to learn to look. A man need not be worth a thousand a year to look. Anyone can look; a child can look. But this is what the text says, Then it says, Look unto ME. 'Ay' said he in broad Essex, 'many on ye are looking to yourselves. No use looking there. You'll never find comfort in yourselves. Some look to God, the Father. No, look to Him by-and-by. Jesus Christ says, "Look unto Me". Some of you say, 'I must wait the Spirit's working.' You have no business with that just now. Look to Christ. It runs, 'Look to ME.'"*
>
> *Then the good man followed up his text in this way: "Look unto Me; I am sweating great drops of blood. Look unto Me; I am hanging on the cross. Look! I am dead and buried. Look unto Me; I rise again. Look unto Me; I ascend. I am sitting at the Father's right hand. O! Look to ME! Look to ME!"*

Spurgeon went on:

> *"When he had got about that length, and managed to spin out ten minutes or so, he was at the end of his tether. Then he looked at me under the gallery, and I dare say, with so few present, he knew me to be a stranger. He then said, 'Young man, you look very miserable.'*

Well I did, but I had not been accustomed to have remarks made on my personal appearance from the pulpit before. However, it was a good blow struck. He continued: 'And you will always be miserable—miserable in life, and miserable in death—if you do not obey my text. But if you obey now, this moment you will be saved.'"

"*Then he shouted as only a Primitive Methodist can, 'Young man, look to Jesus Christ.'*"

"*I did LOOK. There and then the cloud was gone, the darkness rolled away, and that moment I saw the sun...*"

Later in life Spurgeon wryly remarked with a grim smile that the minister who preached the sermon by which he had been converted was a very remarkable preacher for there were three of him, and not one of them resembled the original! Evidently three different preachers had claimed to have preached that vital sermon whereby Spurgeon had come to faith in Christ, but Spurgeon did not recognize any of them!

Charles became convinced of the truth of believer's baptism through his study of the Scriptures and this led him to seek out the Baptists. On 3 May 1850, five months after his conversion, on his mother's birthday, Charles was baptized in the River Lark. It was a Friday and the officiating minister was Rev. W. W. Cantlow of Isleham, a former missionary to Jamaica. Two women were also baptized on that occasion—Eunice Fuller and Diana Wilkinson. Charles had walked 8 miles to the Isleham Ferry, the site of the baptismal service.

On 9 May 1850, six days after his baptism, he made an entry into his diary. He prayed that God would make him *"an eminent servant of Thine and to be blessed with power to serve Thee like unto Thy great servant Paul."*

It was not until 1896, four years after his death, that Mrs. Spurgeon opened and read this diary.

When Charles reached the age of 16, in August of 1950, he went to Cambridge to serve as an assistant at a school run by Mr. E. S. Leeding, where he spent the following three years. He joined St. Andrew's Street Baptist Church where Robert Hall had once ministered, and became very active in the Sunday School and in the Lay Preacher's Association.

The Trumpet Begins to Sound

Charles gained the reputation of being a very successful Sunday School worker at St. Andrew's Street Baptist Church. However, the majority of the church's membership grew to dislike him because of his blunt, outspoken manner. Among the handful of persons who appreciated his qualities, a Mr. Williamson, one of the deacons, predicted that,

> *"Whoever lives to see it, he will become one of the greatest men in*
> . *England."*

This prophecy sounded strangely similar to that made by Rev. Richard Knill of the London Missionary Society when Charles was only 10 years old.

At the outset of his preaching ministry his chief fault was that which is common to most novice pulpiteers: he tried to pack too much into each and every sermon. On 9 February 1851, he preached on the topic of *"Adoption"* at Barton. The outline of this sermon is the very first one that has been preserved. It shows that he based his message on the text, Ephesians 1:5, and had five divisions with no less than 28 subdivisions! In addition to struggling with the issue of being too detailed and attempting to embrace too much subject matter in one sermon, Spurgeon's biggest problem was selecting a text upon which to preach.

At the age of 17, in January of 1852, he became the pastor of the little Baptist Chapel of Waterbeach, which was situated about 6 miles from Cambridge in the very village where Rowland Hill had preached his first sermon. He ministered here until February of 1854 and within a few weeks, membership jumped from 40 to 100.

When he started out preaching at Waterbeach some described him as a *"ragged-headed boy."* Older folk thought him *"uncouth, impertinent, and lacking in reverence."* One member expressed surprise to the leader of a prayer meeting because he had *"called on that rude young man to pray."*

Charles' physical stature was small and his gestures were awkward. However, it was said that when he would rise to preach the people were quite astonished because of his remarkable flow of language and his exceptional Bible knowledge, accompanied by forcible expression and witty illustrations.

On one occasion he noticed that several in his congregation had fallen asleep during the drowsy hours of a Sunday afternoon service. Whereupon Spurgeon shouted, *"Fire! Fire! Fire!"*

The sleepers started from their slumber and asked where the fire was. To this Charles replied, *"In Hell, for sinners who will not accept the Saviour!"*

At another time he said that if it were possible for people to go to heaven without having their natures changed, it would neither add to their own happiness nor to that of the redeemed generally. Then he added that if a thief could get into heaven in an unregenerated condition, he would be a thief still, and would go up and down the golden streets picking the angels' pockets! During the week someone remarked that celestial beings had no use for pockets. The following Sunday the audacious, youthful pastor told his hearers that he had been informed that angels had no pockets so it was necessary for him to correct an error that he had made on the previous Sunday. He would therefore say that the thief in question would probably try to steal feathers out of the angels' wings!

This is only one example of his exuberant humour at that period of his life, which was not always in the best of taste and often got him in trouble with his hearers, marring his earlier ministry. Critics regarded him as *"a mere pulpit buffoon."* Later on, Spurgeon used these stories to warn his students NOT to follow the example which he had set at the dawning of his ministry.

One elderly minister said to him after hearing him preach,

> *"I've been a minister for nearly 40 years and was never more pleased with a sermon in my life; but you are the sauciest dog that ever barked in a pulpit!"*

On another occasion he went to preach for a gentleman who divided his attentions between a flour mill and a chapel pulpit. At breakfast on Sunday morning, his host informed him,

> *"We always provide two eggs for the minister's breakfast on Sunday morning, because the phosphorus feeds the brain; and it looks as though you need it!"*

At the close of the day's service Spurgeon's host summed up his opinion of the youthful preacher:

> *"Young man, let me give you a bit of good advice. You'll never make a preacher; so give it up and stick to your school teaching."*

A Close Brush With Theological Education

At one point Charles considered entering college to undertake theological studies. To this end he scheduled a meeting with Dr. Joseph Angus, Principal of Stepney College, London, (now Regent's Park College, Oxford) who was coming to preach in Cambridge. The meeting was arranged to take place in the home of Mr. Macmillan, the publisher.

Spurgeon was on time and the maid seated him in the drawing room. He waited patiently for two hours. Finally he rang the bell for the maid and discovered that Dr. Angus had been seated in another room and was compelled to leave and catch a train back to London. At first Charles was disappointed, but later, upon reflection, he regarded the mixup to be the result of the over-ruling Providence of God. From that day onward he renounced all desire to get a formal college education.

Called To His Life's Work

The curious manner in which Charles Spurgeon came to the attention of the deacons of the New Park Street Chapel, Southwark, London, is one that deserves mention. Charles was only 19 years old at the time.

He had been invited, along with two other speakers, to address the annual meeting of the Cambridge Sunday School Union held in the Guildhall in 1853. Charles was invited to speak first and then was followed by the two older ministers who were much more senior than himself. Both of these gentlemen indulged themselves in very poor taste by speaking in an insulting and offensive manner concerning the young preacher. With the permission of the Chair, Spurgeon made a brief reply, in which he courteously, but very effectively, turned the tables on his critics.

A Mr. George Gould of Loughton was present. He was so impressed with how Spurgeon handled this situation that when he returned to London he described the incident to Mr. Thomas Olney, one of the deacons of New Park Street Chapel. This in turn led to the invitation being issued to Spurgeon to meet with the deacons.

At first, Charles was convinced that there had been some mixup between himself and perhaps some other Mr. Spurgeon in view of the fact that he was still only a youth of 19. Nevertheless, on 11 December 1853, he went to meet with the deacons. In January 1854 he received a call to come and preach on a six-month probationary basis. His ministry at New Park Street Chapel began in March that year but by the time he had preached only one month of the six-month probationary period, fifty men signed a petition on April 19th demanding a special church meeting be called in order to nullify the probation scheme and to permanently install Spurgeon as their pastor.

On April 28th Charles accepted the unanimous call and ministered to this congregation for 37 years, preaching his final message in June of 1891.

Marriage and Twins

On Tuesday, 8 January 1856, Charles was joined in marriage with Susannah Thompson of Falcon Square. Charles was 21 years old. The ceremony was conducted by Dr. Alexander Fletcher of Finsbury Chapel. The wedding caused a sensation! A group of policemen from the M Division were called upon to prevent traffic accidents. The young couple had their honeymoon at the Hotel Meurice in Paris.

Charles wife, "Susie", was an invalid for most of their married lives and yet she outlived Charles by 11 years. She went to be with Christ on 22 October 1903. The only children they ever had were twin boys, Charles and Thomas, born just over 9 months after their marriage, on 20 September 1856.

In reference to Susannah's ill health, Andrew Melrose, in his 1903 article, "One Who Knew Him Well", wrote:

> "The tenderness and intensity of his love for his wife were pathetic to witness, and we have been struck on many occasions by the boyishness of his delight when she was able to leave the house and sit with him on the lawn, or walk slowly on his arm under the shady trees…On her bad days his distress and anxiety were pitiable to witness…"

A rather humourous incident occurred on the day Spurgeon preached to the vast gathering in the Crystal Palace in 1857. Charles sent a deacon down into the audience to ask his wife to move to another seat where he could not see her, because the sight of her made him nervous!

The Meteor Becomes a Fixed Star

In the afore mentioned biographical sketch written by Andrew Melrose in 1903, the meteor metaphor was used and since then was copied by several other authors when referring to the phenomenon, which <u>was</u> Charles Haddon Spurgeon. Melrose wrote:

> *"It may be fairly said that his career presents some of the most interesting problems that could engage the attention of the religious historian. Meteorlike in the suddenness with which he flashed across the firmament of English Nonconformity, unconventional and bizarre to a degree that startled as much as it perplexed most observers, he did not, like so many religious meteors, blaze up for a moment and then die out into the darkness of a kindly oblivion. The meteor became for a time a fixed star, attractive in its brightness and beneficent in its influence. Possessing the accident of brains, without the incident of learning in any remarkable degree; preaching not merely simple things, but often highly unpalatable truths; strongly opposed, not only by the man in the street but by the religious leaders of the day, Spurgeon not only attracted crowds but formed them into a great congregation. He did not arouse temporary excitement, but attracted a general interest which remained undiminished to the day of his death. His brilliant, if sometimes eccentric, orations, developed into a homiletic literature without parallel."*

> *"His influence was great beyond his own congregation, and tinged the teaching of a thousand pulpits. The interest that his preaching aroused took permanent form in almshouses, orphanages, and a college; while his evangelistic zeal not only filled to overflowing the huge tabernacle which became one of the recognized sights of London, but spread into the distant provinces, establishing missions and building chapels in many a town and village. The influence of the boy preacher from the Cambridgeshire fens stamped itself not only upon the religious teaching but upon the Biblical and social*

thought of the nineteenth century. His friendships included not merely those who agreed with him, but many of the greatest minds of the day, among whom may be mentioned John Ruskin and W. E. Gladstone; and when at last he was stricken down by the illness which terminated his career, the public concern manifested was not merely national, but universal. Such a phenomenon invites and demands study."

A member of the Society of Friends wrote in *"The Friend"*:

"The crowds which have been drawn to hear him, the interest excited by his ministry, and the conflicting opinions expressed in reference to his qualifications and usefulness, have been altogether without parallel in modern times. It was a remarkable sight to see this round-faced country youth thus placed in a position of such solemn and arduous (responsibility), and yet addressing himself to the fulfilment of its onerous duties with a gravity, self-possession, and vigour, that proved him well-fitted to the task he had assumed. In a few weeks the pews, which had been so long tenantless, were crowded, every sitting in the chapel was let; and ere many months had elapsed the eagerness to hear him had become so great, that every standing-place within the chapel-walls was occupied on each succeeding Sabbath; and it became evident that increased accommodation must be provided for the wants of the congregation. Within one year New Park Street Chapel had to be enlarged."

Frederic C. Spurr described his rise to fame:

"He came to New Park Street for that one Sunday, never dreaming that on that day his life destiny was to be decided. In an out-of-the-way building, seated for 1,200 people, he found a morning congregation of less than 200. The place had run down terribly and the leaders were anything but sanguine about the future. But in that chubby-faced country lad they found their Joshua. The sermon that morning settled their future and Spurgeon's. Like a revealing flash it came to the whole congregation spontaneously that here was their man. He went to a nearly empty church building. Within a few weeks thousands of people from all over London were clamouring for admission. So great was the crush that the famous Exeter Hall in the

Strand was hired for one service per Sunday. That became too small, and the daring experiment was made of engaging the Surrey Music Hall for Sunday services. The building seated some seven thousand people, and it was filled to capacity on Sunday mornings."

One accounting of membership figures for the New Park Street Chapel congregation (not to be confused with <u>attendance</u> figures) which was later to meet in the Metropolitan Tabernacle, is as follows:

In the first year of Spurgeon's ministry, 1854	232
January 1855	313
1856	860
1857	4,417
At Spurgeon's death, 1892	5,307

In the newspaper, Globe, on 22 March 1855, a reporter described traffic snarls which were caused by the people crowding to the 6 p.m. service:

"Since the days of Wesley and Whitefield—whose honoured names seem to be in danger of being thrown into the shade by this new candidate for public honours—so thoroughly a religious furor has never existed. Mr. Spurgeon is likely to become a great preacher; at present his fervid and impassioned eloquence sometimes leads him a little astray, and sometimes there is a want of solemnity which mars the beauty of his singularly happy style."

Criticism: Some of it Justified

That Spurgeon made mistakes is a matter of historical record. He admits to it himself. In fact, he used his mistakes as illustrations with which to admonish his students. It is to his eternal credit that within a relatively short period of time he profited from the lessons he learned from his own mistakes. He responded to his critics by setting about to correct those features of his manner and speech which were particularly offensive to many. Good men opposed him and equally good men defended him.

In an article entitled *A Chat About Spurgeon in a Railway Train*, published by James Seaward (London, 1867), which was a fictitious conversation between an imagined clergyman and a farmer, the following commentary on Charles Spurgeon was offered:

> *"Spurgeon, by his funny jokes, amusing stories, positiveness, and other fruits of NOT the spirit, has attracted all the grumblers, hero-worshipers, and dissatisfied in and around all London. They are certainly a motley crew."*

George John Stevenson labeled Spurgeon, when in his 23rd year, as *"a young man who had been almost everywhere spoken against..."* But then went on to say—

> *"...now he is looked upon as the greatest preacher of the age, his sermons are listened to by admiring and approving thousands every week, and they are read in every city, town and village in the land, and more eagerly looked for by their readers than almost any other serial which is conveyed in the bookseller's parcel...By the end of his third year's ministry in London...his popularity was second to that of no other preacher of the age."*

Spurgeon was a punster, possessed irrepressible humour, and had in his eye a "gleam of fun in almost every glance." In those early years his exuberance often brought him into disfavour, particularly with older clergymen. There was a certain tone of familiarity, almost verging on irreverence, in his public prayers. His pulpit attitude and gestures were somewhat exaggerated and theatrical, while his language was often exuberant and unguarded. And because of this, for many years he endured extraordinary abuse and misrepresentation in the public press. For a time this caused him keen suffering and not a little fear that his usefulness might thereby become impaired. But as is so often the case, the public slander heaped upon him only had the effect of bringing more crowds to hear him preach.

One example of his unrestrained humour which breached the borders of good taste, was when an American visiting speaker publicly condemned the use of tobacco. Spurgeon's one great indulgence was his cigars! He never did smoke a pipe nor did he ever have to waste money on his habit because his friends kept him well supplied! Spurgeon responded to the American's comments with a mild protest saying that his visitor had emphasized that we should do all to the glory of God, and Spurgeon confirmed that as in everything else he did, he also smoke his cigars to the glory of God! This received wide coverage in the press and proved to be an unfortunate incident.

In 1856, S. J. Brown published an article in response to the question, *"Why So Popular?"* entitled *An Hour With The Rev. C. H. Spurgeon: The Causes of His Success.* He said that men call Spurgeon the youthful Whitefield.

> *"...the why and the wherefore of such a rage for such a preacher whose vulgar rant, almost blasphemous in its pretended familiarity with the great I AM, passes current with his excited auditory as the realization and complete embodiment of the sublime ideals in the sermon on the Mount and Paul's sermon on Mar's Hill."*
>
> *"...if we can judge by past experience of the duration of popularity based upon such unsubstantial groundwork, it is not likely to be of long existence—the decay of his popularity will be as sudden as its rise and will proceed from one of two causes—either he himself will grow wiser, or, his people will; we think the latter by far the most likely. While he is followed and courted and made so much of, there is not very much hope of his leaving off a style and mannerism which, to use a common phrase, so evidently 'takes'."*
>
> *"In our opinion, his success is but a seeming one, a success as regards himself, and the deacons of his church, but not to the vital interests of Christianity. The old illustration of the rocket and the stick will again be exemplified; his erratic course will end, as where only it could end, in blacker night."*

This particular critic bitterly takes offence at the element of the melodramatic in Spurgeon's style in the treatment of subjects. For example, Spurgeon depicted a sinner approaching the gates of heaven, and Justice saying—

> *"There he comes! There he comes! He spurned a father's prayers, and mocked a mother's tears; he has forced his way downward against all the advantages Mercy has supplied, and now, there he comes! Gabriel! Take the man: The Angel binding you hand and foot holds you one single moment over the mouth of the chasm, he bids you look down, down, down—there is no bottom, and you hear coming up from the abyss 'sullen moans and hollow groans and*

screams of tortured ghosts'—you quiver, your bones melt like wax, and your marrow quakes within you: where is now thy might, and boasting and bragging? Ye shriek, and cry, and beg for mercy; but the Angel, with one tremendous grasp, seizes you fast, and then hurls you down with the cry 'away, away!' and down you go to the pit that is bottomless and roll forever downward, downward, downward, ne'er to find a resting place for the sole of your foot."

"After this," S. J. Brown concluded, *"one would think the force of fancy could no further go."* Brown referred to the above and similar passages from Spurgeon's sermons as *"passages of undiluted buffoonery and impiety."* He attributed Spurgeon's popularity to his making salvation easy and using as an example Spurgeon's own testimony that he had *"looked and lived."*

On the other hand, in the face of such sharp criticism, some of which was justified, there were also those who saw the potential of Spurgeon, defended him and refused to join the chorus of detractors. Among these, the great Thomas Binney stood tall. When he overheard disparaging remarks about Spurgeon coming from a student, at a time when Binney was lecturing in an independent college, he told the students to be quiet and listen to what Spurgeon had to say:

"I, myself, have enjoyed some amount of popularity; I have always been able to draw together a congregation; but in the person of Mr. Spurgeon we see a young man, be he who he may, and come whence he will, who, at 24 hours notice can command a congregation of 20,000 people. Now I have never been able to do that and I never knew of anyone else who could do it."

Again, Frederic C. Spurr confirms our contention that—

"Spurgeon lived down all the calumnies and criticisms where were freely heaped upon him during his early years in London."

Even the PUNCH magazine which had cruelly caricatured him in his early years, made a handsome amends at the time of his death. In the face of hostility, for his own private consolation, Spurgeon took comfort in the fact that every month there were numerous candidates for baptism. There were nearly always conversions at his meetings and great crowds—it was like a continuous revival.

Understanding the Times

In order to gain some insight into the success of Charles Spurgeon it is beneficial to understand the historical context in which he ministered and the condition of London's society in those days. It is difficult for us, who live in an age of rapid transit, computers, highly commercialized sports and entertainment, to visualize the London of yesteryears. There were no railroads, automobiles, air travel, electric lights and what we know now as suburban life. It was just one year before Spurgeon's birth that the very first railroad track was laid in the north of England. Owners of businesses and stores lived right on their own premises where they conducted their daily work. The streets were lit at night by gas lamps. The majority of the masses were poor and the prevailing culture was correspondingly low. Metropolitan Tabernacle, which became the home of Spurgeon's ministry, was situated in a predominately residential area and people had not far to go to reach the church doors. Most of the houses at that time were single-family homes and families were quite large. Public education did not get its first great boost until Spurgeon had already been in ministry for 20 years. The School Board came into existence in 1870.

There were few activities in which the general public could participate on a Sunday in those days. People were not in the habit of going off on an excursion on Sunday nor going into the country over weekends. If a golfer indulged in his favourite pastime on a Sunday he was frowned upon and regarded as a pagan. Families generally stuck together on Sundays, many attending church both morning and evening, and most taking a rest in the afternoon. The family pew was an established tradition. As for Sunday church services themselves, they were bound by convention. Sermons and prayers were lengthy and dull. Sermons were read and droned on about theology as if designed to provoke slumber. Ministers in general were seen as aloof and patronizing. In short, the church was a highly respected and conservative institution in British society.

Then along came Charles Spurgeon...the unconventional in the midst of convention, the diamond in the rough in a context of what was regarded as proper and pious. His messages were lively and humourous in contrast to the read essays of refined ministers. After services people did not sleepily file out the door with a polite nod to their clergyman; they were excited because they had been witnesses to conversions and had been challenged by sermons which were both dynamic and delightful. People longed to see something more genuine, more real than what they had found in the standard church services of that day. They felt they had found it in Spurgeon's ministry.

The Tragedy of Surrey Music Hall and the Triumph of Crystal Palace

Spurgeon encountered the greatest tragedy of his lifetime when he was only 22 years old, married less than one year, and the twins having arrived only one month before the event. The trauma caused by the tragedy had a permanent impact upon his health throughout the remainder of his life.

On 19 October 1856, 12,000 people packed into the Surrey Music Hall in the Surrey Zoological Gardens at Walworth to hear Spurgeon preach. An estimated 10,000 additional people stood outside. Someone in the galley, all of a sudden, shouted, *"FIRE! The galleries are giving way! The place is falling!"*

Panic ensued. Seven people were trampled to death as the crowd tried to escape to the exits and 28 were seriously injured and hospitalized. Many more were hurt. Subsequently the press slandered and vilified him, laying the blame for the incident at his doorstep.

Spurgeon never fully recovered from the emotional trauma of this disaster. He lay for some time in an almost unconscious state in the vestry and was afterwards removed through a private garden and carried home, more dead than alive. To the end of his life he could never hear any allusion to the disaster without manifesting extreme distress and he was always rather nervous when preaching in overcrowded buildings.

As is so often the case, the Lord took the tragedy and turned it around for the good of His servant. It was actually because of this tragedy that his name became famous throughout the world for people began to ask what manner of preacher was this who could draw such a crowd to hear him preach.

One year later, on 7 October 1857, he preached to a crowd of 23,654 people in Crystal Palace on the Day of National Humiliation in remembrance of the Indian Mutiny. Spurgeon was only 23 years old when he preached to this gathering which was reputed to be the largest congregation ever to be addressed by a preacher of the Gospel, in Europe or anyplace else in the world, up until that time.

In addition to the story about Spurgeon asking his wife to move to another part of the building so he couldn't see her, another incident took place in the run-up preparation for this great meeting. Spurgeon had gone to the Crystal Palace a few days prior to the meeting in order to test out the acoustics of the meeting hall. He stood inside the building and lifting up his voice, he cried, *"Behold the Lamb of God which taketh away the sin of the world!"* A workman, painting high up in one of the galleries, heard Spurgeon's quotation from John's Gospel, came under conviction of sin, returned to his home and was converted to Christ!

After this meeting in Crystal Palace was over, Spurgeon slept from Wednesday night all the way through until Friday morning, having been so nervously drained by preaching to this vast crowd.

Metropolitan Tabernacle

It had become clear that Spurgeon had come to stay and that the present church building facility could not contain the swelling crowds. The foundation stone for Metropolitan Tabernacle was laid in 1859, five years after he took up the ministry at New Park Street Chapel. He was 25 at this time. The Tabernacle was erected in Newington Butts and was officially opened for use in 1861. It seated 5,500 people with standing room for another 1,000. It was crowded weekly, averaging 5,000 over a period of 31 years. The Monday evening prayer meeting drew 1,500 persons and a Thursday evening preaching service, 3,000. Spurr acknowledged that there had been nothing quite like this happen in the whole history of Christendom.

In the early part of his ministry Spurgeon preached one to three times a day, ten to twelve times a week, and always to large audiences. The dimensions of the Tabernacle itself were 174' x 81' x 62'. It had two galleries and a schoolroom which could seat 900 beneath the chapel. There was no organ and no choir. The consequence of Spurgeon's refusal to use an organ was that the singing often dragged and fell flat. Singing was led by a man with a tuning fork and Spurgeon compiled his own hymnbook. The style of preaching and the conduct of services were largely shaped by Puritan and Calvinistic teaching.

During Spurgeon's pastorate at Metropolitan Tabernacle, a total of 14,691 persons were received into membership, the vast majority of whom had been converted under his preaching.

George John Stevenson maintained,

"Since the days of the Apostles, no man has ever occupied a more prominent place in the religious world than that now so deservedly held by the pastor of the Metropolitan Tabernacle."

Probably no other congregation in Spurgeon's lifetime ever sent forth as large a proportion of its members as ministers, evangelists, workers of various sorts, and both foreign and home missionaries.

The Pastors' College, Stockwell Orphanage, and Writings

Originally, the Pastors' College was started with only eight students. Rev. George Rogers was the Principal in the 1850's and the student body was drawn mainly from the poor and uneducated class. The College aimed to train preachers rather than scholars.

On 14 October 1873 the foundation stone was laid for the college building behind the church. Classes started there in 1874. Prior to this, classes were held in the basement of the church. Charles Spurgeon stamped his style and theology upon the students and in due course the pulpits of hundreds of towns and villages throughout England were manned by Spurgeon understudies. In his own Baptist denomination his preaching has been described as epoch-making. He set a model for pulpits world-wide, not only for England. The Gospel was more clearly enunciated and there was a firmer insistence upon emphasizing evangelical truths. This was noticeable among the laity as well as among the clergy. Dr. F. W. Boreham is numbered among the graduates of this college. Eventually the college was renamed *Spurgeon College* and was transferred to South Norwood.

Spurgeon was quoted by Frederic Spurr in his publication of 1934, *Charles Haddon Spurgeon*, as having once said,

"The God that answereth by Orphanages, let Him be God."

The Stockwell Orphanage was established in 1869 with the boys' section being completed at that time. In 1879-80 the Girls' section was erected. Spurgeon committed himself to a large number of charities and it was said that he gave away almost everything he ever earned!

Spurgeon read widely. His 12,000 volume library was stored in four rooms of his house. He was also a prolific writer although much of what has been published were actually the sermons which he preached.

Some have reported that he wrote over 160 volumes although because of a measure of overlap the number probably could be reduced to 100. The written form of his published sermons fail to capture the true power and excellence of the preacher's pulpit ministry. Nevertheless, he published a weekly sermon from 1855 to 1892. He also edited a monthly magazine which enjoyed a wide circulation. Reviewing books by the hundreds, he published a 7 volume commentary on the Psalms entitled *The Treasury of David*, prepared two volumes of homely wisdom entitled *John Ploughman's Talk*, and wrote two volumes of proverbs in addition to several small devotional books.

Spurgeon, The Man

It is seldom an easy task to get behind the veil of the projected image of a public figure in order to discover a true picture of his character and personality. In company with Elijah, Charles Spurgeon was very human—a man *"just like us."*

As mentioned earlier, in his younger years his physical appearance was not imposing. He was small for his age, of pale complexion and rather awkward in his gestures. He had thick, black hair which was worn long, parted almost in the middle, and he wore a very high collar wrapped with a tie around his short neck which made him appear anything but dignified. No one would have considered him handsome, in fact, Archbishop Benson recorded his impression after meeting with Spurgeon in Addington: *"He is certainly uglier than I had believed."*

Being of below middle height his stoutness in later years did not enhance his appearance. He suffered frequently from recurring attacks of rheumatic gout which turned him into a partial invalid. He had heavy features with *"a curious inequality in his eyes."* His heavy eyes literally *"beamed with benevolence when he looked at you...there was a gleam of fun in almost every glance, and the impression his looks created was not only that of an honest and kindly nature, but of a genial and witty intelligence."*

(By, *One Who Knew Him*) Indeed, Spurgeon was quick-witted and humourous in the extreme!

When Spurgeon reached middle-age he looked his worst and was often unwell. In the latter part of his relatively short life, he immensely improved his looks when he sported a short beard, and his wavy hair became almost white previous to his death. Observers described him at that time as being neat, well-groomed, and pleasant. James Seaward described him as *"the happiest and the heartiest of men."* Spurgeon was a most pleasant gentleman to have as a companion, possessing a natural and unaffected character.

Although he smoked cigars, he ate in moderation and in later life he became a total abstainer from alcohol believing that this would make him more useful. He had no serious extravagances, with the possible exception of his hobby for collecting rare and costly editions of Puritan writings. From all reports the Spurgeons enjoyed a very happy family · life in spite of the ill health which both of them suffered throughout their lifetime together.

He would never accept any of the degrees which were offered him by American institutions. Nothing amused and annoyed him more than to see himself described in foreign papers as *"Doctor Spurgeon."* (Spurr)

Some regard him as a bonafide genius with a great analytical mind. He was blessed with a prodigious memory, retaining anything he chose to remember out of his vast volume of reading. Though not university-trained he had a wonderful command of the English language and what has been described as a musical quality to his voice which uniquely suited him to oratory.

Occasionally, Charles Spurgeon suffered from periods of deep depression, even to the point of doubting his own personal salvation. The *One Who Knew Him Well* described one such episode.

> *"...he became so impressed with the idea that he was only a waiter and not a guest at the Gospel feast, that he left London and retired to an out-of-the-world village, resolved that he would not preach again until the question was cleared up. On the Sunday he went to a little Methodist chapel where the service was conducted by a local preacher."*

Spurgeon picks up the story himself at this point:

"The tears flowed freely from my eyes; I was moved to the deepest emotion by every sentence of the sermon, and I felt all my difficulty removed, for the Gospel, I saw, was very dear to me, and had a wonderful effect on my own heart. I went to the preacher and said, 'I thank you very much for that sermon.' He asked who I was, and when I told him he turned as red as possible, and said, 'Why, it was one of your sermons that I preached this morning!' 'Yes,' I said, 'I know it was; but that was the very message that I wanted to hear, because I then saw that I did enjoy the very word I myself preached.' It was happily so arranged in the good Providence of God."

Although he often suffered from nervousness in the pulpit, it was not until April of 1891, when, for the first time in 40 years of ministry, he became so oppressed with nervousness in the pulpit that he was compelled to leave and to turn the chairmanship of the meeting over to his assistant to complete the service.

Spurgeon used astringents for his throat such as chili vinegar mixed with water which he sipped occasionally during the service. Beef tea *"as strong with pepper as can be borne"* was his panacea for whatever ailed him!

He was never ordained for he held that an inward call to preach the Gospel which was recognized by Christian people in electing him to serve as their pastor, was a sufficient and true ordination which did not require a formal commissioning and laying on of hands of other ministers.

Spurgeon's Humour

No accounting of the life and ministry of Charles Haddon Spurgeon could be deemed complete without some special mention of his sense of humour. He believed that it was less of a sin to raise a smile than to plunge an audience into sleep!

The following quotations will give the reader some insight into his spontaneous wit and the original character of his humour.

He once described a character who came to apply to enter his college. He said that the applicant's face *"...look like the title page to a whole volume of conceit and deceit...and he had enough assurance for 100 adventurers."*

He once asked his men to open the chapel windows in the middle of a service, because *"the next best thing to the grace of God for a preacher is oxygen."*

He revealed his opinion of committees in the following comment: *"I believe in a committee of three, elected by myself: one of them to be always away, and the other one ill in bed."*

"I've noticed that perfect men usually beat their wives, or perform some other useful service to the community," he said, tongue-in-cheek.

"My pocket is often a type of immutability, for there's no change in it!"

"The first two things that a student should learn when he comes to college are these: First, that he's a fool; secondly, that he's not the only one there."

"Don't put the emphasis on the wrong word, like the student who read, 'He said to his sons, saddle me the ass; so they saddled HIM."

"Here is a riddle for you. If Paul was less than the least of all saints, what size are you?"

"Don't pray for 20 minutes in the prayer meeting and then ask God to forgive your shortcomings."

"It's an awkward experience to preach on the devil and feel full of your subject."

"Don't use hackneyed illustrations. You know the venerable anecdote about the sinking ship and the rescued sailor whispering to his rescuers, 'There's another man! There's another man!' What possible good can be done by such a worn-out illustration—except to give some old maid fresh hope?"

"In preaching, remember that, as a rule, what is new isn't true, and what is true isn't new."

In one of his several biographies the following story was recorded:

"He once dined with several of her late Majesty's judges at the house of one of them, who was a great friend of his. During dinner he remarked with apparent gravity, that a puzzling question had arisen in connection with a member of his congregation about which he would like to have their lordships' opinion. This man resolutely refused to bury his wife. She had been lying upstairs for the last fortnight, and, in spite of all remonstrances, he would not bury her. Was there any process of law by which he could be compelled to do so? The judges present at once bent themselves to the task, and after much quoting of Acts of Parliament, they explained to him the

process by which the man could be compelled to bury his wife. But they were very much taken aback when he remarked, 'I do not think you would succeed for all that, because, you see, the woman is not dead yet!'"

He used to say that certain ministers possessed some of the attributes of divinity, *"for they were invisible all the week and incomprehensible on the Sunday."*

Politically, Spurgeon was a *"pronounced liberal."* He had no sympathy with the pseudo-pietism which regards the duties of citizenship as outside the sphere of religion. At one of the general elections he was returning from the polling station, where he had been to record his vote, when he met an exceedingly pious man to whom he chanced to mention what he had been doing.

"Oh, brother Spurgeon," came the protest, *"how can you do so? Do you not know that the new man does not vote?"*
"No, it was the old man that voted," retorted Spurgeon.
"Yes, but aren't we told to mortify the old man?"
"Well, that's just what I did. I did mortify him. My old man's a Tory, and I made him vote for the Liberals!"

The Prince of Preachers: How to Account for This

Although the biographers of other leading preachers of the 19th century have proclaimed their subjects as the *"greatest"*, the evidence weights our evaluation in the direction of Spurgeon. He was indeed the Prince of Preachers during his lifetime.

George John Stevenson, in his book, *The Prince of Preachers: Charles H. Spurgeon* (London, 1867), wrote:

"As a preacher, he is THE PRINCE; he has no rival: but as a divine, some do not give him a high place."

Such a conclusion, that Spurgeon was an effective evangelist but not necessarily a model *"divine"* did not sit well with all who studied his life. The probability is that his strong individuality, his wide popularity, and his keen sense of humour eliminated him from the category of *"pious saint"* in the minds of many. Perhaps his cigars blocked the path to his elevation to evangelical sainthood!

Taking into account the leading preachers of the day, Frederic C. Spurr gives a comparative summary in the following manner:

> *"In the Mid-Victorian period there were three outstanding personalities in the Christian pulpit of London: Henry Parry Liddon, Canon of St. Paul's; Joseph Parker, of the City Temple; and Charles Haddon Spurgeon, of the Metropolitan Tabernacle. Visitors to London made it their business to hear one or all of these three distinguished men, and often on the same day. Spurgeon's morning congregation was, perhaps, the largest in the whole Protestant world, consisting of more than 5,000 people. Liddon preached at St. Paul's on Sunday afternoons, and attracted as many as 2,500 people. Parker had as many to hear him on Sunday evenings. Naturally people had their favourites. Certain who were devoted to Liddon would not have considered it decorous to attend a Free Church service. In this they were perfectly sincere. Parker attracted great audiences of men, many of whom belonged to the Professions. Students from all Colleges found their way to the City Temple. Parker was known as a preacher to preachers. Spurgeon, on the other hand, was a magnet to draw the 'common people,' who thronged to hear him for forty years save one. Yet in his congregation were always found persons of note in the world."*

> *"Liddon was an apologist of a very high order. He believed himself called to defend the Christian Faith from the assaults of infidelity and scepticism, which, in his time, had become serious, especially the variety emanating from Germany. Parker set himself to expound the whole Bible and apply its principles to common life. Spurgeon was an evangelist from the beginning to the end, but an evangelist of the pastoral order. It were foolish to attempt any comparison between men so diverse in gift, temperament, and ministry. Each had his place and each accomplished a great work."*

> *"It is the strict truth, however, to say that of the three, the name of Spurgeon was the most widely known."*

Professor Cleaver Wilkinson's judgment of him was that *"had he not been a preacher, he might have been the most perfect orator of his time."*

Many have attempted to define the secret of Spurgeon's success but seem to have failed, or at best, were incomplete in their analysis or overly simplistic. After weighing up several factors and discarding them as being non-critical, Spurr attributes Spurgeon's success to his spirit, that he was a man who fervently loved his Lord and possessed a singleness of heart and mind to win men to Christ. Spurr regarded Spurgeon as one of the world's great evangelists.

When Sir William Robertson Nicoll was asked the secret of Spurgeon's power, he replied simply, *"The Holy Spirit."* But as fine and pious as these answers appear to be, they do not give a full and honest answer to the question. Other men and women have also been fervent in spirit, hungered after the souls of men, and have been mightily endued with the power of the Holy Spirit for service, and yet they did not enjoy the marked success that attended Spurgeon's ministry.

Though we too shall fall short of a complete explanation to Spurgeon's power and success, it is fair to say that the answer lies in a coming together of a complexity of factors.

The factor of *timing* has already been touched upon above under the heading 'Understanding the Times.' Spurgeon was the right man, with the appropriate gifts, personality and character qualities, to appear on the non-conformist stage at the right time. The timing was right and ripe both in terms of the life of the church in England, and of the secular society. Spurgeon had come to the kingdom for such a time as this!

Being a mere boy when he started out made him somewhat of a phenomenon in the English pulpit.

> *"The very youthfulness of the preacher added to his attractiveness, and his manifest zeal and transparent sincerity of heart won for him an enthusiastic reception which a staid and experienced divine might have longed for in vain."* (From, *One Who Knew Him Well*)

In the *Greville Memoirs* dated 8 February 1857, the following description appears:

> *"He is certainly very remarkable, and undeniably a fine character; not remarkable in person; in face, rather resembling a smaller Macaulay; a very clear and powerful voice, which was heard through the hall; a manner natural, impassioned, and without affection or extravagance; wonderful fluency and command of language,*

abounding in illustration, and very often of a very familiar kind, but without anything either ridiculous or irreverent. He gave me an impression of his earnestness and sincerity; speaking without book or notes, yet his discourse was evidently very carefully prepared."

Not everyone would agree with the above synopsis of Spurgeon's preaching. There are a couple of points in this description which should not go without challenge, or at least mention, for the impressions of other observers begged to differ. For example, some regarded his manner as being quite irreverent, his gestures theatrical, and his speech unguarded. Others took exception to his use of illustrations from his personal life, and yet others objected to his references to the many people who were coming to Christ under his ministry. At least one biographer felt it was Spurgeon's *"eccentricities and extravagancies"* which drew the crowds to hear him preach.

Within a relatively short period of time the objectionable features of his manner dropped off. His theatrical gestures disappeared and he curbed his humour to some extent. In the early years there was far too much laughter from the audience. In fact, the truth of the matter is, that after about five to six years of ministry in London, he lost some of the *"sparkle"* to his preaching as he went through a period of change and moderation. He now became much more dignified and grave. He did not seek so much to attract crowds as he directed his efforts now to build up his people in the faith. Spurgeon himself recognized that the degree of excellence which he possessed in the beginning, and later on near the end of his ministry, had slackened off. Though there were some ups and downs during this period of adjustment and growth, Spurgeon deserves much credit for opening up his life for Divine pruning that he might be a vessel unto honour in the Master's house.

He demonstrated an intense earnestness. Often his voice would break into sobs and tears would stream down his cheeks as he pleaded with the souls of men to be reconciled to God. In earlier days he preached much on the terrors of the law and indulged in awe-inspiring descriptions of the doom of the wicked, but later he advised his students against this style.

Andrew Melrose recorded that Spurgeon's earnestness burned unabated throughout his life into his later years.

"His earnestness was often terrible. We have seen him preach when in such agony from gout that he could not keep his foot on the ground, but had to kneel on a chair while speaking. But presently, as he warmed to his subject, he would spring to his feet and advance to the front of the pulpit and preach with all his old vigour, regardless of the pain that burned like a fire in his bones. No wonder that such fervour was potent to persuade men."

"Above all, the blessing of the Holy Spirit manifestly rested upon his ministry. One was conscious while listening, of a power and influence that were not due to the force of his argument or eloquence of his utterance."

In 1867, George John Stevenson tried to define the secret of Spurgeon's effectiveness. It is—

"summed up in a few words; it is traceable in the main, to the doctrines which he preaches; to his sincerity, fidelity, honesty and truth...his righteous boldness is traceable to a source which is a tower of strength to any minister, he is a man of truth."

Stevenson went on to acknowledge Spurgeon's

"fine, natural, bell-like voice and his unartificial use of it...But the basis of the whole is unquestionably to be found in his sincere, earnest, piety and in his preaching a personal Christ to be believed on by every sinner who will flee to Him for refuge and pardon."

The British and Foreign Evangelical Review gives us one of the most vivid descriptions of Spurgeon's style in its January 1866 edition; they also seek to define the secret of his success:

"He is himself not only popular, but he represents the popularity of his time. He is as unlike the popular preacher of the past as his Tabernacle, with its stage, pit, and galleries is unlike Westminister Abbey. He is The Times of modern evangelism. Many of his sermons would make good leading articles; and in power, the profusion, and the rapidity with which they are poured forth, we are reminded of the steam-press and the electric telegraph. His pulpit is stript of all its common accessories; and it is very doubtful if the short round figure

of the preacher would be improved by gown and cassock. He is no clerical fop; there is no cant or whining about him, and were it not for time and place, few would suppose from look, tone or style, that they listened to a sermon. The secret of his success arises from a combination of gifts as rare as they are startling and precious. The logical faculty is manifest everywhere, combined with a fancy which brings up images at will, and scatters around the plainest subject in copiousness of apt illustration with amazing skill. Then there is the marvelous memory of the man which seems always ready to supply him with the stores of his reading as they are needed; the sonorous voice, ringing like a church bell; the terse Saxon-English of his style, the volubility of his elocution, joined with that perfect self-control, which prevents it from degenerating into declamation, and imparts to it something of the measured tramp of military precision. The whole structure of his sermons is conversational; but it is conversation through a speaking-trumpet; the speaker is on fire throughout, not with flashes of flame, but in the sustained white heat of the furnace. There is, besides, the world-like tone of his addresses; he has the knack of making his shot tell upon the world. He has got into the way of talking for the Gospel exactly as the world talks against it."

This latter remark, in the view of the author, after studying Spurgeon's sermons analytically, is one of the most perceptive conclusions he has read, in trying to account for the secret of Spurgeon's success as a preacher-evangelist.

Sermon Preparation and Delivery

It bears repeating, that reckoning from the very outset of the sermon preparation process, Spurgeon's greatest difficulty was in the choosing of a text. Multitudes of preachers will quickly identify with this difficulty!

In his 1903 publication, Andrew Melrose included an analysis of the ingredients which made Spurgeon's preaching so great:

1. His command of English was pure and undefiled, marked by simplicity and clarity.
2. He announced his divisions and had a definite plan for his sermons which made them easy to recall.

3. His sermons possessed a perennial freshness due to their Scriptural character.
4. Spurgeon's knowledge of the Scriptures.
5. His keen sense of humour.
6. He was a master in the art of sermon illustration. Spurgeon was an omnivorous reader and a keen observer. He had a practice of turning everything to spiritual profit, even the smallest incidents.

"To tell him any striking fact during the week was often to hear it from the pulpit on the following Sunday as a vehicle of some religious instruction."

Later in life, his two Sunday sermons were prepared after 6 o'clock on Saturday evening. His sermon preparation procedure went something like this:

1. The chief task was to fix upon a text. Sometimes the text would be in his mind for days. At other times the text would come to him at the last moment. Sometimes the text would be suggested to him by trivial incidents. At other times he would ask his friends for texts and their advice as to how to treat the texts. He would not preach unless the texts would *"bite."* He would shut himself into his study Saturday evening and would not leave until the Sunday morning sermon was ready. He gave less attention to the preparation of the Sunday evening message. He would at least decide on its general outline on Saturday night but then he would spend his quiet hour Sunday afternoon to complete it.

2. After he had settled on a text, he would examine the text minutely in the original languages.

3. Next, he would study the context in which the text was couched.

4. He would then consult commentaries but he complained that they usually told him what he already knew, and failed to tell him what he didn't know.

5. Following this he would jot down roughly the main lines of thought.

6. He would next examine his list of published sermons to see if he had already preached from this text. If he had, and his treatment was the same as before, he would either abandon the text, or, adopt a new treatment.

7. Sometimes Mrs. Spurgeon helped by reading aloud extracts from various divines regarding the text, while Charles made brief notes.

8. Finally, his jottings were arranged in order and the outline of the sermon neatly copied on a half-sheet of note paper for pulpit use.

Melrose went on to say, *"Saturday evenings were always times of agonizing prayer to God."*

> *"He preached for forty minutes, on average. He was careful to enunciate every syllable, especially the final ones. There was a slight provincial accent in his speech and he had a curious habit of emphasizing the personal pronouns. One saw no tricks of oratory or efforts after dramatic effect. These were very marked at the beginning of his London ministry but he entirely abandoned them as he grew older. Indeed, he used to speak of them in terms of condemnation in his lectures to ministers and students."*
>
> *"The charm of his oratory lay in its perfect naturalness. He just 'talked' his sermons and the very simplicity of his style was eloquent of the honest convictions of the preacher. But while simple, he was never commonplace. His thoughts were remarkable for their originality, his illustrations were striking and illuminative, and his general style was dignified and impressive. Without any effort, his language rose to the loftiest oratory and when warmed to his subject the words flowed like a majestic flood. When denouncing sin his sarcasm could be withering; when pleading with sinners his voice would be full of tears; when speaking of the wonders of Divine love, his tones became musical in their graciousness."*

In his early years he walked about the spacious pulpit gesticulating freely. In his later years he stood almost still, leaning with one hand on the back of a chair. Sometimes, because of the pain caused by gout he would lean the weight of his body on a chair with one knee as previously noted. The expression of his face and the tone of his voice were animated in the extreme.

One of the earliest descriptions of his preaching we owe to a Mr. Hare:

> *"His voice is clear and musical; his language plain; his style, flowing, but terse; his method lucid and orderly; his matter sound*

and suitable; his tone and spirit, cordial; his remarks always pithy and pungent, sometimes familiar and colloquial, yet never light or coarse, much less profane. Judging from a single sermon, we supposed that he would become a plain, faithful, forcible, and affectionate preacher of the Gospel in the form called Calvinistic; and our judgment was the more favourable, because, while there was a solidity beyond his years, we detected little of the wild luxuriance naturally characteristic of very young preachers. Want of order and arrangement was a fault the preacher soon found out himself, and he refers to it when he says,'Once I put all my knowledge together in glorious confusion; but now I have a shelf in my head for everything; and whatever I read or hear, I know where to stow it away for use at the proper time.'"

The End

During the period 1887-89 the *"down grade"* controversy arose over the straying from orthodoxy of some of the ministers and churches in the Baptist denomination. Spurgeon strongly defended the faith. His own brother, James, was not as conservative as Charles. He had been trained under Dr. Angus. In the end Spurgeon was censured and left the Baptist Union.

On 7 June 1891 he preached his last sermon at the Metropolitan Tabernacle. He was only 57 years old but had become prematurely old, broken in health, white-haired and feeble. His text was I Samuel 30:21-25. The very last words that he ever preached were as follows:

"If you wear the livery of Christ, you will find Him so meek and lowly of heart that you will find rest unto your souls. He is the most magnanimous of captains. There never was His like among the choicest of princes. He is always to be found in the thickest part of the battle. When the wind blows cold, He always takes the bleak side of the hill. The heaviest end of the Cross lies ever on His shoulder. If He bids you carry a burden, He carries it also. If there is anything gracious, generous, kind, and tender, yea, lavish and superabundant in love, you always find it in Him. His service is life, peace, joy. Oh, that you would enter on it at once! God help you to enlist under the banner of Jesus Christ."

On Friday an overpowering headache set in and he hurried home to bed. It was the beginning of an acute attack of Bright's Disease which he endured for 3 months. In the end it was this that caused his death. He suffered long attacks of delirium. The physician's daily bulletin on his health was printed in a prominent place in all newspapers. He improved slightly but the disease was incurable.

Finally, at 11:05, Sunday evening, 31 January 1892, Charles Haddon Spurgeon passed into the Presence of His Lord at Mentone in southern France. His body was brought back to London for the funeral and burial.

Other notable men of God who died at age 57 include John Calvin, William Tyndale, Jonathan Edwards, Jeremy Taylor and George Whitefield.

Funeral services were held at the Metropolitan Tabernacle from 7–11 February 1892. One account recorded that 60,000 people filed past his coffin to pay him tribute. Another account claimed 100,000 attended the funeral. On the coffin the Bible lay open at the text, *"Look unto me and be ye saved all the ends of the earth…"*…the very text which had led to his conversion 42 years before. Ira Sankey sang at the funeral. Spurgeon was buried in West Norwood Cemetery on a slope beside the cemetery chapel. "Susie", his beloved wife, died over 11 years later on 22 October 1903.

Joseph Parker lamented,

> *"The great voice has ceased. It was the mightiest voice I ever heard; a voice that could give orders in a tempest, and find its way across a torrent as through a silent aisle."*

The one whom his earliest critics nick-named *"Punch in the Pulpit"* had become the greatest power-in-the-pulpit the 19th century ever witnessed. Now, at last, he was at rest.

Chapter Eleven

Alexander Whyte

13 January 1836–6 January 1921

Child of Unmarried Parents

Alexander Whyte was born on 13 January 1836 in Southmuir of Kirriemuir (which became the County of Forfar) in Scotland.

His father was John Whyte, who left Alec's mother, Janet Thomson, soon after Alec was born. They never married. Alec grew up in his mother's home whereas John went to the United States and fought for the North in the Civil War. He was captured and imprisoned at Richmond. Eventually his father married in New York, but his wife died, leaving behind one daughter, Elizabeth, who subsequently came to have a large part in her half-brother's heart and life. Alec referred to her as "the friend of all friends to me." John Whyte died in New York on 31 March 1871 when Alexander was 35 years of age.

Late-Starting Family Man

Alexander Whyte married quite late in life. He was 45 years of age when he took Jane Elizabeth Barbour to be his wife on 9 September 1881. Their first daughter, Margaret, was born in July of 1882. They had eight children in all. One of their sons, George, died after only six months of life on 19 August 1885.

Alexander suffered grievous losses within a relatively short span of time. His beloved mother who had bravely raised her son alone, died on 7 June 1882. On her coffin were inscribed the lines:

"Nothing in my hand I bring; Simply to Thy Cross I cling."

One week later he saw his beloved half-sister, Elizabeth Macadam, and her three children off to Canada, and was never to see them again. In 1888, three years after baby George died, Alec received word that his half-sister, his dearest friend, had died in Ontario.

Personal Characteristics and Challenges

Kathy Triggs, in her book *Alexander Whyte: Peacemaker*, described Whyte as having—

> *"a tremendous strength of will. Along the line of duty he is one of the most determined, I would venture to say, one of the most dogged, persons whom God ever created."*

Surely this is so because he had to battle a learning defect all his life which would have eliminated lesser men from ministry. He suffered from a defective verbal memory—he simply could not memorize anything—which resulted in poor performance in subjects like maths, physics and chemistry. This defect also dictated that he must read his sermons.

As for physical appearance, his hair has been described as *"long yellow hair which he flung back with his hand from time to time"* when preaching. Another described the colour of his hair as being red. Whether yellow or red it became white in old age. He had blue eyes and a *"sudden smile."* In the pulpit he wore a Presbyterian gown. His voice, remembered by one who heard him in his early days of ministry at Free St. George's, Edinburgh *"...came to my ear as the sound of the North Sea breaking on the cliff..."*

In the winter of 1882-83, having observed the ruin that drink had caused in the lives of so many, he completely gave up using alcohol and admonished others to do the same.

Also, in the autumn of 1882, he was involved in a serious coach accident in which he was dealt a severe blow to the head resulting in his being bed-ridden for four weeks. We gain some insight into the esteem in which Whyte was held nationally at that time, in that, Queen Victoria herself, while in residence at Balmoral, sent word to inquire into his progress.

His daily routine called for an early start in reading and writing in his study up until 1 p.m. His study was a sacred place to him, the very nerve centre of his activity as a minister. He was very tidy and had an instinct for order. He was a methodical note-taker. He would use a Bible with blank pages interleaved so that he could jot down thoughts as he was reading and make use of them later in sermon preparation. At 1 p.m. he would then have lunch and launch forth in pastoral visitation and congregational work. He preached four or five evenings every week. At 9:45 p.m. he ended the day with brief but meaningful family prayers.

Each year he took two months off in the summer in addition to Christmas and Easter breaks.

In spite of all his success and renown, he suffered periods of deep depression when he would agonize over his alleged *"failure in the ministry."* In December of 1909, when he was 73, he suffered his first heart attack, and a second one in the summer of 1910.

It was Alexander Whyte who coined the phrase *"Catholic Evangelical."* Kathy Trigg wrote:

> *"The well-read, the open-minded, the hospitable-hearted, the spiritually exercised Evangelical, as he is called. He is of no sect. He is of no school…He comes of no movement. He belongs to all sects, and all sects belong to him…How rich such men are in truth and love and hope!"*

In his latter years, Whyte always strove for peace: peace between opposing denominations in a quest for church unity, and, peace between Britain and Germany as the *"Great War"* loomed up on the horizon.

The Shaping of the Vessel

Whyte received his first sense of the spell and power of sacred oratory from sitting under the preaching of Rev. James Dunlop Paxton, Minister of Auld Licht Kirk, from 1843–1846. Also, in 1843, when Alec was only 7 years old, the great Robert Murray M'Cheyne, minister of St. Peter's, Dundee, came and preached at Kirriemuir in the 30th year of his life. He died just three months afterwards. M'Cheyne made a deep impression upon young Alec's heart and mind.

Janet Thomson wanted to make sure that her son had a trade under his belt, consequently from 1849 to 1854 Alec took an apprenticeship in a shoemaking business under James Ogilvy. He told his mother that he would *"serve his time"* but then afterwards he was going to become a minister.

Alec took what in those days was a common route to gain entrance into university, by commencing to teach at a school in Padanaram in 1854. The following year he taught at Free Church School at Airlie which is five miles west of Kirriemuir. David White tutored him at that time.

Alexander Whyte got his first opportunity to speak publicly in a Sabbath School in Kirriemuir, where he also joined a debating society.

From 1858 to 1862 he studied at King's College, Aberdeen. During that period, in 1859, a revival swept over the north of Scotland among the clergy and laity alike, but was mainly guided by laymen. Alec's life was touched and empowered by this revival blessing.

Alec was appointed missionary at Kinnoir in 1861 taking up residence at the Huntly Free Church mission station which had been erected by the Duchess of Gordon in 1860.

From 1862 to 1866 he studied at New College, Edinburgh.

He served as assistant to Dr. John Roxburgh, in Free St. John's, Glasgow, from 1866 to 1870. On 7 June 1866, he was licensed to preach by the Free Presbytery of Edinburgh. His fame as a preacher began to spread, and on 27 December of that same year, he was ordained.

Free St. George's, Edinburgh

Alec received a call from Free St. George's, Edinburgh, to become a colleague of Dr. Candlish. He began his ministry there in the afternoon service of 9 October 1870. Unexpectedly, in 1873, Dr. Candlish died, and from the end of that year Alexander Whyte became the church's sole minister. An interesting footnote here is that Whyte laboured for 22 years alone before obtaining a colleague to share the burden of responsibility at Free St. George's.

One month after Candlish died, Moody and Sankey arrived in Edinburgh, and Alexander Whyte became very involved in the crusade and was affected by it. In 1874 they experienced revival.

From 1876 to 1881, the Free Church passed through another period of struggle over the issue of freedom of the Church to function without

State interference. There was the famous "Robertson Smith Case." Robertson Smith published a new interpretation of the Pentateuch which was brought into dispute. Whyte stood on the side of Smith stating that Smith had the freedom and right to hold to his own views. In the end Smith was removed from the Hebrew Chair at Aberdeen College. Whyte did not agree with the results of Higher Criticism—he merely defended the right of scholars to pursue legitimate inquiry and study.

During that same period of history, Whyte was part of a small deputation from the ministers of the Free and the United Presbyterian Churches, which presented an Address to Mr. Gladstone, over breakfast, on 23 May 1878. In the Address they thanked Gladstone for his firm stand on behalf of the oppressed Christian peoples in the Turkish empire, and for his stand against the forces which were dragging Britain towards a second Crimean War. Whyte's sympathy for the suffering Armenian people became a permanent, life-long interest.

In the Spring of 1881 the University of Edinburgh conferred a D.D. on Whyte and on 9 September of that year, after 45 years of bachelorhood, he married Jane Elizabeth Barbour, as recorded earlier. It was during the 1880's that he became friends with Joseph Parker.

On 19 May 1898 he became Moderator of the Free Church of Scotland. Gladstone died on the very first day of that Assembly. In October of the year 1900 the United Presbyterians and the Free Church united. From 1909 to 1916 Whyte served as the Principal of New College, Edinburgh.

In 1916 he resigned from Free St. George's. He had ministered there for 46 years!

The Preaching of Alexander Whyte

In the biographical sketch of John Henry Jowett we note that while Jowett studied at the University of Edinburgh, Whyte, above all other preachers, was Jowett's favourite. He commented:

> *"Few preachers brought home to their audience the sense of sin so deeply as Dr. Whyte. One could not listen to him without feeling the pressing need of a Gospel."*

Whyte's preaching was marked by forthrightness—a directness of speech. He is best known for his sermons on Bible characters. He had a most vivid and lively spiritual imagination, especially in the development of those Bible personalities. He once wrote that to have imagination was to have *"eyes and a heart for the unseen and the spiritual."*

> F. B. Meyer wrote in his volume entitled, *Expository Preaching: Plans and Methods,* "*Biographical preaching has found a chief exponent in our day in the masterly analysis of character given by Dr. Whyte of Edinburgh, laying hold of the salient features and characteristics and enforcing them for imitation or warning.*"

Whyte's use of his vivid imagination in the elaboration of the personality traits, sins and foibles, of Bible characters, would take him far beyond the actual information provided in the text itself. Once Whyte determined that he had discovered the central evil or attribute of a Bible character, he then would push far beyond the boundaries of revelation to describe the person's character or behaviour. For example, in describing Michal's reaction to seeing her husband, King David, dancing before the Ark of the Covenant, Whyte said,

> "*At the despicable sight, she spat at him, and sank back in her seat with all hell in her heart.*"

This statement is not how the Bible states her actions but it is the fruit of a vivid imagination which seeks to characterize Michal's reactions. It is in this imaginative characterization that Whyte departs from what we might understand as being correct hermeneutics.

In another sermon on Ham, (concerning which we shall comment further in the section entitled *Fertile Imagination*) once Whyte determined that Ham's heart and character were blacker than tar, he launches forth on a gripping description of Ham's vileness. Whyte envisioned an old, wicked reprobate of a man, boiling a pot of pitch to daub onto the ark, and he saw Ham always hanging about the hollow where the old man worked:

> "*The black asphalt itself was whiteness itself beside that old reprobate's heart and life. Now Ham, Noah's second son, was never away from that deep hollow out of which the preparing pitch boiled and*

smoked. All day down among the slime-pits, and all night out among the sultry woods—wherever you heard Ham's loud laugh, be sure that lewd old man was either singing a song there or telling a story. All the time the ark was a-building, and for long before that, Ham had been making himself vile under the old pitch-boiler's instructions and examples. Ham's old instructor and exemplar had gone down quick to hell as soon as the ark was finished and shut in. But, by that time, Ham could walk alone."

Later in the description of Ham's evil heart, Whyte sees Noah's sons tending to the animals inside the ark:

"The pairs of the unclean beast that Ham attended to with his brothers were clean and chaste creatures of God compared to Ham. For Ham could neither feed those brute beasts, nor bed them, nor look at them, nor think about them without sin. More than one of those abused beasts will be brought forward at the day of judgment to bear testimony against one of their former masters. From a little boy Noah's second son had been a filthy dreamer. The best and the holiest words his father could speak had an unclean sense to his son. Every vessel in the ark and every instrument held an unclean association for Ham. Within all those steaming walls the only brute beast was Noah's second son."

In this one example, once Whyte determined that Ham's essential character was vile, he then set forth in the most imaginative detail to paint an image of Ham that was blacker than black!! We shall have more to say about this particular sermon later on.

Whyte treated Bunyan's characters as he did Biblical characters. There is a published work of Whyte's in four volumes, entitled, *"Bunyan's Characters."*

No matter what our judgment might be regarding Whyte's method of interpreting the Scriptures, his preaching was accompanied with mighty conviction of sin and great numbers of men and women found Christ as a result.

On one occasion he astonished a group of Edinburgh's poor slum-dwellers, when he announced that he had found out the name of the wickedest man in Edinburgh and that he had come to tell them of his discovery. Then, bending forward, he whispered, *"His name is Alexander Whyte."*

Whyte went to a great deal of trouble in his sermon preparation, giving much attention to style and to the very selection of words. *"He studied his favourite exponents of good English style* (such as Hooker, Bunyan and Newman) *and modeled his own upon their example,"* wrote Triggs.

Whyte once remarked,

> *"I would have laziness held to be the one unpardonable sin in all our students and in all our ministers."*

Though his sermons were usually read, his delivery was not wooden and his voice captivated the attention of his audience.

Whyte had a heart for the welfare of young people and for forty years he conducted classes for young women and young men.

Death

This great Scottish preacher passed on to his reward on Thursday, 6 January 1921.

Chapter Twelve

Frederick Brotherton Meyer

8 April 1847–28 March 1929

Birth and Upbringing

F. B. Meyer was born at Lavender Terrace, Wandsworth Road, London, on 8 April 1847. He was the grandson of John Sebastian Meyer of Worms, Germany, who, in the earlier half of the 18th century, established himself in London as a sugar refiner. Frederick's mother died when he was only six years old.

He studied at Brighton College where his family had moved in 1855. While still in his mid-teens his pastor at Brighton, Dr. Brock, had told him that one day he would become a minister and by age 16 he was convinced of the Lord's leading to enter the ministry. He was baptized by the Rev. David Jones on 2 June 1864 at New Park Chapel in London.

During his early years Meyer sat under the preaching of such notables as Joseph Parker, Charles Spurgeon, Landels, and Thomas Binney.

In October of 1869 he entered Regent's Park College and on 1 December 1869 earned a B.A. at London University. M. Jennie Street published a biography of Meyer in 1902 in which she wrote that it was surprising to discover that very few of his classmates it Regent's Park anticipated his future prominence. In fact, Street called him *"one of the least known men in the world!"*

Early Ministry and Marriage

In 1868 he began his pastoral ministry at a Baptist church in Richmond. In 1870 he became Associate Pastor to the Rev. Charles M. Birrell at Pembroke Chapel, Liverpool. A. Chester Mann said that it was from Birrell that Meyer learned to preach expositionally.

While at Pembroke Chapel, on 20 February 1871, at 23 years of age, he married Miss J. E. Jones of Birkenhead. In May of 1872 Meyer took up the pastorate in York, at a Baptist Church on Priory Street. When the Meyers moved to York they already had an infant daughter, the only child of their marriage. Later in life they were to have two grand-daughters and one grandson who was killed in the war at Vimy Ridge.

Dwight L. Moody and Ira D. Sankey

F. B. Meyer is inseparably identified with the first evangelistic mission of Moody and Sankey in Great Britain. This association influenced Meyer in a rather significant way in future years.

D. L. Moody, and his family, along with Ira D. Sankey, arrived in Liverpool on 17 June 1873. Plans for this proposed mission were very uncertain and Moody began to believe that God was closing the door on the whole venture. That very evening, while going through his own pockets in the Adelphi Hotel, he found a letter he had received just prior to his departure from New York. It was from Mr. Bennett, Secretary of the Y.M.C.A. in York. Moody had met this gentleman years before somewhere in the West. Moody sent a telegram to Bennett immediately, whereupon Bennett fired back a reply asking for dates for a conference. Moody shot back a message, "I will be in York tonight!" Moody arrived in York at 10 o'clock that very evening.

On the following Sunday a Congregational pulpit was opened to him and Moody preached his first sermon. The people were aloof and expressed a "positive disfavour."

In a few days time they went round to visit F. B. Meyer, who was pastoring the Priory Street Baptist Chapel, York. At the time of their first meeting, Moody was 36 years old and Meyer, 26. To Meyer's credit, and to the spiritual benefit of Great Britain, Meyer received Moody with open arms. It was then in Meyer's church that Moody and Sankey began their triumphant tour. Meetings were conducted for five weeks in Meyer's church resulting in several hundred professions of faith. From there, Moody and Sankey went to Sunderland where even larger meetings were held.

An unusual and prominent feature of the Moody mission in later days was the establishment of the *"All-Day Meeting."* This concept came together as Moody and Meyer walked up and down Cowley Street. The

All-Day Meeting began at 11 a.m. and continued for six hours. The program proceeded according to the following general format:

1st hour:	Confession and prayer.
2nd hour:	Hour of praise.
3rd hour:	Testimonies concerning the fulfilment of God's promises in the lives of believers.
4th hour:	A witness meeting for young converts.
5th hour:	Bible Address by D. L. Moody.
6th hour:	Resolved itself into a Communion service led by F. B. Meyer and three other city ministers.

The very novelty of the service attracted considerable attention and in the end the strategy was deemed to have been an unqualified success. Meyer later testified of a little noon-time prayer meeting which was conducted on a Monday in 1873. The first of these was led by Mr. Moody in a small, ill-lit room on Cowley Street. Meyer wrote:

"It was the birth-time of new conceptions of ministry, new methods of work, new inspirations and hope."

Moody also referred to the vestry of Priory Street Baptist Chapel, York, when he spoke in Manchester, calling it that little room *"from which the river of blessing for the whole country had sprung."* During these meetings Meyer caught a vision of wider, non-denominational ministry and he never looked back.

One story emerging from those days was that of Moody suddenly receiving a strong impression, in the midst of tea-time at home, that he was to preach his sermon on heaven, which later became quite famous. He got up from the table and walked three miles to fetch his sermon notes.

F. B. Meyer has left us with descriptions of Dwight L. Moody:

"He was a good man for whom one might dare to die."

He said that Moody was thoroughly natural and that there was no limit to his inventiveness. He would create naive resolutions to difficult problems, and succeed! Moody was most in his element when ministering to men. *"Strong natures were strongly influenced by him."*

"What an inspiration when this great and noble soul first broke into my life! I was a young pastor then in the old city of York, and bound rather rigidly by the chains of conventionalism. Such had been my training, and such might have been my career. But here was revelation of a new ideal. The first characteristic of Moody's that struck me was that he was so absolutely unconventional and natural. That a piece of work had generally been done after a certain method would probably be the reason why he would set about it in some fresh and unexpected way. That the new method startled people was the greater reason for continuing with it, if only it drew them to the Gospel. But there was never the slightest approach to irreverence, fanaticism, or extravagance; everything was in perfect accord with a rare common sense, a directness of method, a simplicity and transparency of aim, which were as attractive as they were fruitful in result."

It is claimed that Moody taught Meyer to be himself and not to strive to be a copy of anyone else. Henry Drummond called Moody, *"the greatest human I ever met."* At some point along the way, Moody was responsible for the founding of the Bible Training Institute in Glasgow.

The author has taken this much time to speak of D. L. Moody in relation to F. B. Meyer, for had Moody not come across the pathway of Meyer, we might never have taken note of Meyer's contribution to the history of the English Church. A significant contribution may have been non-existent. In fact, Moody's impact upon several of the men who are the subject of this book's attention, was profound.

Victoria Road, Leicester

In 1874, F. B. Meyer responded to a call to the pulpit of Victoria Road Church, Leicester, where he sailed into some stormy waters. On 5 May 1878 he preached his last sermon there having resigned over the tension which was caused by his own evangelistic zeal.

Continuing in Leicester

Meyer was persuaded to remain in Leicester by some of his supporters and began preaching in the Museum Buildings. The Paradise Mission, a local city mission, which was started while he pastored Victoria Road Church, was handed over to him.

On 23 September 1878 they started a *"Church of Christ"* with the objective to reach people outside of ordinary Christian agencies.

A most intriguing look into F. B. Meyer's character and activities, is afforded us when we learn that Meyer assisted unskilled, unemployed men, by selling firewood. He drove a van around Leicester selling firewood and on its side was written, *"F. B. MEYER: FIREWOOD MER-CHANT."*

Melbourne Hall

In 1881 he began meeting in the newly built Melbourne Hall which could comfortably seat 1,200, and could hold up to 2,000. He established Sunday Schools with up to 2,500 scholars in attendance. At one point they were conducting up to 83 different meetings of various sorts on a weekly basis at Melbourne Hall.

Hudson Taylor, founder of the China Inland Mission, ministered there, as did two of the famous *"Cambridge Seven"* who had volunteered to go to China—Stanley Smith and C. T. Studd, the renowned cricketer. F. B. Meyer was greatly inspired and challenged by the devotion of these young men which led to a spiritual crisis in his life.

The year was 1881. Meyer talked with Smith and Studd at 7 o'clock on a grey November morning. *"The talk we held then was one of the most formative influences of my life,"* wrote Meyer. The men challenged Meyer to be willing to be MADE willing to yield up everything in his heart and life, and to trust Christ for victory over sin. They urged Meyer to take a definite step of faith and obedience. Afterwards, Meyer wrote the following account of his encounter with God:

> *"Very memorable was the night when I came to close quarters with God…There were things in my heart and life which I felt were questionable, if not worse; I knew that God had a controversy with respect to them; I saw that my very dislike to probe or touch them was a clear indication that there was mischief lurking beneath. It is the diseased joint that shrinks from the touch and tender eye that shudders at the light. At the same time I did not feel willing to give these things up. It was a long struggle. At last I said feebly, 'Lord, I am willing to be made willing; I am desirous that Thy will should be*

done in me and through me, as thoroughly as it is done in Heaven; come and take me and break me and make me.' That was the hour of crisis and when it had passed I felt able at once to add, 'And now, I give myself to Thee: body, soul, and spirit; in sorrow or in joy; in the dark or in the light; in life or in death, to be Thine only, wholly and forever. Make the most of me that can be made for Thy glory.' No rapture or rush of joy came to assure me that the gift was accepted. I left the place with almost a heavy heart. I simply assured myself that He must have taken that which I had given, and at the moment of my giving it. And to that belief I clung in all the days that followed, constantly repeating to myself the words, 'I am His.' And thus at last the joy and rest entered and victory and freedom from burdening care, and I found that He was molding my will and making it easy to do what I had thought impossible; and I felt that He was leading me in the paths of righteousness for His Name's sake, but so gently as to be almost imperceptible to my weak sight."

John Henry Jowett spoke of this event:

"Dr. Meyer has told us that his early Christian life was marred and his ministry paralyzed just because he had kept back one thing from the bunch of keys he had given to the Lord. Every key save one! The key of one room was kept for personal use, and the Lord shut out. And the effect of the incomplete consecration was found in lack of power, lack of assurance, lack of joy and peace. The joy of the Lord begins when we hand over the last key. We sit with Christ on His throne as soon as we have surrendered all our crowns and made Him sole and only ruler of our life and its possessions."

Keswick Conferences

The Keswick movement originally emerged out of previous conventions which were conducted at Oxford and Brighton. F. B. Meyer became closely associated with Keswick and served as one of its leaders. It was in 1887 that Meyer walked out into the hills around Keswick, in the darkness of the night, and prayed to receive the Holy Spirit's fulness by faith.

"Before I first spoke on the platform I had my own deeper experience, on a memorable night when I left the little town with its dazzling lamps, and climbed the neighbouring hill. As I write, the summer night is again casting its spell on me. The light clouds veil the stars and pass. The breath of the mountains lead me to yearn for a fresh intake of God's Spirit. May we not count on the Anointing Spirit to grant us a fresh infilling when we are led to seek it? May we not dare to believe that we have received, even when there is no answering emotion? Do we not receive by faith? These were the questions which a few of us had debated far into the night, at a prayer meeting convened at which a number of men were agonizing for the Spirit."

"I was too tired to agonize, so I left that prayer meeting and as I walked, I said, 'My Father, if there is one soul more than another within the circle of these hills that needs the gift of Pentecost, it is I: I want the Holy Spirit but I do not know how to receive Him and I am too weary to think, or feel, or pray intensely.' Then a Voice said to me, 'As you took forgiveness from the hand of the dying Christ, take the Holy Ghost from the hand of the living Christ, and reckon that the gift is thine by a faith that is utterly indifferent to the presence or absence of resultant joy. According to thy faith, so shall it be unto thee.'"

"So I turned to Christ and said, 'Lord, as I breathe in this whiff of warm, night air, so I breathe into every part of my being Thy blessed Spirit.' I felt no hand laid on my head, there was no lambent flame, there was no rushing sound from heaven: but by faith, without emotion, without excitement, I took, and took for the first time, and I have kept on taking ever since."

"I turned to leave the mountain side, and as I went down, the tempter said I had nothing, that it was all imagination, but I answered, 'Though I do not feel it, I reckon that God is faithful.'"

When he got back to his place of lodging he became very agitated, walking up and down saying,

"Can I have been wrong and waiting until now? Has my life hither to been lacking in power?"

His hostess prayed with him and he went to his bed without joy— but the very next morning his heart was filled with a settled peace.

Afterwards, in a letter written in that same year to *The Baptist*, he invited fellow ministers to unite in prayer in the early morning of each Lord's Day *"to seek a fuller enduement of the power of the Holy Spirit for themselves and for their brethren."*

Dr. W. Y. Fullerton reported that *"no one was more helpful at a Convention and no personality more spiritually effective"* than was F. B. Meyer. He said that Meyer—

> *"was not a passioned orator…rarely carried away by his feelings… but when speaking in the power of the Spirit the very quietness of his style was deeply impressive. His chief gift was his sympathy, his power of getting into touch with his audience and carrying them along with him. He could speak out unpleasant truths boldly and fearlessly, but he never gave offense."*

Meyer became known as one of the most effective speakers at Keswick.

Four Separate Pastorates in Two Churches

F. B. Meyer has the distinction of having served four pastorates between two churches. In 1888 he accepted a call to Regent's Park Church, London, and served there for four years.

In 1892 he went to Christ Church, Westminster Bridge Road (in the same year that Spurgeon died). While at Christ Church he had up to 4,000 scholars in 8 separate Sunday School he organized. Dr. F. W. Boreham was in his Bible Class for Young Men on Saturday afternoons. For approximately 15 years at Christ Church, he systematically preached through the Old Testament in the mornings and through the New Testament in the evenings, each Lord's Day, commencing at Genesis, chapter 1, and Matthew, chapter 1, respectively. In the 15th year he was still only 2/3's the way through each Testament.

In 1909 he returned to Regent's Park and then in 1915 returned once again to Christ Church where he remained until 1921.

During this period he became involved in various ministries and responsibilities outside of his pastoral duties. In 1891 he first visited the Northfield Conference in New England, U.S.A., at D. L. Moody's invitation. In 1902 he was elected the first ministerial President of the National Sunday School Union. He was elected President of the Baptist

Union in 1907-1908, and in May of 1907, he became President of the Sunday School Convention in Rome. In 1904, and, from 1910 to 1920 he was President of the Free Church Council. Meyer holds the distinction of being the first Principal of All Nations Bible College. In 1911 he received an honourary degree of Doctor of Divinity from MacMaster University in Hamilton, Ontario, Canada.

Northfield Conference

Special mention should be made of F. B. Meyer's impact upon Mr. Moody's Northfield Conference in New England. One anonymous writer recorded the following impressions of Meyer's first summer ministry at Northfield in 1891:

> *"As a preacher, Mr. Meyer ranks very high in the best qualities of power and effectiveness. He is a man 'mighty in the Scriptures,' saturated with Bible facts and truths...His style is free, unconstrained, and direct, and is marked by great simplicity, united with a certain effective chasteness of diction and action and with yearning earnestness, suggesting the possession of much reserved power; and all penetrated with a spiritual unction which may be felt but cannot be described. Of all the great teachers and preachers whom Mr. Moody has brought from afar to his annual Conferences at Northfield, no one has more thoroughly won all the hearts than F. B. Meyer."*

It should be quickly noted that this was written several years in advance of the coming of G. Campbell Morgan to Northfield in 1896. Under the biographical section dealing with Morgan we have related how Morgan's popularity began to eclipse that of Meyer's and how Meyer had to guard his own heart lest he be crippled with jealousy.

A. Chester Mann described Meyer's surprising effectiveness as a Gospel preacher to the unconverted at Northfield:

> *"...those who had known him as a speaker at Mildmay Hall in London, or at Keswick...had regarded him, possibly, as having a mission for Christians only—as bearing a message dealing specifically with the deepening of the spiritual life—were more than mildly surprised at Northfield. For Mr. Meyer proved himself not only a*

*speaker of singular power on subjects such as those just referred to,
but as a proclaimer of a vibrant Gospel message to the unconverted."*

Also, in 1891, Rev. W. H. Bocock of Flatbush, New York, gave this
description of Meyer at Northfield:

*"...no one can deny that he is a man of exceptional power...slender
and fragile in build, bent over at that time with lumbago, with a
small head and face, peaked and thin..."*

"The Mystic Saint of Devotional Preaching"

M. Jennie Street wrote that it was a venerable deacon of Duke Street
Chapel who taught F. B. Meyer how to preach. Meyer regarded his
own pastor, Rev. C. M. Birrell, as an excellent model for expository
preaching, as well as the preaching of John Knox, who set an example
for many Scottish preachers to follow. Meyer always extolled the
virtues of expository preaching because of the variety of truths and
emphases this method provides, and that it prevents indulging in fads
and pet peeves or hobby horses as well as guards against the neglect of
broad tracts of truth. He also cautioned against preachers becoming
too detailed in their exposition, teaching them to get to the point of
each passage, because men did not want to *"stop to count every petal on
a daisy."*

Rev. W. H. Bocock said that many London preachers were drawing
crowds but that the leading quality of Meyer's drawing power was
primarily spiritual in nature and that his secret was in his consecration
to Christ. A. Chester Mann described him as a—

*"Saintly, mystical, lovable man...his sermons healed the wounds of
the heart. His preaching was near, intimate and personal...he shed
the light of the eternal on the common ways of life...No other man I
ever listened to was so completely able to hold my unflagging attention as was F. B. Meyer...No preacher in Protestant Christendom
excelled him in the art of presenting finished material. Nothing
crude, broken, ill-considered, half digested, or amateurish, found
place in his pulpit efforts."*

Meyer remained an *"incorruptible Evangelical"* throughout his life-time, emphasizing the Cross of Christ for 60 long and strenuous years. Meyer has a *"blood-earnestness"* though a tranquil style of delivery. He *"felt the truths he uttered."*

He had the soul of a poet and his intensity emerged out of his own experience of spiritual depth and reality. Spurgeon said,

> *"Meyer preaches as a man who has seen God face-to-face."*

Joseph Parker referred to Meyer as his *"father confessor."* Once he said of him:

> *"Here is my friend, Mr. Meyer. He always has a new scheme—the sweetest and brightest thing ever seen in the market-place. He calls upon me before 9 o'clock in the morning, having risen a great while before then, and he always gets younger and younger. He is to me a most welcome visitor: he brings a benediction with him, a better air than earth's poor murky climate, and he never leaves me without the impression that I have been face-to-face with a man of God."*

In *John O'London's Weekly*, the following article on Meyer appeared in the 12 July 1924 edition:

> *"His body is tall and spare, alert and straight. The face is pale and clean shaven, the beautifully molded features combining to a wonderful degree a look of dignity, peace and holiness. Solemnity (not gloom) is the prevailing expression, but frequently the face lights up with the most winning of smiles. There is something wonderfully sympathetic and fascinating in the character and personality of Dr. Meyer. He loves the beauty of the world, he loves animals, and above all, he loves little children. These things he never succeeds in concealing from us, however hard he may try, and they peep out from every sermon or address that he delivers."*

Often when Meyer was asked what he would do to revive a decadent Church, he would quote Phillips Brooks, who had replied instantly to this question, with *"I would preach a missionary sermon and take up a collection!"*

While in America, one man was so impressed with Meyer's deeper life preaching that he followed him to the next city and got a room in the same hotel where Meyer was staying. He ate in the diningroom at the next table to Meyer in order to observe him. At the end of this time the man burst into the study of Dr. Curtis Lee Laws and declared that F. B. Meyer *"failed in no particular."*

Meyer had remarkable powers of concentration and filled every waking hour with work. One of the features of his ministry was the brevity of his public prayers.

Thomas Phillips, Principal of the Baptist College, wrote:

> *"He wove a spell over the audience...he is not so learned as Dr. Clifford, not so human as Mark Guy Pearse, not so consecrated as Hugh Price Hughes—he is undoubtedly one of the great preachers of the generation."*

Canon E. C. Earp of Saskatoon, said:

> *"His measured sentences proceed from thought to thought carrying his hearers with him along a mental pathway from which none can err. He brings tolerance and calm as he declares the everlasting purposes of the Eternal God. Around him is an indescribable air of gentleness and goodness...there is no striving after effect, the grand simplicity of his message makes its own appeal. His sincerity is as clear as the light and is an unconscious revelation of the soul within."*

Hugh Sinclair gave his impressions of Meyer:

> *"His preaching is expressive of his personality, suggesting spiritual fastidiousness, and a sweet, sun-washed serenity of soul. So simple and intimate is his utterance that many hearers will scarcely divine the art that conceals art, but the practiced will soon realize with what consummate ease and subtle mastery of effect he handles speech and thought, and how enchantingly he plays upon an instrument whose limitations are known and accepted by him."*

Rev. J. Havergal Sheppard wrote,

> *"He possessed that rare quality of pious personality that impressed you with the mystic more than the minister, the saint than the scholar, the priest than the prophet...His deliverances were devotional rather than didactic."*

Dr. John McDowell, Secretary of the Board of National Missions of the Presbyterian Church in the U.S.A., said,

> *"Meyer held the people in the hollow of his hand as he spoke to them of the deeper experiences of the Spirit and led them, as it were, on to the tablelands of the Kingdom, where the atmosphere is rarer, and the vision of the Highest is made clearer to the eyes of the soul."*

Mann maintained that at least part of the reason for Meyer's success was that he always remained simply himself, that he was forever an Englishman who did not pick up a single American pulpit-mannerism. On 2 September 1921, *The Presbyterian Banner* printed the following:

> *"With him, all roads lead to the Cross of Christ. If one were to ask him where exists the centre of the universe, I am sure he would answer quickly, 'Where Jesus is.'"*

When three United Presbyterian ministers were asked what about Meyer impressed them most, replied: (1) simplicity (2) saintliness (3) Scripturalness.

> *"However, while there is evident style in the sermons of this British divine, there is little reference to art or literature or philosophy, or even science as she unfolds herself in nature. The Bible interprets the Bible, and, like the early apostles, he is ever proving 'out of the Scriptures that Jesus is the Christ.'"*

Meyer liked to show "foregleams" of Christ in and through the lives of Bible characters. In F. B. Meyer's book *Expository Preaching: Plans and Methods*, he quoted Principal Rainy who wrote the following passage to students at the Madras College:

"We possess nothing so precious, we value nothing so much; we have no source of good so full, fruitful, and enduring; we have nothing to compare with the Lord Jesus Christ. To Him we bear witness...'Whom we proclaim,' cried the apostles..."

In this same volume Meyer went on to write,

"The main objective of the Holy Spirit in the present age is to glorify Christ. He withdraws Himself from observation with an infinite modesty (if we may use that word) but as light proceeding from an unseen source, He casts its full radiance on the face of 'the man, Christ Jesus.'"

Home at Last

On 28 March 1929, only a few days short of being 82 years of age, Frederick Brotherton Meyer died in a nursing home in Bournemouth. His beloved wife passed away in the same home only two months before. They had been married for 58 years.

Chapter Thirteen

John Henry Jowett

25 August 1863–19 December 1923

Heritage and Early Influences

John Henry Jowett was born in the industrial town of Halifax, Yorkshire, on 25 August 1863, the fourth child and third son of Josiah and Hannah Jowett. Both parents were from farming backgrounds. Their home was in a section called Claremount, about a mile out from the centre of Halifax. Josiah ran a tailoring and drapery business out of a room on the second floor of their home.

John was studious in disposition as a lad and possessed a delightful sense of humour. During his youth, one person who exerted an enormous influence upon his life was Dr. Enoch Mellor, pastor of Square Church, Halifax, a great preacher in his own right.

In September of 1882, John was sent by the Halifax church to Airedale College as a probationer to study theology in preparation for the Congregational ministry. He won the "Brown Scholarship" within one year. Scottish Dr. Andrew M. Fairbairn was Principal at the time. Jowett had just turned 19. He spent seven years at the College and the University of Edinburgh, commencing studies at the latter institution in 1883.

While in Edinburgh, the city itself was a veritable "university of preaching." Notable preachers occupied the pulpits of the city, such as Dr. Alexander Whyte, Free St. George's; Dr. Matheson, the blind preacher, at St. Bernard's; Dr. Walter Smith, the poet-preacher, at Free High Church; Dr. John Pulsford, Albany Street Congregational Chapel; and Dr. Landels, Dublin Street Baptist Church.

Jowett's favourite preacher was Alexander Whyte. Of him he wrote,

"Few preachers brought home to their audience the sense of sin so deeply as Dr. Whyte. One could not listen to him without feeling the pressing need of a Gospel."

At the University Jowett was greatly impressed by Dr. David Masson's lectures on literature. This opened up to him the works of such writers as Milton and Bunyan as well as the great English classics. He was also influenced by Calderwood, and especially by Henry Drummond. Of Drummond he once said:

"I was deeply interested in his simple, unaffected, manly addresses. He rarely dealt with intellectual difficulties, but he fearlessly handled the bald, practical problems and temptations of a young man's life. Many and many a time Drummond sent me home to my knees."

In 1887 Jowett was graduated with a Master of Arts degree and subsequently spent two terms, during 1888-1889, at Oxford during the period when Mansfield College was being built. Lectures were given in rooms in High Street. Arthur Porritt reported that Jowett's studies at Oxford made very little impression upon him!

Newcastle-on-Tyne

St. James Congregational Church in Newcastle-on-Tyne issued a call to Jowett in 1888 but it was not until October of 1889 that he preached his first Sunday there. On 19 November 1889 he was ordained. Jowett ministered at St. James for six years and his fame began to spread, people referring to him simply as *"Jowett of Newcastle."* During his time there the church membership doubled.

Carr's Lane, Birmingham

On 6 October 1895, Jowett preached his first sermon at Carr's Lane, Birmingham, succeeding the great Dr. R. W. Dale. Carr's Lane Chapel seated 1,500 persons and operated four large Sunday Schools. The church paid much attention to young men and women, possibly a legacy left behind by Dr. Dale. Fortunately, Dr. Dale had also left behind a very competent group of individuals who cared for the administration of the church.

It was at Carr's Lane that Jowett gained recognition as *"the greatest living master of the homiletical art."* We recall from the biography of R. W. Dale that John Henry Jowett acknowledged that the experience of having to follow Dale in the Carr's Lane pulpit had a profound impact upon his own life and preaching ministry. He testified that it saved him from becoming merely a *"pretty preacher."*

In Jowett's first sermon at Carr's Lane he said:

> *"I stand today in the line of an illustrious succession. I have to take up the work of a man who moved with rare and reverent intimacy among the greatest truths of the Christian religion. This pulpit has never been belittled by the petty treatment of small and vulgar themes. The familiarities of the pulpit here have been sublimed...I feel my poverty most when I remember the purity and the altitude of spirit which gave possibility to his profound spiritual discernment. To be able to enter as he did into the burning bliss of the eternal light required a consecrated and thrice-purified soul. But then it is my joy and my encouragement to know that I serve the same King, the same resources of grace are open to me, the same Holy Spirit of Christ is pledged to sanctify me and to lead me into the light of truth. I believe I have the same sympathy of a loyal and warm-hearted people. On these I shall lean, and with these I dare to face the labours of tomorrow with a quiet and trustful courage."*

After a visit to Carr's Lane, Sir William Robertson Nicoll wrote:

> *"The great simplicity, reality, sympathy and tenderness of the prayers moved one strangely...of the startling wealth and beauty of Dr. Jowett's diction, the incisiveness of his contrasts, the overwhelming power of his appeals, it is impossible for me to write adequately...,. in Dr. Jowett, everything preaches. The voice preaches and it is a voice of great range and compass, always sweet and clear through every variety of intonation. The eyes preach, for though Dr. Jowett apparently writes every word of his sermons he is extraordinarily independent of his manuscript. The body preaches, for Dr. Jowett has many gestures, and not one ungraceful. But above all, the heart preaches. I have heard many great sermons, but never*

one at any time which so completely seized and held from start to finish a great audience...Above all preachers I have heard, Dr. Jowett has the power of appeal..."

During Jowett's tenure at Carr's Lane, the Digbeth Institute came into being. Although Albert Peel says that it was founded in 1906, Arthur Porritt, Jowett's biographer, claims it was on 16 January 1908 that this recreational centre *("billiards without Devilry")*, and mission to the poor, was formally opened.

All told, Jowett preached 16 years at Carr's Lane, from 1895 until 1911. In May of 1906 he was elected Chairman of the Congregational Union at the age of 41. Although some claim he was the youngest ever to hold this post, the facts reveal that R. W. Dale held this distinction, being only 39 when he was elected in 1869.

In contrast to his predecessor, Dr. Dale, Jowett remained detached from political controversies. He refused to be drawn in and thereby he escaped being detracted from his principle preaching ministry where his gifts really lay.

In 1909 Jowett was invited by William R. Moody to preach to the Northfield Conference which is located in the heart of New England in the U.S.A., at a point in Franklin County where the State of Massachusetts touches the borders of New Hampshire and Vermont. One story emerging from that ministry was of a converted *"down-and-outer"* from Jerry McCauley's mission who attended an early morning prayer meeting held somewhere in the woods out from Northfield. Just before Jowett preached, this man prayed—

"Oh Lord, we pray for our brother. Now blot him out! Reveal Thy glory to us in such blazing splendour that he shall be forgotten."

From March 1910 until March of the following year, Jowett served as the President of the National Free Church Council. In 1910 the University of Edinburgh conferred on him the Doctor of Divinity degree.

Fifth Avenue Presbyterian Church, New York

On 2 April 1911 Jowett began his ministry at the Fifth Avenue Presbyterian Church in New York City. His arrival in New York was regarded as the *"event of the week"* by the local press. Large crowds assembled to hear this master of the pulpit art, including church dignitaries from a wide range of denominations, missionaries, rabbis, and actors. During his sojourn in the United States he served as an unofficial ambassador on behalf of his native England.

During this period, while visiting back in England in 1915, he contracted neuritis which in turn caused insomnia.

Westminster Chapel, London

Jowett once wrote while in the United States, *"Give me that grey, misty, cloudy island England, first and last."* When the renowned G. Campbell Morgan resigned from Westminster Chapel, London, John Henry Jowett was called to replace him. Prime Minister Lloyd George himself, wrote to Jowett, urging him to return to England to inspire the nation during the ensuing rebuilding period following World War I. On 19 May 1918 Jowett formally commenced his ministry at Westminster. His four years here proved to be difficult ones as his health began to deteriorate. In 1920 he suffered fatigue, weight loss and fainting fits which finally culminated in a complete breakdown.

Throughout his time at Westminster Jowett stressed social and international concerns. His final months during 1922 were given over to a peace campaign. Since some of his schemes proved to be unworkable, he honestly admitted to Randall Cantuar, the Archbishop of Canterbury, *"I am more of a bugler than a captain!"*

In 1922 he suffered from anaemia and eventually resigned after preaching his final message on December 17th.

Personality and Habits

Throughout his ministry Jowett habitually started his working day at 6 a.m. except for the final year of his life. He kept no diary. In this he was similar to Dr. Dale who kept no diary up until the age of 60. Harold Murray described Jowett as having a certain shy reserve. *"He hated the familiar stranger who plunges into an undesired conversation."* He was possessed of a deep, personal humility and spirituality.

Personally, Jowett was not impressed with the design of Westminster Chapel, claiming that the people who sat in the galleries *"seemed to belong to another planet."*

It would probably come as a surprise to many who were acquainted with some of his more doctrinal sermons that Jowett acquired a wonderful capacity to speak to children. Every six weeks he devoted the entire Sunday morning service to children at St. James Church, Newcastle-on-Tyne.

Frank Morison wrote, that behind the rhetoric, epigram flowing into epigram, fertile and suggestive thought—

> *"there lies the genius of a severe and ordered mental discipline."* He was a great *"disregarder of the unessential...He stands preeminently for the eternal principle that if you look after the big things, the little things will look after themselves. He refuses to be drawn into petty and irrelevant issues."*

Jowett was regarded as a national as well as a denominational possession and treasure. Dr. Gore First Bishop of the Diocese in Birmingham said that Jowett represented *"ideally the combination of the Christian prophet with the Christian citizen."* He had a spirit of broad toleration which allowed him to work cooperatively with men who held widely differing beliefs. Frank Morison believed that his greatest contribution was to the *"temper of the age"* rather than to its thought.

Reflections on the Master-Preacher's Style

Morison contended that—

> *"with absolute certainty, he has given us a new revelation of the possibilities of the preacher's art...he is one of the indisputably great preachers of our own generation."*

Morison went on to say that while pulpit ministry was generally on the decline—

> *"Dr. Jowett has been drawing vast audiences in England and America by a series of sermons and addresses sustained with an astonishing degree of spiritual and imaginative power. It is in the technique of his art that he possesses such certain and unfailing mastery."*

Harold Murray referred to Jowett as *"the silver-tongued preacher."* It is claimed that Jowett was the first Non-conformist since the Commonwealth, to preach in a Cathedral. John Harries, biographer of G. Campbell Morgan, commented on Jowett's sermon preached at the 3rd Mundesley Bible Conference, calling it, *"one of those great sermons of his that hold the memory for a lifetime."* When Dr. Jowett preached G. Campbell Morgan's induction sermon at Westminster Chapel in November of 1904, his sermon is again referred to as a *"memorable sermon"* on the topic *"Destructive Heresies."*

These remarks beg the question as to why his sermons were so fixed in the minds of his audience that they remained in their memories until the end of their days. Not discounting the noteworthiness of the quality of his voice, nor the spirituality and force of his personality, most of those who were qualified to make analytical comment would attribute his success to his style and technique. Morison wrote that next to his spirituality, Jowett owed his reputation to two qualities: (1) he was a *stylist* in preaching of a high order, and (2) his distinctive emphasis was on the *practical* rather than the theological. As a stylist, Jowett stood almost alone in his day.

> *"It is in the technique of his art that he possesses such certain and unfailing mastery...To many, the attraction is in the purely external mechanism of his art. The soft and modulated voice; the wealth of illustration, both in thought and gesture; the novel and colloquial treatment; the frequent epigram; the rapid flow of succinct and highly compressed thought—these are the qualities which go to make up the subtle thing we call style."*

In addition to this brief analysis of Jowett's style, let us attempt the following description of Jowett's technique, feature by feature.

(1) The Centrality of the Redemptive Theme

In Jowett's Yale Lectures published in 1912 he had this to say about the perils of choosing themes from the realm of economics or politics:

> *"I am in no doubt about my position as a citizen, and of my duties and privileges in the life of the nation. I must not be an alien to the commonwealth, living remote and aloof from its travails and throes.*

My strength must be enlisted in the vital, actual forces which, through tremendous obstacles, are seeking the enthronement of justice and truth. I can also conceive it probable that critical occasions may arise when it will be the duty of the pulpit to speak with clarion distinctness on the policy of the state or nation. But, even with these admissions I can clearly see this danger, that the broadening conception of the preacher's mission may lead to the emphasis of the Old Testament message of redemption. Men may become so absorbed in social wrongs as to miss the deeper malady of personal sin. They may lift the rod of oppression and leave the burden of guilt. They may seek to correct social dislocations and overlook the awful disorder of the soul. It seems to me that some preachers have made up their minds to live in the Old Testament rather than in the New, and to walk with the prophet rather than with the apostle and evangelist...In the fascinating breadth we may lose centrality; things that are secondary and subordinate may take the throne."

Jowett maintained that attention to secondary matters can impair one's spiritual sensitivities and vision, resulting in a loss of power to unveil the unsearchable riches of Christ.

Dr. Gore, Bishop of Oxford, warned that we are *"seeking refuge from the difficulties of thought in the opportunities of action."* Jowett warned, *"You cannot drop the big themes and create great saints."* He urged that we preach the great apostolic themes. We are not just to give good advice but rather to preach Good News! We are to preach on the great texts...

"whose vastnesses almost terrify us as we approach them...We may feel that we are but pygmies in the stupendous task but in these matters it is often better to lose ourselves in the immeasurable than to always confine our little boat to the measurable creeks along the shore. Yes, we must grapple with the big things about which our people will hear nowhere else; the deep, the abiding, the things that permanently matter."

(2) Highly Cultivated Literary Form

To his task Jowett brought a very high degree of perfection—*"...the external mechanism of spoken thought."* Jowett combined a high caliber of literary skill with *"an apparent ease of spontaneous thought."* Morison said that men would listen to him preach, not so much for the content of his sermon as for *"the exquisite joy of hearing their own language as it should be spoken."*

Jowett used all manner of literary devices: metaphor, analogies, contrasts, comparisons, epigrams, and repetition.

W. Y. Fullerton, in his biography of F. B. Meyer, compared the preaching of Rev. C. M. Birrell of Pembroke Chapel, Liverpool, to that of Jowett:

> *"Birrell's plan of sermonizing was something like Dr. Jowett's in later years. Every sentence was polished and balanced. Then the written discourse was committed to memory and recited in the pulpit."*

Jowett left nothing to chance. He studiously selected every word for its appropriate use. His sermons were written in full and were delivered substantially as they had been written. He insisted on writing out, word for word, polished phrase by polished phrase, his entire manuscript.

> *"I feel that* for me, writing a sermon is absolutely necessary to exactness of thought and expression."

The consequence of this, according to Morison, was that *"his utterances abound in literary artifices which would be quite impossible to extemporaneous speech."* Though Jowett prepared a full manuscript, Morison claimed that after five minutes into preaching the audience would be unaware of its existence.

(3) Order and Logic

Jowett's preaching was marked by order, charm and logic. He appealed to the reasoned judgment of men.

(4) Every Message Had a Purpose

Jowett said that one should be able to state in written form the purpose, or, mission of a service so that if an angel asked as he went into the pulpit one could tell him clearly what that purpose was. *"Who keeps one end in view makes all things serve."* He stuck to his purpose and preached for a verdict.

(5) Hypnotic Manner of Delivery

> *"Dr. Jowett's style does not consist so much in the substance of his sermons as in the manner of their delivery. Not a little of his wonderful influence over his congregation is due to the almost hypnotic effect of his personality while preaching. He has a kind of psychological power of thought projection which creates an atmosphere which is congenial to him. You soon discover that his personality is even more eloquent than his voice. There is a fascination in his manner which enlists your interest even though your judgment pronounce against him. It is this quality which is missed by those who only know him through his printed books."*
>
> *"There is nothing in the manner of the grand port, no highly sustained periods of dramatic power—nothing but an atmosphere of quiet interest as the speaker unfolds his thought which deepens into stillness as he reaches the point to which he has been leading up. Some of his most impressive passages are delivered almost in an undertone, which, however, he contrives to make audible throughout the entire building. It is then, apparently, that he has the greatest command of his own thought."* (Morison)

He spoke in a quiet conversational manner, now rising to a height of rhetorical power, but then recovering *"the brilliant half-conversational manner of which he is such a perfect master."* His major points were underscored with a low voice.

(6) Speaking in Pictures

Jowett believed that,

> *"The deepest truths come to men most readily in pictorial form. The imagination can grasp with certainty what the undisciplined mind cannot, from sheer inexpertness, lay hold of at all."* He carried his audience *"back to the picture book and nursery stage of their spiritual experience. He contrives to teach them much the same lesson as his more academic friend, but he accomplishes it by interesting them*

in the pictures and leaving them to imbibe the truth which they represent." (Morison)

Thus Jowett's style was a return to simplicity in the sense that it stood as a protest against *"the artificiality of dogmatic theology."* His pictorial technique used to illustrate practical, every-day truth, stood in contrast to theological and philosophical abstractions.

> *"He delights to take some great ruling principle of life, drawn frequently from an obscure text, and then to conduct his hearers on an imaginary tour of inspection revealing the principle at work in the varied departments of science, philosophy and life."* (Morison)

Jowett excelled in what John Morley called *"the imaginative treatment of the common-place."* His mind was a *"veritable storehouse of illustration and metaphor, drawn chiefly from the broad ways of nature."* He was quick to draw analogies between what his quick, keen eyes saw in nature, and his own deeper philosophy of the soul.

> *"The ability to present an argument with lucidity and grace, to describe a mental picture with precision and just that touch of emotion necessary to make it live in the minds of the hearers, is the haunting dream of all whose business it is to clothe their thoughts in spoken word."* (Morison)

This was unquestionably Jowett's distinctive and unrivaled gift.

Death

W. Y. Fullerton made reference to the fact that Jowett wore himself out meeting the demands of his admirers. At the relatively early age of 60 years, John Henry Jowett passed into the Presence of his Lord on 19 December 1923, exactly one year and two days after he had preached his final message at Westminster Chapel.

Chapter Fourteen

George Campbell Morgan

9 December 1863–16 May 1945

A Preacher's Son

G. Campbell Morgan was born in the village of Tetbury, Gloucestershire, on 9 December 1863, to a Baptist minister, Rev. George Morgan, and his wife, Elizabeth Fawn Brittan. Rev. Morgan had been the pastor of a Baptist church in Herefordshire but under the influence of the teachings of the Plymouth Brethren, and particularly of George Muller, he resigned his living with the Baptists in order to start a faith mission in a hired hall in Tetbury.

When the family was in Cardiffe during Morgan's boyhood, in the years 1870-71, Morgan wrote about his early attempts at preaching as a 7 to 8 year old lad:

> *"I had one living person in my audience and quite a number that were not alive. I preached regularly there, week after week, and time after time, to my sister and her dolls. It was then that there was born within me the passion to become a preacher."*

In the early, impressionable age of 8 years, Morgan remembered finding an antiquated book on his father's bookshelf, entitled, *"Todd's Lectures to Children."* Dr. Todd taught parents to never teach their children that they *"had souls"* but to rather emphasize that they had bodies. His point was, that a child should be taught that he is a spiritual being, a soul who happens to possess a body.

This may seem like a fine distinction to the reader, but for some reason this passage, read when but an eight year old child, never left Morgan's memory throughout his lifetime.

His father used to take him to hear many different preachers during his youth, and he later testified, *"It was thus that the passion for preaching took possession of me."* He preached his first sermon when he was only 13.

Teacher Training in Birmingham and the Eclipsing of His Faith

At the age of 16 Morgan began to train to become a teacher. During this period, leading up to his twentieth year, he was faced with the teachings of Darwin, Huxley, Tyndall, Spencer, and Bain, which all worked toward the eclipsing of his faith. There came a moment when he was sure of nothing at all! He became confused and perplexed.

Finally he put aside all books, which either supported or denied a Christian world-view, and went out and purchased a new Bible.

> *"That Bible found me. I began to read and study it then in 1883. I have been a student ever since and I still am."* (Written by Morgan in 1938)

Morgan emerged from two years of spiritual eclipse and never looked back.

In 1883 he joined the staff of the Jewish Collegiate School, Birmingham, and became a teaching *"Master"* even though he did not have the benefit of formal academic training for this task. During those years he learned much from the headmaster, a Jewish rabbi, and continued on there until 1886.

The Influence of Dwight L. Moody and Ira D. Sankey

The year 1883 was significant in Morgan's life for another reason. This was the year when D. L. Moody and Ira D. Sankey visited Great Britain for their second U.K. mission. They preached and sang for three weeks in Bingley Hall, Birmingham. The Town Hall and several church buildings in the vicinity were used for overflow meetings. While Moody preached in Bingley Hall—

> *"Sankey went round in a cab or carriage lent by some friend, to the other meetings, singing at each in turn. He would return to the central meeting in time to help in the enquiry room which he did with great delight and profit."* (Jill Morgan)

Jill Morgan, the wife of Morgan's oldest surviving son, gave this description:

> *"Ira D. Sankey was never a performer; he was a prophet in song. He was not a musician anxious to attract attention to himself; he was a minister of Jesus Christ, determined to direct attention to his Master. By nature, gifted with a voice of remarkable strength and sweetness, by the grace of God that gift was consecrated and used to the glory of the Lord in ways of which he never dreamed in his earlier years."*

Little could Morgan suspect at that stage in his earliest association with D. L. Moody, how profoundly his life would be affected and directed by the influence of, and connection with, this American evangelist. In later years Morgan wrote:

> *"...it is one of the greatest privileges of my life to come very near to him in the ripest years of his life...he had an influence upon my life that I should find it hard to measure."*

Moody and Morgan became great friends and we shall outline their association further in this biographical sketch. One day, R. W. Dale said to Morgan in Dale's study,

> *"I think I have only known one evangelist that I felt had the right to speak of a lost soul." Morgan asked, "Who was it?" Dale replied, "It was D. L. Moody, and it was because he never spoke of the possibility of a man being lost without tears in his voice."*

From Mission Preacher to Popular Conference Speaker

From 1886 to 1888 G. Campbell Morgan ministered as a mission preacher. Early on he learned the valuable lesson that one could not violate the laws of health and be successful as a preacher. Often his meetings were followed by half-nights in prayer. He became exhausted and his lowered resistance would often result in a sore throat. On occasion he would eat too much before a service.

"I suffered in my speaking tonight from eating a good dinner. D.V., no more of them!"

He wrote this in 1886 and adopted the rule of eating sparingly before preaching for the rest of his life.

In 1888 he received a terrible blow when he was rejected by both the Methodists and the Salvation Army. Just two days prior to being informed of the Methodists' decision he met his cousin Annie, who went by the name, Nancy, who had come for a visit. Campbell was already courting another girl whose affections cooled, possibly as a result of the rejection of Campbell by the Methodists. Campbell and Nancy became increasingly attached to one another which led to a proposal, by letter, in the month of June.

"I can only ask to share the life of a wandering evangelist," Campbell wrote.

Nancy replied, *"If I cannot start with you at the bottom of the ladder, I would be ashamed to meet you at the top."* (From Jill Morgan's biography of G. Campbell Morgan)

They were married on 20 August 1888 in a little country chapel at Market Drayton. Thus began 58 years of a wonderful married relationship. Four sons and two daughters were born into their home. The eldest son entered the Episcopalian ministry and the remaining three sons became Presbyterian preachers. In fact, in 1933, their youngest son, Dr. Howard Morgan, succeeded his father in the pulpit of the Tabernacle Presbyterian Church of Philadelphia, PA, which had been G. Campbell Morgan's only U.S. pastoral charge. One of his daughters, Kathleen, traveled with her father for seven years in the U.S. and Canada.

In due course G. Campbell Morgan was accepted into full-time ministry and ordained by the Congregationalists in 1889. Subsequently, he pastored several churches:

1889-91	Stone, Staffs.
1891-93	Rugeley, Staffs.
1893-97	Westminister Road, Birmingham
1897-1901	North London, New Court Church, Tollington Park

When he first arrived in Birmingham he was welcomed by the great Dr. R. W. Dale who was then in the sunset years of his Carr's Lane ministry and his life. (He passed away on 13 March 1895.)

It was quite characteristic of Dr. Dale to take the time out of his very full schedule to welcome a younger colleague to his city. In a conversation between the two preachers Morgan made mention of the fact that he was virtually untrained for the ministry. Dr. Dale immediately retorted,

"Never say that you are untrained. God has many ways of training men. I pray that you may have much joy in His service."

In 1896, while still at Westminster Road, Birmingham, Morgan received his first invitation to come to Northfield Conference in New England to address the famous conference established by Dwight L. Moody. Contrary to Moody's usual practice, he invited Morgan to come, sight-unseen, not only to preach at Northfield, but also to give lectures at his Institute in Chicago.

Northfield Conference, New England, U.S.A.

John Henry Jowett once said of G. Campbell Morgan,

"I never can decide whether Morgan's greater opportunity lies in a settled pastorate, or in a wider ministry in many lands."

D. L. Moody, himself, wrote,

"Campbell Morgan is the most remarkable man I have ever had at Northfield."

As stated above, Morgan made his first appearance at Northfield in 1896. In a sermon Morgan preached at Westminster Chapel on 11 May 1906, entitled, *My Friend*, Morgan described how he felt when he first landed in New York. He said it was the most lonely moment in his life. When he stepped from the steamship on to the wharf, there were hundreds of people meeting their friends, but no one was there to meet *him*. He said that there was not one familiar voice nor face and that he just stood there feeling *"desolately lonely."* Somehow he managed to make his own way to the home of friends.

A word about Northfield and the famous conference is in order. Northfield is situated on the banks of the Connecticut River and was reputed to be one of the most beautiful colonial villages in New England. As previously described, it is located in Franklin County at a point where the borders of the three states of Massachusetts, New Hampshire, and Vermont touch each other. It is the birthplace, the early home, the place of residence in later years, the scene of the close of the earthly life, and the final resting place of Dr. D. L. Moody. Moody was the first in America to put forward the idea that during vacation periods, school and college buildings should be utilized by conferences and schools of Christian training. In 1880 he had convened a meeting of Christian workers in his home near the campus of the Northfield Seminary for Girls which he had founded in 1879, and this was when the Northfield Conference idea was born. At the beginning 300 workers gathered for training. In later years, from early June to late August, a total of 10,000 were trained in a series of seven assemblies over the three-month summer period. Almost every man and woman in attendance was either a preacher, a teacher, or a student looking forward to some form of Christian service.

Each year in August, up until the death of Dr. Moody in 1899, and beyond, Morgan was invited back to preach in the Northfield Conference and to be the Northfield Extension Lecturer, going from coast to coast in both the U.S. and Canada, holding Bible Conferences.

When Dr. Moody died on 22 December 1899, his son, William R. Moody, came to London to ask G. Campbell Morgan to come to East Northfield to carry forward the work that his father had left behind.

At about this time, near the end of his ministry at New Court Church, Tollington Park, in the year 1900, and before he took up his full-time responsibilities on the other side of the Atlantic, Morgan suffered a serious throat problem which eventually led to surgery. His doctors ordered him to complete silence for two months.

Joseph Parker preached at the farewell service at New Court Church, and F. B. Meyer organized the meeting. It is rather interesting that F. B. Meyer himself, was very much involved in the Northfield Extension work, and Morgan's work was now to become an enlargement of both F. B. Meyer's efforts and that of H. W. Pope.

Morgan did this work at Northfield from 1901 to 1904. He conducted conventions, each from seven to ten days, in populous centres all over the country. The objectives were two-fold: (1) the deepening of interest in Bible study, and (2) the promotion of wider fellowship among Christian workers of every grade.

In the summer conference periods at Northfield itself, he conducted three consecutive conferences: (1) for students, with approximately 700 men in attendance; (2) a Young Women's Conference attended primarily by members of the Y.W.C.A.; and (3) the General Conference of Christian Workers which was regarded as the Northfield Conference proper, conducted in the first two weeks of August.

John Harries gave his personal evaluation of the contribution to Northfield of G. Campbell Morgan:

> *"Perhaps it would be well within the bounds of conservative statement to declare, that Campbell Morgan's service to Northfield is the most important ever rendered it by any man, with the bare exception of its founder (D. L. Moody)."*

G. Campbell Morgan's name became permanently linked to the Northfield Conference and his participation in the Conference's ministry extended over a period of 34 years.

In 1904, Dr. Charles I. Schofield summed up Morgan's American ministry by quoting Joseph Parker's characterization of Will Moody coming to England to urge Morgan to come to Northfield, calling it *"flat burglary."* *"Dr. Morgan has conquered all hearts on this side of the water."* He described Morgan's ministry in one word—*"vital."*

An interesting sidelight is the account of F. B. Meyer's reaction to the growing popular appeal of Morgan at Northfield. The biographer of F. B. Meyer, A. Chester Mann, records what Meyer disclosed to Rev. J. Havergal Sheppard in a private conversation at Northfield in 1902. Sheppard was the first of Dr. Barnardo's boys to enter the Baptist ministry. Meyer said:

> *"When I came to Northfield at first, I delivered the popular addresses, and the people were saying, 'Have you heard Meyer?' Now...I am delivering the devotional addresses and Morgan is delivering the more popular messages, and people are asking, 'Have you heard Morgan?' The self-life has been tempting me to jealousy, but I have crucified it by asking all my friends to hear Morgan, for he is really wonderful. This is the only way to become a real overcomer!"*

While in the United States Morgan drew large crowds in such places as St. Paul, Minnesota; Dayton, Ohio; Seattle, Washington; Atlanta, Georgia; Wilkes-Barre, Pennsylvania; and St. Louis, Missouri. In December of 1902, Dr. and Mrs. Morgan were received at the White House in Washington, D.C. by President Theodore Roosevelt. He became an ardent golfer, played tennis, and took up horseback riding in Chicago in a seven-week period in 1902. In this same eventful year, he was honoured with a Doctorate of Divinity degree by the Chicago Theological Seminary.

Westminster Chapel, Buckingham Gate, London: 1904–1917

By 1904 the work at Westminster Chapel had sunk to a low ebb. Harold Murray, who wrote a sketch of Morgan's life and ministry in 1938, reported that Westminster was nearly empty and bankrupt. Many prominent preachers had declined to respond to a call to come and pastor the work. Dr. A. E. Guthrie described the Chapel as a *"white elephant."* We recall that J. H. Jowett was not at all impressed with the building saying that the people in the galleries *"seemed to belong to another planet."* In partnership with Rev. Albert Swift, who became Morgan's closest friend *"they revived a forlorn hope."*

John Henry Jowett preached a memorable sermon on the occasion of Morgan's induction service in November of 1904. The subject: *"Destructive Heresies."*

Morgan is most renowned for his ministry at Westminster, which was rendered within two separate time-frames: 1904–1917, and then again, 1933–1943. The most outstanding feature of the first tenure, and what became the very heart of the ministry, was the Friday night Bible School which averaged anywhere from 1,400 to 1,800 people. This Bible School was *"the dream of his heart come true"* according to Don M. Wagner. Pastors, Sunday School teachers of all denominations attended, including some Roman Catholics. A modern Sunday School was another noteworthy part of the work. Morgan's preaching method was expository, as always. It took him three years of Sunday mornings to exposit the Gospel of Matthew and two years to cover the Book of Acts. One tenth of Westminster's income was set aside for missionary work. Morgan preached monthly on the great mission fields of the world. During the winter he taught a course of monthly lectures dealing with the principles of foreign missions. One of his most unforgettable missionary sermons was preached on 19 January 1906 on the subject of *"China"* in which he decried Britain's actions which resulted in the wide-spread use of opium among the Chinese people. Because of the Opium War and its terrible consequences, Morgan held that Britain had a double responsibility toward China.

> *"Oh, China, and China's millions, and China's wail! We have a two-fold responsibility; Christ has sent us with His Evangel; we must go. Our nation has sent the curse; we must wipe it away."*
>
> *"Never talk of murdered missionaries,"* thundered Morgan, *"without also talking of murdered Chinese for British revenue. Don't talk with disdain when Chinese call you 'foreign devil.' If I were Chinese I would say there are a thousand devils within you!"*

When war broke out, people were sitting on the window ledges. The Chapel was crowded out. Extra chairs were brought in and people sat on the rostrum steps.

Morgan became known henceforth as *"Campbell Morgan of Westminster"* on the same order as people referred to *"Dale of Carr's Lane"* and *"Parker of City Temple."*

Mr. F. A. Atkins wrote,

> *"…it is an interesting fact that Dr. Morgan's ministry attracted many people seldom seen in any other Non-conformist place of worship."*

A list of dignitaries included three or four members of the Cabinet, Lord Armistead, Lady Tullibardine, who became Duchess of Atholl, Lord Acton, Lord Halsbury, and Lord Northcliffe. Added to these better known persons were journalists, judges, doctors, editors, and members of Parliament. It is a compliment to Morgan's character that he was also loved by children and he loved them in return.

Jill Morgan recorded that during this period Dr. Morgan developed nervous twitches in his face and eye.

Other Involvements While at Westminster

The Mundesley Bible Conference (Mundesley is pronounced by dropping the 'de' and saying the rest—'Munsley') was established in 1906. Mundesley-on-Sea was a pretty little village on the East Anglian coast, midway between Cromer and North Walsham in the County of Norfolk. It boasted only 600 inhabitants. It is about three hours from London and very accessible to the Midlands. Morgan bought a home there and began conferences. Bible lectures were delivered every morning, followed by a missionary and workers conference. The afternoons were entirely taken up with recreation such as cricket, lawn tennis, golfing, and there were the beach and the sea. A meeting tent had been destroyed by a gale and Morgan's American friends paid to replace it. The last conference was held at Mundesley in 1914. In 1915 the conference was held at Westminster Chapel, and in 1916, at Llandrindod, Wales.

From 1911 to 1914 Morgan served as President of Cheshunt College, Cambridge. He helped to raise funds for the new buildings.

Itinerant Ministry

During World War I, Morgan preached throughout England and France in an itinerant ministry and also helped to train workers at Mildmay Centre for the Y.M.C.A. After the war he itinerated in the U.S.A. and Canada. In his lifetime he crossed the Atlantic a total of 54 times.

After leaving Westminster Morgan held a brief pastorate at Highbury Quadrant Congregational Church, from 1918 to 1919. In 1918 his health demanded a change of climate according to Harold Murray.

In 1919 he returned to America and from that year through to 1929 he ministered widely in Bible Conference work throughout 38 states, all the Canadian provinces, and most of the larger cities, some more than once.

In 1925 he delivered a series of lectures at the Biblical Seminary, New York, on the topic, *"Preaching"* with a subtitle, *"Preparation for Expository Preaching."* Those lectures are now printed in a small 90-page volume.

From 1927 to 1928 he taught at the Los Angeles Bible Institute and from 1929 to 1932, he held a three-year pastorate in Philadelphia, PA, at the Tabernacle Presbyterian Church, teaching also at Gordon College of Theology and Missions in Boston. (Don M. Wagner claims that Morgan was at the Presbyterian Church up until 1933.) It was during . this time in 1931 that Morgan suffered attacks of amnesia for short periods.

Return to Westminister Chapel: 1933–1943

Morgan returned to Westminister Chapel in 1933 to assist Dr. Hubert Simpson. In 1934 he assumed full charge and continued ministering there until 1943. In the summer of 1935 he experienced a breakdown of health. In later years Dr. Martin Lloyd-Jones became his Associate and eventually his successor at Westminster Chapel.

In 1936 Morgan celebrated his Diamond Anniversary as a preacher. He had kept a careful record of his preaching engagements ever since 1886 and when he calculated the number of sermons preached by the time of his Diamond Anniversary, the number stood at 23,390. He, of course, preached many times since that time. Morgan also kept a complete diary since 1885, in contrast to John Henry Jowett who never kept a daily journal.

On the occasion of his Jubilee, Morgan said,

> *"I crave today more than I ever did in my life, with a greater longing than I ever felt, to know that men and women are praying for me."*

Harold Murray reported that Morgan still preached with extraordinary power at age 75, which brings us to the year 1938, but in that same year, his doctor ordered him not to preach more than once a Sunday.

Prolific Writer

The British Museum contains over 70 volumes authored by G. Campbell Morgan. He published his Bible notes, sermons, and commentaries.

The Prince of Expositors

Dr. Morgan's rare gift was to distill and condense large portions of Scripture, from chapters to entire books, and to make the central message of those portions understandable to his hearers, step by step, point by point. While others would bog down in detailed minutiae, Morgan would capture and explain the big picture, the heart and main point of the passage.

In Don M. Wagner's book *The Expository Method of G. Campbell Morgan*, Dr. Morgan's process of sermon preparation is explained in a brief chart:

THE FUNDAMENTAL PROCESS

	A. Activity	B. Result
I Survey	Read	Impression
II Condense	Think	Outline
III Expand	Work	Analysis
IV Dissect	Sweat	Knowledge

In the order set forth above, Morgan would first of all read an entire Bible book 40 to 50 times to gain an overall impression of its central message. Then he would design an outline to express in the briefest possible way the content of the book. For example, the book of Genesis can be broken down into three simple parts: Generation, Degeneration, Regeneration. Next comes the expansion phase which is very much like a repeat of the outlining phase. Each main division is isolated and broken down into its own outline. Morgan would quietly work through each sub-division, analyzing, dissecting and outlining. During the condensing phase he constantly looked back to his conclusions and analysis he discovered in the first Survey stage, and during the Expansion phase he would do the same. In the Dissecting phase it is just plain hard work—sweat, in other words—and which yields the prize of knowledge. His crowning technique was the ability to select the truly significant details of a passage and to bring to bear upon key words the root meaning of the Greek language. His method spared him and the audience from wordiness and allowed him to get to the heart of the matter quickly.

Morgan stuck strictly to the context method of interpreting Scripture:

"A definition of 'context principle' indicates that the hypothesis contains a great deal more than that which appears on the surface. Context principle is the interpretation of a given passage in the light

of the text which surrounds it, diminishing in importance as one proceeds from the near to the far context. Two fundamental processes are involved in putting this context principle to work: they are analysis and synthesis. Analysis takes apart and classifies or describes each part; synthesis assembles the parts in a logical order. The important, fundamental process, therefore, is the correlation of parts to a whole, and explains the reason for Morgan's insistence on "survey" for general impression, because it makes possible the correlation of the various parts. One further important factor is the order of importance of the contextual materials. It is the use of this principle that makes Morgan's method expository. Without this principle Bible study becomes something other than expository." (D. M. Wagner) The real key is "the correlation of a passage of Scripture to its textual connections."

Morgan always lamented the way chapters and verses were assigned to the sacred text.

"In study, the first thing to do is forget chapter divisions…over and over again, the chapters, as they are arranged for us, begin at the wrong place."

"Unquestionably, Dr. G. Campbell Morgan was the outstanding expositor of the first half of the 20th century," wrote Don M Wagner.
Dr. John H. Jowett commented:

"His one aim is to let the Bible tell its own eternal message. In that kind of work, he has a genius which is incomparable."

To this, Morgan's son, Rev. K. J. Morgan, responded by saying that it was more work than genius, and that no man ever worked harder than his father.
With few exceptions, topical preaching was almost foreign to Morgan. He consistently held to the context principle in Biblical exposition. He believed that—

"the indiscriminate use of widely separated texts is the exact technique of those sects who use the prestige of the Bible to sell their

*unbiblical, religious ideas, many of them boldly furnishing interpre-
tative context."*

Rev. J. P. Stephens, M.A., of Camberley, said, *"As a preacher he had no
superior. In pulpit and on platform he was master of his craft."* Jill Morgan
described him as being *"virile and dynamic in the pulpit"* and that there
existed an *"intangible atmosphere of union between teacher and taught."*
Mr. F. A. Atkins described Morgan as a *"lively personality"* and that he
had an *"explosive method of expressing himself."*

A prominent newspaper journalist wrote of Morgan's ministry in
London, Ontario, Canada:

> *"Speaking with a power that must be akin to that of Peter's on the
> Day of Pentecost, this kindly-looking man becomes a human
> dynamo, and beyond all else tremendously fervent and deeply in
> earnest. He is not an apologist, but a trumpeter."*

John Harris wrote,

> *"At no point of his intellectual equipment is Campbell Morgan bet-
> ter served than by his imagination. He does not make pictures, he
> sees them."*

Arthur Marsh accounted for Morgan's great appeal by crediting it to
the following:

(1) his impeccable adherence to method
(2) his insistence on expository preaching
(3) the central factor in his ministry is the Divine, the Living
    Word. His great intellect was ever subservient to the Word

Journalists tried to describe Morgan in the pulpit: *"a truly notable
pulpit figure...almost without peer."* They described his voice as *"beautiful."* One article read: *"...as the beautifully elastic, alternately strident or
nasal, or gentle, or persuasive voice, sweeps the entire gamut of emotions..."*
One journalist credited Morgan as being *"...the most consistently popular preacher in the English speaking world during the past 30 years."*

Wilbur Smith felt that Morgan possessed two distinct New Testament gifts in that he was both a teacher and a prophet. After hearing Morgan preach on one occasion Smith wrote:

"We felt a tenseness, a magnetic pull, a lift, an atmosphere saturated with terrific intensity...I have been moved by others, in one way or another, but no Bible teacher in the world, in the 20th century, could cast over his audience without flash, without show, that mystic spell that Campbell Morgan (did) when he was at his best."

Wagner described the *"intangible atmosphere"* created by Morgan's personality, his clarity of expression, his compelling logic, and his keen understanding of the Bible itself. These factors accounted for his popularity. Wagner held that Morgan was *"first and foremost a Christologist."* He claimed that Morgan was strongly influenced by dispensational teaching. He was a premillennialist who saw Israel and the Church as being distinct, the one from the other.

Another journalist described Morgan as follows:

"A striking figure—tall, gaunt, smooth-faced; a head disproportionately large; a heavy mass of dark wavy hair, worn rather long and falling over the left temple and forehead; a keen, intellectual face; a bright quick eye, which flashes with passion or wells with emotion; a resonant voice, which now blazons like a trumpet, then, pleads in plaintive and irresistible pathos. His pulpit style is animated, his gestures numerous but never exaggerated and peculiarly graceful. A magnetic man—a man to draw an assembly and, having drawn it, to hold it prisoner at his will."

Yet another journalist attempted to paint a verbal picture of Morgan's physical appearance and the spell he cast over an assembly:

"He is tall—very tall, and very thin. His forehead is high, and over one side of it tumbles thick black hair beginning to be shot with grey. His complexion is swarthy...His features are very long, almost equine...something of Lincoln in them...But once he begins to preach, one forgets his angularities, his arresting, almost strange appearance. He is a master of assemblies, and one lies under his spell."

G. Campbell Morgan never resorted to gimmicks and what some would term *"popular preaching."* His sermons consisted of 50 to 60 minutes of close-fitting, elaborate argument.

> *"He will not attempt to overpower you with rhetoric or entertain you with ancient anecdotes, or surprise you with dexterous illustrations, or dazzle you with brilliant quotations. Not at all. But he will—for nearly an hour—build up a solid, sustained, carefully-thought-out and apparently unanswerable argument, which you would not expect to be irresistibly attractive. Still, people crowd to hear it from Los Angeles to London, from the sunny Gulf of Mexico to the muddy Mersey."*
>
> *"His thoughts,"* continued Harries, *"are clothed in language that a child can understand. This simplicity of speech is seasoned with a humour that relieves the strain of thought while it flashes new beauty on the truth itself."*
>
> *"Dr. Morgan never hampers himself with a manuscript and relies for the order and arrangement of his material upon a truly marvelous memory."*

At this point it should be noted that Morgan himself revealed that he took a very carefully prepared *"brief"* into the pulpit with him although it never contained whole sentences.

Morgan always preached for a verdict. He claimed that the closing note to any sermon, should be, *"Thou art the man!"* Concerning the closing appeal, Morgan once said,

> *"I choose in the pulpit, and you cannot help me. You must choose in the pew, and I cannot help you. God help preacher and people alike to choose aright!"*
>
> *"I think conviction is the true secret of Christian preaching,"* he ventured.

Morgan never took theological uncertainties into the pulpit. He preached what he knew with assurance. He held that the preacher was a messenger not a speculator.

> *"The preacher does not go to speculate and if he speculates before he goes, he had better not take the results of his speculation or he may*

have no living, vital message. I would remind you in this connection
of something Goethe said of preaching: 'If you have any certainties,
give them to us. We have doubts enough of our own.'"

Morgan never sought his messages by listening to the voices of the age. He did listen to those voices but he did not get his messages from them.

"Mark well the distinction. Our business is not to "catch" the spirit of the age, but to know it and CORRECT IT!" (Spoken to the Eastern Baptist Theological Seminary, Philadelphia, PA, on 3 February 1930)

Morgan, The Man

Jill Morgan made the rather unique comment that G. Campbell Morgan had *"a wonderful talent for friendship"*—a veritable *"genius for friendship."* As already mentioned, Rev. Albert Swift, his assistant at Westminster during Morgan's first tenure there, became his closest friend. Numbered among those who became very dear friends, were Gypsy Smith, F.B. Meyer, and Dwight L. Moody.

Morgan admitted of himself that he was somewhat shy and withdrawn.

"I don't think my friends would describe me as unsociable, but I cannot bear near me anybody who creates in me a feeling of restraint. I am slow to make friends, or to talk with strangers. What would suit me would be a house buried in the woods, a quick transit to a crowded church—and back to the woods!"

He was conscious of, and affected by, the numbers of the crowds. A large crowd inspired him, and conversely, empty pews dampened his spirit.

As noted above, he enjoyed sports—golfing, tennis, and horseback riding—and he did NOT enjoy deacons meetings! *"He would prefer to preach 3 sermons a day rather than spend half an hour at a deacons' meeting discussing who ought to keep the keys to the doors."* (From Jill Morgan's biography on GCM)

Morgan could not easily tolerate fools. The story is told of one incident where a certain *"brilliant young pastor"* drew large crowds by advertising such topics as, *"Popping the Question," "The Price of a*

Haircut," and *"Two Lumps of Sugar, Please."* By mistake on the part of a printer, the bulletin gave Dr. Morgan's sermon topic as, *"That's My Weakness Now,"* a topic which was to have been the young pastor's the following Sunday.

In introducing Dr. Morgan, the youthful pastor smilingly explained that the visitor would not preach on the topic announced, but that he himself would do so on the following Lord's Day. Amidst the general laughter that the explanation evoked, Dr. Morgan stood up and looking solemnly over the great audience, said with vibrant reverence, *"Hear the Word of God."* He made no apology. No pleasantries. The effect was tremendous, unforgettable. Deathly silence followed. Dr. Roberts added, *"It was an effective rebuke to flippancy."*

Morgan held some very insightful and practical views. One concerned the bestowal of gifts of the Spirit.

> *"But while it is true that the gift is bestowed, and is not merely a natural endowment, it is also perfectly certain that the Spirit of God never bestows a spiritual gift for service except upon men who have natural endowments that will enable them to use it. There is nothing in the economy of God out of joint and out of place. There is perfect harmony between God's first creation and the bestowment of special spiritual gifts. The new birth does not mean the death of everything essential and noble in the first birth, but its life. So also when God bestows the gift of the apostle, or the prophet, or the evangelist, or the pastor and teacher upon a man, the gift will be bestowed upon men who have natural aptitudes and fitness and endowments for their work."*

Morgan went on to say that he had never known of a case where a man who had no gift of speech whatsoever, having become a great preacher.

> *"A gift is a spiritual quantity and quality bestowed by the Head of the Church at His own will through the Holy Spirit upon those who are naturally endowed to receive it. That is the fundamental truth concerning the vocation and the force and the power of the Christian ministry."* (From *Evangelism: A Study of Need and Opportunity,* by G. Campbell Morgan, 1904)

Homegoing

G. Campbell Morgan died in London on 16 May 1945. He was 81 years of age. He was survived by his wife, Nancy, three of his four sons, and two daughters.

PART III

Common Characteristics Which Produced Greatness

What common characteristics and attributes did these men possess which made for their lives and preaching to have such uncommon impact in their day?

Were they merely the product of their times? Were they simply "the only show in town" prompting people to be drawn to them out of sheer boredom? Were they religious entertainers whose dynamic preaching was much preferred over the droning recitations of rectors and canons of the State Church?

Did the political and economical liberal tendency of the noncon-formists strike a warm chord in the hearts of forward thinking people who longed for change and progress in Queen Victoria's England? Did the skepticism of the State Church toward these popular preachers actually contribute to their popularity amongst the masses?

All these are legitimate questions, and each one nips around the edges, but fails to resolve the main issue. However, to suggest that these men were merely the products of their times inasmuch as there was nothing else to do on a Sunday except to go to church and listen to them, is ludicrous, when we consider the ministries of thousands of clergymen who also laboured in those times. With hundreds of churches in the greater London area, why is it that during a certain period of history large crowds gravitated to City Temple, Metropolitan Tabernacle and St. Paul's Cathedral? And why would Thomas Binney squelch students' criticisms of Spurgeon by saying that Spurgeon could instantly draw a crowd of 20,000, anytime, any place—something he himself could not do?

Could physical attributes account for their greatness? Almost uni-formly, firsthand witnesses tell of the magnificent voices with which each man was endowed, but on balance, there was nothing uniform about their height, weight, shape or facial appearance which would excite any unusual degree of fascination. However, the rich quality of their voices does support G. Campbell Morgan's conviction that the Holy Spirit grants spiritual gifts to those who are already possessed of natural endowments which predispose them to receive and make use of those spiritual gifts.

None of the men under consideration was particularly well connected with men of prominence who could advance their standing in British society. How then do we account for their uncommon visibility and place in church history?

Let us engage in a quick review. Regarding the matter of physical health and mental toughness, the record reveals that a high percentage of the preachers upon whom we are focusing our attention suffered from bouts of depression. R. W. Dale suffered from severe depression and mental terror in his earlier years of ministry. Joseph Parker was a most complex personality with an undeniable ego problem which masked a deep sense of insecurity. Though he was accounted by some to be the greatest pulpit orator of his day, he was of a melancholy nature, and could put in a dull performance if he had to use a manuscript. He seemed to be haunted by the fact that his father was born illegitimately. In spite of phenomenal success he lacked self-confidence and stood in constant need of reassurance and of the stimulation of crowds. When his second wife, Emma, died, he sank into a period of emotional and spiritual eclipse for a season.

Even the great G. Campbell Morgan was somewhat dependent upon a good crowd to call forth the best in him for preaching. Morgan was never robust in health. He suffered from a throat problem and manifested facial twitches. In later life he experienced brief attacks of amnesia.

Charles Spurgeon was regarded as rude and saucy when first starting out as a boy-preacher. Most of his life he was plagued by rheumatic gout, often preaching with one leg kneeling on a chair. He eventually died of Bright's disease at the early age of 57. His wife, Susannah, was an invalid for most of their married lives. Spurgeon also suffered from depression, and at least on one occasion, seriously doubted his own salvation.

Alexander Whyte endured periods of deep depression and often agonized over his "failure in the ministry." From his youth he was blighted with a defective memory which caused him to perform poorly in maths, physics and chemistry. Whyte's past also had its skeleton in the closet: his parents never married. Soon after his birth his father abandoned Whyte's mother, Janet Thomson, and Alexander was raised in her home. His father fought for the North in the American Civil War and eventually died in New York in 1871. Because of Alexander Whyte's defective memory, he usually read his sermons.

John Henry Jowett suffered from neuritis which caused insomnia. In later life he became thoroughly exhausted, lost weight, experienced fainting fits, developed anaemia, and in 1920 his health completely broke down. Though he seemed to be of flawless character, sometimes his schemes were impractical and impossible to carry out.

Henry Parry Liddon was dogged by violent headaches. Though his facial beauty was declared "faultless" the rest of him was unimpressive and he became quite portly in later life. In can be generally concluded that he normally preached too long! Liddon also suffered from rheumatism.

Alexander McLaren was of a retiring nature—a bit of a recluse. He suffered terribly throughout his life from stage fright. When he started out in the ministry he refused to wear the ordinary ministerial dress and had no sense of how to combine colours in his wardrobe. His preaching was considered "novel" and many feared that he would depart from sound doctrine, mainly due to his vivid imagination. As when Joseph Parker's wife, Emma, died, so when Mrs. McLaren died, Alexander could not face friends for a fortnight and many thought he would never preach again.

F. B. Meyer, one of Britain's most saintly preachers of yesteryears, was forced to resign from his pulpit charge at Victoria Road, Leicester, because of the tension caused by his evangelistic zeal.

I have taken the time to summarize previously cited weaknesses or shortcomings of these men, to illustrate the point that the "treasure" of the Holy Spirit was indeed encased in "earthen vessels." These vessels of clay were flawed and frail. As James wrote of Elijah in chapter 5 verse 17, that he was a man "just like us," so we can also conclude that Spurgeon was a man "just like us." The same could be said of the others. These were not gods, but mere men, and their genius did not exempt them from experiencing frailties and failings.

Still, the historical record stands: these were *"the men who moved the masses"* in their day and we seek to know why this was so, in spite of their limitations and shortcomings.

Before attempting to resolve this issue, we must report that not all are agreed that these men, most of whom were classified as "dissenters" with the exception of Liddon, brought great benefit to the cause of Christ. Erik Routley, in his book, *English Religious Dissent*, (Cambridge, University Press, 1960), does not really give full marks to the influence of the dissenting preachers of the Victorian era. He confesses that they indeed had a powerful intellectual and political influence in their day, but he goes on to write:

> *"The worst aspect of all this was the tendency to treat the preacher much in the same fashion as the film-actor is now treated and to regard public worship as something like a respectable public entertainment.*
>
> *"There was, with all the pomp and circumstance of the new-rich non-conformity, a softness at the centre which too often made the new Puritans content with cheap but pretentious buildings, second and third rate music, and a sentimentality in popular religion which a realistic 20th century generation has justifiably rejected."*

He pointed out that there was a tendency for wealthy employers to attend the large Congregational churches while their mill-hands attended Methodist missions.

> *"Non-conformity has in this present century paid dearly for its follies, and the unhappier aspects of Victorian non-conformity have been too widely celebrated both by historians and by anti-clerical novelists to need labouring here."*

There is nothing veiled nor subtle about Routley's bias against non-conformity and I am not sure that his case is strengthened by citing the writings of anti-clerical novelists! Eternity will reveal the fairness and accuracy of Routley's judgments and criticisms. I suggest that the debate is far from over on the issue of cheaper buildings as opposed to the enormous cost of building and maintaining well-constructed and elaborately decorated cathedrals. As for second and third-rate music, the church to this day has not outgrown its usage nor is the Established Church of Great Britain free from resorting to little choruses in even its morning worship services. As for *"sentimentality in popular religion"* I am not sure at whom this accusing finger is pointing, but I suggest that an injection of sentiment might not be the worst thing which could happen to some congregations which are currently held fast in the grip of a paralyzing atmosphere of sterility and death.

Routley maintains that non-conformity has paid dearly for its follies. However, there was one feature in several non-conformist churches and in a few of the congregations of the Established Church, which cannot be fitted into the category of "folly." I speak of the preaching of the men whose lives and work I have been researching. No matter how the public may or may not have treated them, no matter what the faults were in their overall approach to ministry, no matter how historians may judge them generally, when the preaching of each man is placed under close scrutiny, the critics have need to cease their much speaking, lay bare their heads, and take their shoes from off their feet, for they do indeed stand upon holy ground!

This era referred to as *"The Golden Age of Preaching"* is justly designated. The preaching was not perfect by any means. At least one of these men in our study broke nearly every sound homiletical principle ever agreed upon by teachers of the homiletical art. Joseph Parker's homiletics were abysmal and yet he was hailed by Alexander Whyte as the *"ablest man now standing in the English-speaking pulpit"*..."*a preacher's preacher"*, and *"a preacher of extraordinary power."* Thus, these were not perfect preachers, perfect in the art of preaching, but their preaching bore a God-given weight of greatness to the end that the preachers themselves have been called, *"The Men Who Moved the Masses."*

In the main, the content of their messages was marked by greatness. They majored on major truths. They adhered to the centralities of the Christian faith. Having something important to say, combined with their individual styles, they established a rapport between themselves and their audiences to an exceptional degree. They ever worked at developing their craft. Liddon was a life-long student of homiletics. Dr. R. W. Dale delivered lectures at Yale University on preaching. At age 58 Dale re-evaluated his preaching and effected major adjustments to his style and content thereafter. Jowett laboured over every word, every phrase of his sermons in his preparation, carefully polishing each phrase and painstakingly selecting each illustration. G. Campbell Morgan's son insisted that his father's expository preaching was the product of hard work and not of genius.

Some have questioned why I would want to spend these years in researching these men of God and their sermons. Some have prematurely concluded that the results of such research would be irrelevant to our present-day pulpit requirements. My conclusion is decidedly to the contrary. These men, though dead, yet speak to us, and model for us preaching skills which are wholly applicable to our present-day pulpit ministries. Features and elements of truly great preaching are perpetual, applicable to any generation. These are the features which I shall seek to underscore in this last section of this book.

Accounting for greatness is a difficult task. Two preachers once tried to analyze the greatness of the person and ministry of Joseph Parker of City Temple, London. William Adamson wrote:

> *"The late Professor Drummond, and one of Scotland's most able preachers, walked the streets of Edinburgh for hours one night after hearing him (Parker) preach, endeavouring to define the secret of his powers and popularity, but failed to satisfy themselves that they had found a solution of the problem."*

It is virtually impossible to attribute the greatness of any one of these men to one identifiable factor. All the biographers struggled with this issue as they tried to account for each preacher's greatness. Always the answer was the same: the best that authors could do was to list a number of factors which contributed to the whole, but even then a final pronouncement on the subject escaped them. There were considerable similarities between these men and there were obvious differences. It can be generally stated that the hand of God rested mightily upon them, but so was His hand upon many others! These men came to the Kingdom in an era which was marked by peculiar characteristics, and they brought to their task a set of peculiar, personal qualities and spiritual gifts—a different package of gifts in each case. God was well pleased to bless them to an extraordinary degree. But who can fully account for these things? *"The wind bloweth where it listeth…"*

Let us now make a modest attempt to identify those common, personal characteristics which resulted in such uncommon impact through their preaching ministry. As a backdrop and foundation to all of our considerations, I am convinced that the Sovereignty of God and His peculiar anointing upon these men to direct and enable them in their generation, are two factors which eclipse all others in accounting for their extraordinary accomplishments and influence. But there are human factors of style, manner, language usage, conscientious study and preparation, and of spirit and personality, which added fuel upon which the Holy Spirit's fire fell.

Chapter Fifteen

Individuality Intact

On the basis of my research, I conclude that God uses, to an extraordinary degree, unique personalities who have managed to retain, even salvage, their individual characteristics in spite of the neutralizing effects of life's experiences, training and education. There is no doubt in my mind that one of the principal reasons why the preachers in our study had such an uncommon impact upon the spiritual life of the U.K. in their era, is that they never abandoned nor compromised their unique individuality for the sake of church politics, nor for any other reason.

A concern, which has often been voiced in recent generations, is that university education followed by seminary training, has tended to produce in its graduates much of a sameness in thought, style and manner of expression. The academic exercise has been like a giant mower which has cut the lawn of graduates down to the same height, it is said. People in the pew have even claimed that they can accurately guess which seminary trained their Sunday morning guest preacher. Graduates of some seminaries have an uncanny likeness to one another in the way they dress, in their mannerisms, their gestures, their cool, analytical and cerebral approach to communicating the message, and in their overall style. This may be an unfair generalization and exaggerated depiction of these graduates, but the complaint persists, nevertheless.

No one could ever lay such a charge against the men in our study. No matter how well they were educated, no matter which route their academic pursuits had taken, one fact remained the same: *their individuality of personality remained intact*. In discipline of thought and in style of expression, each was his own man. They were not imitators of other men's mannerisms. They did not take their cue from the secular press nor from the sermons of their contemporaries. They put their own individual stamp and seal upon everything they did and said.

In today's ecclesiastical world, the more we have tended toward the adoption of corporate structures within denominational life, the farther away we have distanced ourselves from granting opportunity to *"rugged individualists"* to make their mark. Fiery prophets are replaced by individuals gifted with smoother, gentler manners. To be different and distinctive is less valued than to be conformist and *"in line."* If the prophets of old were to resurface in our denominations we would indeed stone them, so to speak!

The great preachers of the Victorian era retained their individuality of personality and style, and this quality of their life and work greatly enhanced the impact of their ministries. Each man in this study could be described as *"an original"*—a *"one of a kind."* They would never settle for allowing other men to do their thinking for them.

Each man's individuality, when analyzed, was made up of varying ingredients. Spurgeon, for example, was endowed with a most unusual and exuberant sense of humour which consequently spiced much of his sermon content. Therefore it can be concluded that Spurgeon's intelligence, plus study, plus humour, plus imagination, plus spirituality, plus who knows how many other qualities, resulted in a certain individual style which was peculiar to Spurgeon. Other men tried to imitate Spurgeon, but Spurgeon imitated no one.

This is not to say that these men did not learn from the work and manner of other men. Liddon was said to have been influenced to some extent by the French masters of oratory and that his personal style reflected that fact. Spurgeon greatly admired the preaching and work of George Whitefield. Alexander McLaren claimed that it was when he sat under the ministry of Thomas Binney that he learned to preach. But having acknowledged all of that, when these men are carefully studied, one discovers that they were carbon-copies of no man. They were originals. They were master-craftsmen. Their individuality remained intact.

As noted previously, Spurgeon's reply to R. W. Dale when Dale was trying to recruit him to take over the Chair of the Lyman Beecher lectureship at Yale University, reflects both Spurgeon's humour and his own self-awareness of his individual contribution in the work of the Kingdom. He replied, *"I sit on my own gate, and whistle my own tunes, and am quite content."*

We should quickly point out that retaining one's own individuality is not synonymous with a stubborn, independent, non-cooperative mind-set which refuses to function amiably within the Body of Christ. R. W. Dale was nominated President of the International Council of Congregational Churches in 1891 and was foremost among his peers in his day in shaping the lives and ideals of younger ministers. Dr. Jowett preached G. Campbell Morgan's induction sermon at Westminster Chapel in 1904. Among Dr. G. Campbell Morgan's various involvements were his service on the Governing Board of the London Missionary Society, his tenure as Vice-President of the Board of the Women's Christian Medical College at Ludhiana in Punjab, India, as well as being one of the founders of the Evangelical Union of South America. F. B. Meyer was instrumental above all other clergymen in opening the door for D. L. Moody's initial crusades in Great Britain. The Rev. R. Shindler devoted a page and a half in his biography of Charles Spurgeon (see pages 269 & 270) to recording a remarkable list of various agencies which originated and operated out from Spurgeon's Tabernacle which involved his people in a wide range of ministries to the poor and to the unconverted. Spurgeon and his congregation constituted a red-hot centre of evangelistic outreach and compassionate ministry to the poor. As noted in the biographical section, several of the men in our study served as elected Chairmen of their denominations at one time or another. John Henry Jowett was elected Chairman of the Congregational Union in 1906 as was R. W. Dale before him in 1869. Jowett also served as President of the National Free Church Council from March 1910 to March 1911.

Suffice it to say, that these "men who moved the masses" though individualists and strong personalities, were nevertheless very much involved in their denominations, in their communities, and from time to time, with each other. They were not individual islands unto themselves. Their world, their interests, their concerns reached well beyond their immediate pulpit charge. On balance we must admit that Alexander McLaren was more withdrawn by nature and Joseph Parker was somewhat of a lonely individual with few friends.

Chapter Sixteen

Fertile Imagination

To some degree their fertile imaginations were encouraged by their individuality and independence of thought. Being mimics of no man, their imaginations were constantly activated to find in their natural environment, human nature, and in history, apt illustrations to illuminate the texts upon which they were expounding. John Henry Jowett was a master at first seeing with his mind's eye some phenomenon in nature, and then in his verbal description of what he saw, weaving through the fabric of the image, golden threads of Biblical truth. He was quick to draw analogies between what his quick, keen eye saw in nature, and *"his own deeper philosophy of the soul."* Ever thereafter, the hearer would remember the Scriptural truth whenever the beautifully described landscape, or other image, was conjured up in his memory. Jowett's hearers were enabled to see what Jowett first saw in his fertile imagination. His fiery, vivid imagination acted like a branding iron upon their memories. John Henry Jowett excelled in what John Morley called, *"the imaginative treatment of the commonplace."*

Fertile imagination gives birth to originality. Dr. R. W. Dale wrote that originality *"was a pearl of great price: we were willing to sell all that we had to buy it."* A. W. W. Dale said of Dr. Dale,

> *"As a student he went to the foundation of every subject he touched, and examined it on every side, and carefully as his opinions were formed, he would on the slightest provocation revise them again. Needless to say, he was an independent thinker, and on some points reached conclusions in which he met but little sympathy from those most attached to him."*

John Harris wrote of G. Campbell Morgan,

"At no point of his intellectual equipment is Campbell Morgan better served than by his imagination. He does not make pictures, he sees them." Morgan insisted that the first vital ingredient to sermon preparation was "first-hand work on the text." He insisted that before any authorities were consulted that the preacher must grapple personally with the text and subject. "To turn to commentaries first is to create a second-hand mentality."

William Adamson said that Joseph Parker presented *"his conceptions rather in the setting of the imagination than in the framework of the logical faculty."* The power of his preaching lies in the contact of a mind of perpetual and amazing originality with the sublime truths of the Gospel. He was gifted to discover *"the principles which lie behind what seems the poorest detail, and which resolves all things into a unity."*

Adamson said of Spurgeon,

"His track is his own and the jewels he lets fall in his progress are from his own casket. This will give a permanent value to his works when the productions of copyists will be forgotten."

In like manner, Alexander Whyte developed a *"lively spiritual imagination"* especially in his treatment of Bible characters. G. F. Barbour said that Whyte had *"the right exercise of imagination in preaching."*

Observe a classic example of individual thought in connection with the text and the vivid use of imagination employed by Alexander Whyte when he preached his sermon on "Ham" in Edinburgh, published in 1896. We referred to this sermon in Whyte's biography section. The text was Genesis 9:22: *"…and Ham saw his father and he told his two brothers without."* From this text Whyte concludes that Ham was essentially a sensual man, a base character.

In his introduction he describes how Ham, as a young man, was evilly influenced by an old reprobate who boiled the black pitch for the construction of Noah's ark. The pitch-maker was an evil man whose heart was blacker than the pitch he boiled. The wicked reprobate died in the flood and went immediately into Hell, but Ham lived on and walked alone. Whyte referred to Dante who met his old schoolmaster in Hell as he passed through on his way to Heaven but such an experience was not yet to be for Ham, as he had yet to break his father's heart. Ham should have been raised in Sodom and Gomorrah. The midnight streets of the cities of the plains was his proper place. He was a filthy dreamer. Everything he looked upon, beast or sacred temple object, had unclean associations for him. He was the only true brute beast within the steaming walls of the ark.

Sensuality takes a most tremendous revenge on the sensual sinner. Cicero said, *"If you begin to think about forbidden things you will never be able to think about anything else."*

Whyte proceeds—

> *"There was a woman who clung to the door of the ark which was in the side thereof; and the woman cried and prayed. Ham! She cried. Ham, my husband! She cried. Ham, my destroyer! Preacher of righteousness! She cried, Open the door! Where is thy God? Open thy door and I will believe. Throw out thy son Ham to me, and I will take him to Hell in my arms! Is there a woman within these walls, or are they all she-wolves? And she dashed her head against the shut door. Mother of Ham! Wife of Ham! Sisters of Ham! She cried. My mother's blood is on his skirts. My own blood is on his hands! Cursed be Ham! And the ark shook under her words and her blows. And Ham, Noah's second son, listened in the darkness and through the seams of pitch. And then he kneeled in prayer and in thanksgiving, and he blessed the God of his fathers, that she had gone down, and that the waters still prevailed."*

What imaginative depiction of evil, of a heart that is blacker than pitch!

It was Dr. Whyte's contention that all the mechanisms of sermon preparation must be *"fused by the glow of personal experience and lit up by the flash of imagination"* if the message were to become living and powerful. Barbour goes on to explain:

> *"And, during the long, solitary walks of his holiday seasons, not less than in the silence of his study, Dr. Whyte, of set purpose, let his imagination pierce through and through the subjects or the characters regarding which he had in mind to preach. This deliberate and conscious cultivation of that which he regarded as "nothing less than the noblest intellectual attribute of the human mind" brought its abundant reward. For long years he carried out his own precept, "Let your imagination sweep up through the whole visible heavens,*

up to the heaven of heavens. Let her sweep and soar on her shining wing, up past sun, moon, and stars." (From Whyte's sermon on *Imagination and Prayer*).

R. W. Dale once described Alexander McLaren's preaching, making reference to his exercise of imagination, as follows: *"Dr. McLaren is a great preacher: he sees what he says."*

It is appropriate to repeat here what Dr. R. W. Dale had to say about the importance of imagination:

> *"If your imagination is vigorous, you will so use these words as to restore to the worn coin the sharpness of the original impression, and to the canvas, the brilliance and the richness of the original colouring. The difference between vivid and languid speaking depends very largely upon the extent to which the imagination contributes in this way to the expression of thought."*

Chapter Seventeen

Masters of the English Language and Metaphor

In his book, *The Upper Room*, Bishop J. C. Ryle cited an Arabian proverb: *"He is the best speaker who can turn the ear into an eye."* With their vivid imaginations, the preachers in our study *"saw truth,"* and by the masterful use of the English language they turned the ears of their hearers into eyes!

It should be of no surprise to us, (1) that individuality with its habit of independent thought, (2) vivid imagination, and (3) the ability to uniquely express what is seen with the mind's eye, should be linked together in a triplet of golden qualities adorning the master-pulpiteer. These men were masters of metaphor. Many had studied other languages and were able to draw upon literary resources written in languages other than English, but of critical note is the fact that they were masters of their own mother tongue and able to express themselves through picturesque speech. The author can recall British preachers coming to minister in North American pulpits from time to time, and how riveting, refreshing, and spell-binding it was to listen to the Word of God expressed with such artistry and beauty as well as spiritual power.

The style of each preacher in our study was distinctly his own, but the one common strand which ran throughout the preaching ministry of all of these men, was their superb use of the English language. The author has read and analyzed the sermon manuscripts of all of these men by the hours, weeks and months, and whereas one may be able to fault their homiletics or hermeneutics on occasion, one still must generally conclude that their use of the English language was on the highest level. Being able to see and illustrate truth within the burning crucible of one's fiery imagination is one thing, but to be able to express it artfully so that it sears its impression into the minds and hearts of the hearers, is quite another matter. Men like Spurgeon and Jowett could say things in the heat of inspiration which would fasten in a hearer's mind and heart for a lifetime!

It is no wonder that a general malaise in education coupled with an abandonment of standards and absolutes in our day should finally creep its way into our pulpits in the form of mediocre and grammatically inaccurate speech. Our expressions are like blunt instruments rather than razor-sharp scalpels. Verbally we blunder and stumble our way forward with the fond hope of doing healing surgery upon the souls of men. We do not give due credit to the fact that God communicated His message to us in the form of language—not by communicating mere spiritual impressions nor by exciting our emotions with external visual images. Contrary to the opinions of far too many, *language matters!* And when you link together individuality and independent thought, with a vivid imagination, along with the skilled, artful ability to express truth which imagination has illuminated, we end up with a powerful combination which the Holy Spirit can utilize to produce a profound impact upon our hearers.

Take note: we are not talking about language for language's sake. Not at all. We are talking about language which makes the presentation and penetration of truth like a glorious sunrise in the hearts of men; language that ignites the soul to embrace life-changing truth; language that serves as a drum-beat and bugle-call to the soldiers of Christ who have lingered by their campfires far too long.

The mastery of language is part and parcel of the "craft" of preaching. We must accept the fact that preaching is not only a calling, it is also a craft. Every preacher worthy of his keep must not only study to accurately understand the truth of the Scriptures, but also perpetually work at ever improving his craft and ability to express the truth in a manner which will captivate and motivate his hearers.

This will not be a popular point in this study because the mastery of language *implies work* whereas most people want magic! We instinctively seek the revelation of some "secret of success" to turn our ministry on to an upward path. We hope that the secret will take only moments to grasp and set us on a course to sure, long-term triumph.

One of the interesting features of our study has been to note how our pulpiteers were educated by various means, many being unconventional, and yet all reached an elevated plain of English language ability. Not discounting their formal academic training, in the main, these men were self-educated. Earlier we noted how R. W. Dale read widely in English, German, French, Greek and Hebrew. He studied the speeches of great secular orators and the sermons of outstanding preachers of the past and present and urged theological students to study the sermons of a very lengthy list of preachers who ministered in the British Isles or on the continent. He read the works of ministers from all denominations and insisted that if we must preach then we ought to learn to preach well. And a large part of that undertaking, I insist, is avid attention to the language medium by which we articulate God's message. *It is presumptuous to assume that the anointing of the Holy Spirit shall render unnecessary the industry required to master our own mother-tongue.* The same principle applies to those who preach the Gospel cross-culturally in a foreign language. To expect fullness of blessing to result from preaching in a language which we have only half-heartedly studied is an insult to both God and man. Language matters, whether it be our own or the dialect of some foreign people-group.

The Holy Spirit never intended to negate nor replace our industry. He comes to guide, to enable, and to bless our industry. If indeed we have been called to be communicators of the Gospel then surely we need to give attention to the medium of language whereby we endeavour to communicate that Gospel. Language matters.

"The deepest truths come to men most readily in a pictorial form," wrote Frank Morison in his book *J. H. Jowett, M.A., D.D.: A Character Study,* (James Clarke & Company, London 1911). *"The imagination can grasp with certainty what the undisciplined mind cannot, from sheer inexpertness, lay hold of at all."*

Jowett carries his hearers *"back to the picture book and nursery stage of their spiritual experience. He contrives to teach them much the same lesson as his mere academic friend, but he accomplishes it by interesting them in the pictures and leaving them to imbibe the truth which they represent."* With great industry Jowett transformed the pictures he saw in his mind's imagination into language, which he then used to recreate the pictures in the minds of his audience.

It should be no surprise to us that this was the method of Jesus Christ as evidenced in his teaching by parables and references to natural phenomena.

These men who moved the masses painted unforgettable pictures with words and could so relate the pictures to Biblical truth, that afterwards, the truths could be recalled when the vivid pictures so skillfully etched upon their memories, were revived and conjured up.

It is not the intention of the author nor the objective of this book to teach English but it may be useful to refresh our minds with some definitions of figurative and picturesque speech.

A figure of speech is comprised of a word or phrase that describes one thing in terms of another and is not meant to be understood or applied literally. Such figurative language always employs an imaginative comparison between seemingly and otherwise unlike things. The most common forms of figurative speech are simile, metaphor, and personification. In explaining metaphor, Sheridan Baker defines four levels, in his book *The Practical Stylist* (Harper and Rowe, Publishers, New York, 1981): they are (1) simile (2) plain metaphor (3) implied metaphor, and (4) dead metaphor. For example, "Suppose you wrote, 'he swelled and displayed his finery.' You have transferred to a man the qualities of a peacock to make his appearance and personality vivid. You can choose one of four ways to make this transfer:

1. Simile: He was *like* a peacock/He displayed himself *as* a peacock does/He displayed himself *as if he were* a peacock.

2. Plain metaphor: He was a peacock.

3. Implied metaphor: He swelled and displayed his finery/He swelled and ruffled his plumage/He swelled, ruffling his plumage.

4. Dead metaphor: He strutted. The art of resuscitation is the metaphorist's finest skill. Simply add onto a dead metaphor enough implied metaphor to get the circulation going again. "He strutted" by itself, is a dead metaphor which means to "walk in a pompous manner." The word can be understood very concretely. But then add onto it some implied metaphors...ie..."He strutted, swelling and ruffling his plumage" and you have revived the picture of a proud peacock.

Baker goes on to write that some of the best examples of the reviving of dead metaphors are found in proverbial cliches. See for example what Thoreau does in his journal with "spur of the moment."

"I feel the spur of the moment thrust deep into my side. The present is an inexorable rider."

A metaphor, then, is a figure of speech that connects two basically dissimilar items through some striking similarity. With the exception of simile, metaphors do not use connective words such as like, as, than, or resembles. (See *Elements of Literature*, Holt, Rinehart and Winston, Harcourt Bruce & Company, 2000)

The preachers also used analogy. Analogy is an extended comparison between two objects, ideas, or situations. Analogies can serve many purposes. An analogy often helps to explain unfamiliar terms by comparing them to more familiar ones. An analogy can also persuade an audience to accept the truth of one idea by comparing it to something else that is obviously true. (See *Appreciating Literature*, Macmillan Publishing Company, 1987.)

Examples of Picturesque Speech

Let me randomly lift a few examples of picturesque speech from some of the sermons of a few of these Victorian era preachers.

John Henry Jowett preached on the topic *"The Dayspring"* based on the text Luke 1:78,79 and published in 1901. He was illustrating why the coming of Jesus was as the dayspring, the dawning of the day.

> *"Not the full day, but the spring of the day, the light-fountain, Heaven's East! Even the tenderest eye can bear to look at the dawn! How sore and distressing and bewildering it is, in the hours of darkness to have flashed upon your eyes the harsh glare of the gaslight! We say, "Turn it down a little." The little light is a better minister than the big one. "Turn it down a little until I have become accustomed to it." That is the principle. "I have yet many things to say unto you, but you cannot bear them now." The children of the night must march into the noontide through the softer splendors of the dawn."*

It would be correct to say that Jowett will not merely say, for example, that the night is dark. He will rather place you in that darkness and cause you to feel the fear, the bewilderment, the isolation of darkness, and he will make you hear the sounds of the night that excite fear. For example in his sermon *"Under His Wings"* based on Psalm 91:4-6, he makes us feel the *"terror by night:"*

"...many things become terrifying through the medium of the night... in the night, faint sounds laden with alarming significance...creaking furniture, suggestive of the openings of coffins, stirring of windows by the moving night-air suggestive of unfriendly approach...the scratching of a mouse at the wainscot becomes fraught with all manner of hostile invasion."

Jowett's mind was pregnant with vivid images whereby he made his hearers' inner souls *feel* the truth and *visually see* the truth, as well as understand it.

When illustrating the dangers of the daytimes of our lives, in contrast to the terrors by night, he said in this same sermon *"Under His Wings,"* commenting on the *"arrows that flieth by day,"* he said:

"Enemies may be begotten of sunbeams as well as the darkness...the rays of light may become the arrows of death...how often it happens when men come into the clear happy light of favour, some better part of their being is slain...When a man's life passes into the full blaze of a fierce prosperity, the bloom and beauty of his spirit may be easily wasted and destroyed. His leaf may wither."

Near the end of this sermon he extols the solid foundation of God's truth as being our surest defense rather than a reliance upon our feelings. He said, *"At once I pass from loose stones to compact rock."* (The loose stones, representing our feelings, and the compact rock, being, God's truth.)

In Jowett's sermon on *"What Is Worldliness?"* he drew the analogy between physical and spiritual health. He maintained that the best defense against the spiritual disease of worldliness is to possess spiritual health.

"The ONLY defense against an ill contagion is exuberant health. It is the man who is run down who becomes the victim of pestilence...we must be possessed by the plentitude of spiritual life...this is life...to know Jesus...'I am come that ye might have life and have it more abundantly.' It is in this abundant life that we find the secret of moral security...familiarity with Jesus makes a man invincible against the world."

In his address to the Free Church Congress meeting in Cardiff, Jowett used images of playing and toying to warn preachers against toning down their condemnation of sin. He feared that sin had become less loathsome and that the preachers' repulsion to sin had become relaxed.

> *"Can we now toy with terrors before which our fathers shrank aghast?"*
> *"If sin has become a commonplace, our preaching has become a plaything."*
> *"If we think lightly of the disease, we shall loiter on the way to the physician."*

Jowett painted one of his most memorable images in his sermon *"The First Things"* preached at the Fifth Avenue Presbyterian Church in New York City and printed on 31 January 1917. His text was Matthew 6:33 *"Seek ye first the Kingdom of God..."* and he described his first visit to Mount Blanc. He saw the mountain as a *"monarch"* dominating the entire landscape. Wherever he went he could look back over his shoulder and see the grand mountain. Even when he returned to his living quarters he could see the stately landmark when he glanced out of his window. Mount Blanc was the first and last thing a traveler sees and remembers afterwards when traveling in the region. Jowett saw the commanding presence of Mount Blanc as being akin to seeking the Kingdom of God and His righteousness as the centre and focus of our lives. In every situation of life, the mountain of God's Kingdom and righteousness dominates.

In a sermon published in 1909 entitled *"Our Blessed Dead"* Jowett pictured the works that *"follow"* the blessed dead as being likened to a retinue, a group of attendants, which follow the blessed dead into the glory of Heaven.

> *"They enter the land of glory like monarchs with princely retinues, and their retinue is the radiant assemblage of good works which they have done in their pilgrimage through time."*
> *"And the glorious retinue of some of our earthly obscurities will be a matter of great surprise when the secrets of men are revealed."*

When illustrating the need for a radical and deep cleansing from sin, Jowett said in his sermon *"The Disciple's Theme"* published in 1905—

> *"...he suggests more than the washing out of old sins, he means the removal of an old affection; more than the removal of a pimple, he means the purifying of the blood!"*

Jowett preached on *"The Unbelief of the Fool"* from the text, Psalm 14:1 *"The fool hath said in his heart, There is no God"* and described how the fool's character determined the fool's wish. The fool does not believe in God because he does not WANT to believe.

> *"Our wishes rise as naturally and as inevitably out of our being as sweet fragrance exhales from a rose, and a noisome stench from a cesspool." "As we are, we wish; as we wish, we think; as we think, we judge...this fool has the cesspool in his heart, he is ungodly at the core..."*

In his message *"They That Wait"* he took the text Isaiah 40:31 *"...they that wait upon the Lord..."* and applied it to England's present circumstance caught up in World War I. He emphasized that this particular text had, in a sense, been waiting to be applied to national life at such a time as they were now experiencing.

> *"It seems as if the word had been patiently waiting for the circumstance, like a lock for its appropriate key, to unlock its imprisoned significance."*

Jowett stressed the necessity of prayer in the lives of those who are admonished to *"abide in Christ"* in his message *"Abiding in Christ"* based on the text, John 15:5 & 7.

> *"Take a blown-out taper, the only remnant of whose flame is a swiftly blackening spark, and plunge it into a jar of oxygen, and the dying ember will revive and regain its lost ascendency. And take a soul whose fire of vitality is blackening down into depression and pessimism, and immerse it in the reviving breath of the Holy Spirit,*

and aspirations will kindle again, and black depression will change into radiant hope. That is the very ministry of prayer, to keep the spirit of man in the oxygenating fellowship of the Spirit of God; and if we neglect the ministry, and cease to keep the communication open, we can no more be saved from spiritual depression and unrest than men who are immured in ill-ventilated chambers can save themselves from physical lassitude and perilous sleep. If we would abide in Christ, we must 'pray without ceasing.'"

When Jowett preached on *"The Power of the Cross"* he made the following profound statement, simply but richly endowed with imagery:

"We are never going to have grand trees of righteousness until they are rooted in a rich soil of reverence."

Charles Haddon Spurgeon was hailed as a genius by Frederic C. Spurr. Though Spurgeon was not university nor seminary-trained, he became a Latin scholar, was familiar with his Greek New Testament, read very widely, spoke more than one modern language, was possessed of a prodigious memory, and had an *"amazing mastery of Anglo-Saxon speech."* Professor Cleaver Wilkinson declared that if Spurgeon had not become a preacher *"he might have become the most perfect orator of his time."* Compared to Jowett's lofty illustrations and figures of speech which were of the most refined character, Spurgeon spoke more the language of the common man in the street and his word-pictures had a more earthiness-quality to them. He was often blunt and humourous. Jowett was a pastor, whereas Spurgeon was an evangelist through-and-through even though he pastored what became a prominent church. Let us listen in to excerpts from some of Spurgeon's sermons to hear examples of his use of picturesque speech.

In his sermon entitled *"The Talking Book"* preached on 22 October 1871 at the Metropolitan Tabernacle in London, he took the text, *"When thou awakest it shall talk with thee."* Proverbs 6:22.

"Have we not seen a text, as it were, plume its wings, and fly from the Book like a seraph, and touch our lips with a live altar-coal? It lay like a slumbering angel amidst the beds of spices of the sacred Word; but it received a divine mission, and brought consolation and instruction to your heart."

In Spurgeon's message on *"Waters to Swim In"* taken from the text Ezekiel 47:5, in one brief statement he illustrated the potential of sinners to allow God to bring them to spiritual maturity.

"The clay of the pit may yet be built into a palace for a king."

And again—*"He lifted us as beggars from a dunghill and set us among princes."*

In the same message he commends the work of George Muller with orphans, and uses the imagery of water, swimming, and floods to illustrate his point.

"How blessedly our friend Mr. Muller of Bristol swims! What a master swimmer he is! He has had his feet off the bottom many years, and as he swims, he draws along behind him some 2,500 orphan children, whom, by God's grace, he is saving from the floods of sin, and bringing, we trust, safe to shore."

In his summation to this message he urges upon his congregation to have greater trust in order to attempt greater things for God. He urges them not to walk with their feet safely on the sea-bottom, but to give themselves to the waters—*"waters to swim in"*—to launch out into the deep in exploits for God.

"'I have nobody to help me.' Oh, I see, you are all for walking on the bottom. Brethren, it is 'waters to swim in.' Cannot you swim without any help except the help of the All-in-all? See how the arch of heaven stands without a pillar. See you yon lamps of heaven, how they burn? Who gives them oil? See how they are swung in heaven without a golden chain to hold them in their place. Yet they flicker not; neither do they fall from their sockets; neither doth the arch of heaven tremble. May the Holy Ghost teach us to trust."

"We are not trustful enough of the invisible God. We are young eaglets born of God to mount up to the sun, but we stand shivering by the nest, not daring to try our callow wings. Young eaglets, trust the invisible ether: trust it and rise aloft. It shall bear you up, and ye shall not fall...He shall rise highest who can trust most."

In October of 1875 Spurgeon preached on *"There go the Ships"* from Psalm 104:26. He urged his hearers to go on the voyage of life with a *"fixed, earnest, weighty purpose."*

> *"Here you are, young man: you certainly were not sent into this world merely to wear a coat, and to stand so many feet in your stockings; you must have been sent here with some intention."*

In this same message he pictures himself as a ship which bears emigrants to Glory.

> *"Thank God I have sometimes had my decks crowded with passengers who have from my ministry received the Gospel! The Lord has brought them on board, and oh, I trust before I die, He will give me thousands more who will have to praise the Lord that they heard the Gospel from these lips! May we be emigrant vessels, bearing souls away into the gloryland."*

On July 1st, 1880, Spurgeon preached on *"Elijah Fainting"* from I Kings 19:4. He treated this subject with great compassion and understanding, and counseled his audience not to condemn themselves if . after a time of exhilaration they experienced a time of depression. He said that this was quite natural and common.

> *"...as natural as the retirement of the sea after its waves had kissed the cliff."*

On Sunday morning, 18 September 1881, Spurgeon preached on *"The Pentecostal Wind and Fire"* and lamented that services were rarely interrupted with expressions of praise.

> *"We gather the pinks of propriety instead of the palm branches of praise. God, send us a season of glorious disorder! Oh for a sweep of wind that will set the seas in motion and make our ironclad brethren, now lying so quietly at anchor, to roll from stem to stern!"*

When Spurgeon preached to his Sunday morning congregation at Metropolitan Tabernacle on 26 February 1882 on the subject *"The*

Dream of Pilate's Wife" he emphasized that God gets to the consciences of men by thoughts which come unbidden and abide upon the soul. He cited how Balaam was stopped by an angel in the way, and how Ahab was met by Elijah and cried, *"Hast thou found me, O mine enemy?"* In Matthew 27:19 Pilate's wife sends a warning to her husband to have nothing to do with Jesus for she had suffered many things that day in a dream because of Him.

> *"Often does conscience pounce upon a man when the sweet morsel of sin has just been rolled under his tongue, and he is sitting down to enjoy it; the visitation of conscience turns the stolen honey into bitterness and the forbidden joy into anguish."*

On 23 August 1885 Spurgeon preached on *"The Dying Thief in a New Light"* from Luke 23:40-42. He underscored the necessity of believers making an open confession of Jesus Christ as Saviour and establishing a public identification with God's people.

> *"Soldiers of Christ must wear their regimentals; and if they are ashamed of their uniform, they ought to be drummed out of the regiment. They are not true soldiers who refuse to march in rank with their comrades."*

He warned that many professing Christians get into trouble because they are not true and honest to their convictions. At the workshop they do not *"run up the flag"* at the first and so find it difficult to run it up afterwards. He admonished converts to make a clear stand for Christ right from the beginning, but if they are *"sneaky"* they will be in for a rough time.

> *"His life will be that of a toad under a harrow, or a fox in a dog-kennel, if he tries the way of compromise."*

In the book *"Spurgeon: An All Round Ministry"* Spurgeon urged that the fundamentals of the Christian faith be often repeated to the benefit of the congregation. He compared such a practice to old-fashioned farming:

"Repeat the fundamentals, too; often if you can. In the days of old-fashioned farming, they dropped three beans into the hole. And why? One is for the worm, another for the crow, and number three perchance would grow. Let us be liberal with the seed, for the evil powers are liberal with worms, and crows, and thorns. Let others go forth to shine; you are sowers, and must 'go forth to sow.' Repeat yourselves if necessary." (Pages 308, 309)

Spurgeon declared the goodness of God in his message *"A Visit to the Tomb"* by noting how God gives us something better when He takes away from us some good thing. He uses the comparative value of precious metals to make his point.

"They expected to find Him; He was gone. But then the grief must have been taken out of their hearts when it was added, 'He is risen.' I gather from this, that if God takes away from me any one good thing, He will be sure to justify Himself in having so done, and that very frequently He will magnify His grace by giving me something infinitely better...The Lord never takes away a silver blessing without intending to confer on us a golden gain. Depend upon it, for wood He will give iron, and for iron He will give brass, and for brass He will give silver, and for silver He will give gold. All His takings are but preliminaries to larger giving."

Joseph Parker preached a series of messages on *"I have seen"* texts, describing the reactions of God to what He has seen. In his message *"Memorable Sights in Life, Part II"* he commented on the text *"I have seen the blood of Naboth"* from II Kings 9:26.

"We have an eye for blood. We breed and train our bloodhounds, and great wonders they are in a small way, but the Lord has a nostril for blood, an eye for that murderous redness, for that revolting stain."

He went on to describe how we shed *"bloodless blood"* through the use of a murderous tongue, whereby we murder a man's reputation, slay a trustful, loving heart, and murder a heart that was once filled with hope.

"…a wound that leaves no red scar behind it, a stiletto so fine, so keen, that it pierces the heart without almost touching the skin."

Joseph Parker used the image of a fireplace grate to emphasize the need for Heavenly fire in his sermon *"What is the Gospel?"* published in 1903.

"What say you? Here is a grate, and here you have paper and wood and coals. The wind is blowing from the northeast; go and warm yourself at that grate. You instantly reply, How can we? It is a grate, and it has paper and wood and coal in it; but we cannot warm ourselves at it. Why not? Because it is not lighted. What do you want, then? A match. Strike the match, set fire to anything that will first take it and that will hand it on to the next, and that again to the next, and presently the whole grate shall glow with a generous and hospitable warmth. So it may be in our churches. We have fuel enough; what fuel we have! B.A.'s, and M.A.'s and B.D.'s and D.D.'s—go and warm yourself, if you can. You say—I cannot. Why cannot you? The fuel is good. Certainly, most excellent fuel; then why don't you warm yourself? Because it is not lighted. Exactly! We want Heaven's own spark, we want Pentecostal fire! Then our preaching shall be the preaching of a Gospel, and our Gospel the revelation of a kingdom through a Cross. Amen."

In addition to metaphor and other forms of picturesque speech, these preachers used highly imaginative and bold descriptions to make their point. **Alexander Whyte** in his sermon *"Michal, Saul's Daughter"* published in 1898, described Michal's reaction to seeing her husband, David, dancing before the ark:

"At the despicable sight she spat at him, and sank back in her seat with all hell in her heart."

He went on to describe Michal:

"Michal, with her heart full of war, and her mouth full of wicked words, and her whole after-life full of remorse and misery for that evil day in her house in Jerusalem. Michal is a divine looking glass for all angry and outspoken wives."

In describing Lot's love for Sodom in Whyte's sermon on *"Lot: God Delivered Just Lot"* published in 1896, Whyte said:

> *"Lot knew quite well both the name and the character of that city lying in the rain and sunshine below. He had often heard his uncle praying and plotting with God with all his might for Sodom. But Lot had no fear. Lot did not care. His cattle were already up to their bellies in the grass around Sodom, and that was heaven upon earth to Lot."*

In describing the imperfect nature of our human love which still retains *"the lingering remains of our own evil nature,"* **Alexander McLaren** said in his 1859 sermon, entitled, *"The Holy Spirit, The Earnest of the Inheritance."*

> *"Our love is blended fire and ice…"*

In McLaren's message on *"Weights and Sins"* preached in Union Chapel, Manchester, in 1859, he portrayed besetting sin as being serpent-like:

> *"…it waits, lurks, seeks to coil about us…"*

He went on to explain how the *"weights"* which need to be cast off, can be legitimate things which have been perverted:

> *"Man can distill poison out of God's fairest flowers…"*

In clinging to some of God's endowments to a wrong degree or in a wrong manner, we turn them into a weight:

> *"We make them all sharp knives with which we clip the wings of our heavenward tendencies, and then we grovel in the dust."*

McLaren preached a missionary message entitled *"Christ and the Heathen World"* on 27 April 1864 in Surrey Chapel, London. He described the Lord's penetrating gaze into the darkness of the heathen world, discovering those whom He has called out to be His own:

"He sees the gold gleaming in the crevices of the caves, the gems rough and unpolished lying in the matrix."

In the same missionary message McLaren revealed how that it took long years of labour to prepare the beginnings of God's work in the heathen world. It is slow going at the first but eventual success may come swiftly.

"The preparation may be as slow as the solemn gathering of the thunder clouds, as they noiselessly steal into their places, and slowly unheave their grey billowing crests; the final success may be as swift as the lightning which flashes in an instant from one side of the heavens to the other. It takes long years to hew the tunnel, to make the crooked way straight, and the rough places plain, and then, smooth and fleet, the great power rushes along the rails!"

McLaren described the terrifying disappointment of pursuing satisfaction in sin, in his message *"David's Cry for Pardon:"*

"Sin misses the aim if we think of our proper destination. Sin misses its own aim of happiness. A man never gets what he hoped for by doing wrong, or, if he seems to do so, he gets something more that spoils it all. He pursues after the fleeing form that seems so fair, and when he reaches her side, and lifts her veil, eager to embrace the tempter, a hideous skeleton grins and gibbers at him!"

In his message *"So Did Not I: A Word to the Young"* he visualized how some people had carelessly gone forth into life from his church as being like a pleasure boat, and had made shipwreck of their lives.

"Like some pleasure boat that runs out of harbour with a careless crew, flags flying and laughter sounding, and before she has well cleared the port is smashed to pieces on the black shelf of rocks, half hid by the sunny waters as they break over it in dancing foam."

McLaren painted a word picture in his sermon *"The Eagle and its Brood"* of how God makes us uncomfortable where we are, in order to push us forth into His will:

"The straw is pulled out of the nest and it is not so comfortable to lie in; or a bit of it develops a sharp point that runs into the half-feathered skin, and makes the fledgling glad to come forth into the air."

In 1898 McLaren preached on *"A Father's Discipline"* in which he showed how some portions of Scripture lie dormant upon the page until some dark night falls upon the soul and the verses previously unnoticed and unapplied, shine forth to encourage and guide us.

"They may be long unnoticed on the page, like a lighthouse in calm sunshine, but sooner or later the stormy night falls, and then the bright beam flashes out and is welcome."

McLaren questioned himself and his audience to see if he, along with they, had nurtured a habit of continual occupation of thought with God, in his message *"The Course and Crown of a Devout Life:"*

"When I take off the brake, does my spirit turn to God? If there is no hand at the helm does the bow always point that way? When the magnet is withdrawn for a moment, does the needle tremble back and settle itself northward?"

In the same message he compared the life and end of Enoch with the life and end of himself and his congregation:

"Enoch was led, if I may say so, round the top of the valley, beyond the head waters of the dark river, and was kept on the high level until he got to the other side. You and I have to go down the hill, out of the sunshine, in among the dank weeds, to stumble over the black rocks, and wade through the deep water; <u>but</u> we shall get over to the same place where he stands, and He that took him round by the top will 'take' us through the river; and so shall we 'ever be with the Lord.'"

The saintly preacher, **F. B. Meyer**, in his message *"Joseph's First Interview with His Brethren"* described the mysterious workings of memory by likening it to an old-style camera:

"...(memory) conducts its operations in perfect mystery. The room is shuttered from all human gaze; the camera is covered by a black veil...Nothing has ever passed athwart it that has not left a record on its plastic slabs."

Meyer saw Joseph's brothers as icebergs heading toward a blessed end in the hands of Joseph, in his sermon *"Joseph's Second Interview with His Brethren."*

"Those men were like icebergs floating down into a gulf-stream of warm and sunny love."

In his message *"Joseph Making Himself Known"* Meyer compares the pleading of Judah for the welfare of his young brother Benjamin, to the pleadings of Christ on our behalf before the Father.

"But if a rough man (like Judah) could plead like this, think, ah! Think what must not those pleadings be which Jesus offers before the throne. What moonbeams are to sunshine, what the affection of a dog is to the passionate love of a noble man, that is the pleading of Judah compared to the intercession of our Great High Priest."

G. Campbell Morgan's command of the English language was superb but he used picturesque speech to a lesser degree than those preachers cited above. However, in his message *"The Laodicea Letter"* published in August of 1902, he quoted Keith, applying the analogy of physical health and sickness to the spiritual condition of church goers in Sardis and Laodicea:

"Sooner would a man in Sardis have felt the chill of death was upon him, and have cried out for life, and called for the physician, than would a man of Laodicea; who would calmly count his even pulse, and think his life secure, when death was preying on his vitals."

In Morgan's famous sermon on *"China"* preached on 19 January 1906 in which he condemned his own country and government for their part and responsibility in the Opium Wars, he warned:

*"China is waking...either a yellow peril or a golden sunrise!...
depends upon influences brought to bear upon her...if wakening
hurried by sword, fire, battle...she may in madness turn on those
who exploited her...if helped by the Gospel, she will yet free herself
from the evils inflicted upon her...:"*

In Morgan's message *"Backsliding"* preached on 27 April 1906, he
referred to those who were cooling in their affection for Christ and
sliding back from commitment as being on a...

"...trackless burning desert of degradation."

Morgan claimed that luxurious and extravagant living was detri-
mental to robust spiritual life. In his sermon *"How to Fight the Devil"* he
said:

*"We are calling things necessary which our fathers referred to as
luxuries...when you have found the simplest form of eating and
clothing and recreation you have found the place of strength."*

*"Half the men who have ever seen me on the subject of being mas-
tered by some evil thing against which they are pretending to
fight—if I could pull them out of the place where they are and give
them a plank bed and feed them on porridge and water for six
months, I could cure them!"*

In that same message Morgan warned believers to be careful about
the companions they choose:

*"Shun absolutely and forever any friend who in any way
brushes the bloom off your modesty."*

In his application of this message on how to fight the devil he contrasts the use of spurs vs. the use of a sword:

*"Believe me, you will prove your heroism in this fight more truly by
the use of the spurs with which you hasten from the place of evil
than by your attempt to use your sword in direct and immediate
controversy with evil. Begin your fight by putting as great a*

distance as you can between yourself and that temptation. If you are going to win you must burn your bridges behind you when you start out under Jesus Christ."

In his message entitled *"My Friend"* based upon Proverbs 18:24, Morgan uses the time of year and the conditions of the weather to describe when it is conducive to discover true friends:

"...it is difficult in June days to distinguish between acquaintance and friend...one must wait until November and December...you can't discover them when the sky is blue...You will find them when the sky is overcast and Euroclydon beats the deep into fury, and you are in peril."

"When I face difficulty, give me my one old friend, though a rough and curious specimen of humanity, rather than one hundred butterflies who are round me while the sun shines and are gone when storms lower."

Dr. R. W. Dale was a theologian, philosopher and apologist of the first rank. I am amazed, as I review his sermons preached in the latter half of the 19th century, of how timeless and profound his thinking was. He courageously tackled subjects from which lesser men would flee, and those subjects were so fundamental to the church that his sermons sound as though they were preached only yesterday. His views on such controversial subjects as the use of music, the place of women in the church, ministry to the poor, the responsibilities of the rich, for example, are as relevant today as they were one and a half centuries ago. In later years he even condemned himself for having too often preached above the ability of the average person in his congregation to comprehend, and he set about to correct that fault. However, when one studies his sermons preached over several years, one stands in awe of his insight and his brave but brilliant treatment of the most difficult issues. His pronouncements were analytical, penetrating, and bore the ring of truth. His sermons were captivating, not because they were delivered in any flowery style, but because of the sound logic of his arguments. He had the capacity to completely engulf an issue, with its many facets, and declare his conclusions on the basis of careful thinking, broad exposure to the writings of others, and always founded squarely on the Word of God. But having said all of that, Dale also used some choice analogies and metaphors to illuminate his subject matter.

When Dale preached on the topic *"The Perils and Uses of Rich Men"* (published in 1867) he declared that he, himself, was safe from the perils of rich men for many a long year to come. In fact, he said he would *"be much obliged if someone would tell him how to get rich soon!"* He went on to say in his introduction—

> *"…but this Week-day Sermon on 'The Perils and Uses of Rich Men' is about as worthless to me as a paper on the Dangers of Alpine Ascents to a gouty old gentleman of seventy, or as Mr. Jeavon's book on our Coal Supply to an inhabitant of the planet Mercury."*

In this same sermon he decried the explanation of a certain writer who sought to understand why God permitted rich men to exist at all. The writer postulated that rich men were meant *"to be the prey of the poor. The poor are God's eagles to beset, infest, and strip the rich…"*

In another Week-day Sermon entitled *"The Seventh Commandment"* based on Exodus 20:14 *"Thou shalt not commit adultery"* he counseled those already married, but in a union that was less than hoped for originally, that each partner endeavour to make marriage *"a truer and better thing."* They were to understand that there was good in every man or woman.

> *"You do not root up the rose tree in your garden because through the dreary months of winter there is neither beauty upon it nor perfume; you do not despise it because it looks so bare and ungracious; you think of the shining weeks of summer, when it crowns itself with loveliness, and fills the air with sweetness. The life out of which all this springs is in it all the winter through."*

R. W. Dale's sermon *"The Education of the Conscience"* in which he expounded upon the great text, Philippians 4:8 *"Finally, brethren, whatsoever things are true, whatsoever things are worthy of honour and reverence…etc…think on these things,"* Dale used various word pictures to explain what the Apostle meant.

> *"St. Paul means that the mind of a Christian man is to be the home of noble, lovely, and heroic conceptions of moral character and*

conduct…Rich people adorn their homes with fine paintings…marble statues depicting energy and grace…How do we fill the galleries of memory and imagination?"

He went on to ask, if, in fact, our minds are vacant?

"That is impossible. Our minds are occupied with whatever is carried in to them—noble or ignoble, charming or repulsive, precious or worthless."

"The very poorest of us may fill the mind with forms of immortal majesty and beauty; and this is what St. Paul tells us to do in the text…(Dale then repeats the text, Phil. 4:8)…These are the paintings with which the walls of the mind are to be hung, these the costly marbles, these the priceless gems, which we are to collect from all countries and from all ages, and make our own."

Dale then went on to draw the contrast between minds which are adorned with the positive virtues enumerated in the text, and minds which are filled with negative images. He once had visited a medical museum and since then he could not expel from his mind the horrible things he had seen.

"…there are minds, instead of galleries of art, are rather like a medical museum, a dreadful place, with wax models of hideous and disgusting deformities from which human nature suffers."

Henry Parry Liddon preached on the subject *"The Aim and Principles of Church Missions"* on Tuesday, 27 November 1860, at The Church of St. Mary Magdalene, Munster Square, London. To emphasize the Biblical teaching that there is no second chance offered to sinners to repent after death he said:

"There is no repentance in the grave or pardon offered to the unholy dead.
    The tree will lie as it falls…"

In the same message he described the all-too-obvious wretchedness of the poor, by saying—

"The snow buries the glacier and the treacherous abyss, but with the poor, there is nothing covered or hidden...there is no disguise for their wretchedness."

Listen to Liddon's masterful description of the Apostle Paul's view of man in this same sermon:

"St. Paul, too, had his view of human kind, but it was not that of the man of pleasure, nor yet that of the general or the politician, not that of the poet or the painter. He saw in every child of Adam that which was more noble and precious than the most precious and noble of material and earthly prizes: he looked not at the temporary accidents of man, not at his race, or lineage, or possessions, or position,—he scanned not the beauty of his bodily form, nor yet the endowments of his understanding. He put all these aside, as things for which he had neither sympathy nor appreciation: he knew that birth is but a disposition of Providence, that means and position become worthless in a last illness, that the earthly body will one day slough off like the shell of some chrysalis bursting into a higher life, that all knowledge which is not spiritual is surely destined 'to vanish away." He gazed intently, perseveringly down, 'till he encountered in each man his real self—the undying spirit which underlies voice, and look, and stature, and means, and acquirements, and position, and all that mass of accidents which overlay and intercept it from the general view. And yearning over the multitude of men thus penetratingly, he prayed and struggled that he might save some of them.

"I say some of them;—not all, not even many, but some. (Liddon's text was I Corinthians 9:22 "That I might by all means save some...") He might have said one: for that any sinful child of Adam should be God's instrument, not for influencing, not for improving, but for saving one soul, is a signal and astonishing act of God's grace and mercy."

In Liddon's message on *"Jonah"* he described old age which brings with its years a better understanding of things eternal.

"It is when the clouds are gathering, hour by hour, more and more thickly over the sky of time, when the pulse of strength is sensibly ebbing, and the distant horizons of eternity are coming more and

more distinctly each moment into view, that the real importance of the lessons of Jonah's history become apparent."

On Good Friday, 11 April 1873, Liddon preached on *"The Fruitfulness of Death"* based on the text *"...except a corn of wheat fall into the ground and die, it abideth alone: but if it dies, it bringeth forth much fruit."* He described how pride had so thoroughly infected every man's soul.

"Are we not, you and I, constantly thinking about our good qualities, constantly rating ourselves higher than others; feeling annoyed when we hear others highly spoken of; defending our opinion even in indifferent matters with obstinacy, because it is our own opinion; assuming a quiet air of superiority in conversation as if there could be no sort of doubt about our right to assume it; desponding when our efforts do not succeed, as if we had some kind of chartered right to command success; rejoicing in showy work which attracts admiration rather than in quiet unostentations work only to God and the blessed spirits in Heaven; anxious that men should see, anxious that they should remark upon, our good qualities—anxious, perhaps sincerely anxious, to improve and become virtuous, not because God wills it and to promote His glory, but chiefly at any rate that in the contemplation of our new attainments our vanity might have something more to feed upon. He Who knows us knows that it is hard to be really humble."

In his message on *"The Barren Fig Tree"* Liddon compared the Lord's ultimate approval of our fruitfulness over against man's flattery of our labours in this present life.

"Let us be quite sure that it is better that God should own the fruit of our lives by-and-by, than that men should pay compliments to the leaves here and now."

On the second Sunday after Easter in 1876 Liddon preached his renowned sermon on *"The Virtue of Elisha's Bones."* He put forward the question, *"What does the past do for a nation?"* His answer was that the recollection of past glories and triumphs can have the effect of rekindling a depressed and degenerate nation, even as the corpse touched the bones of Elisha and revived. (See II Kings 13:20,21 which was Liddon's text.)

> *"A degenerate posterity asks itself why, with the same blood flowing in its veins it should be incapable of the virtues of its ancestors. The corpse of national life, the languid pulses of national thought, are brought into contact with the past; they touch the bones of Elisha, and the country may yet revive and stand again on its feet."*

In his unforgettable message entitled *"The First Five Minutes After Death"* based on I Corinthians 13:12 *"Then shall I know, even as also I am known"* Liddon sought to reveal how man would reflect upon his earthly life once he was out in eternity:

> *"Each man's life will be displayed to him as a river, which he traces from its source in a distant mountain 'till it mingles with the distant ocean. The course of the river lies, sometimes through dark forests which hide it from view, sometimes through sands or marshes in which it seems to lose itself. Here it forces a passage angrily between precipitous rocks, there it glides gently through meadows which it makes green and fertile. At one while it may seem to be turning backwards out of pure caprice; at another to be parting, like a gay spendthrift, with half its volume of waters; while later on it receives contributory streams that restore its strength; and so it passes on 'till the ebb and flow of the tides upon its bank tells that the end is near."*

Dramatic Portrayal and Repetition

In addition to apt illustrations, metaphor, simile, and allusion, other literary devices were employed by our pulpiteers such as the dramatic portrayal of a scene or event, or by the rapid, repetitious use of an identical phrase or an identical grammatical structure, such as—

This was his destiny;

This was his reason for living;

This was his high calling;

This was his life's work;

This was his dream;

And this was its fulfilment!

In the Joseph Parker section of the biographies we referred to Parker's stinging and shocking public rebuke of the Turkish Sultan. In spite of the massacre of the Armenians, Germany's Kaiser referred to *"My friend the Sultan"* in an after-dinner speech. Let me quote a larger section of Parker's sermon so that the reader may catch a clearer glimpse of the dramatic and bold language which Parker employed:

> *"When I heard that the Kaiser went to the East, and after a dinner— hear this, for there is no more solemn word in the speech of Christianity—when I heard that the Kaiser went to a dinner, and in an after-dinner speech, said, 'My friend the Sultan," I was aston- ished, I could have sat down in humiliation and terror. The Great Assassin had insulted civilization, and outraged every Christian sentiment, and defied concerted Europe. He may have been the Kaiser's friend; he was not yours, he was not mine, he was not God's. Down with such speaking! And let every man's voice be heard on this matter; then the Liberals may come back to power. So long as any man can say, 'My friend the Sultan," I wish to have no commerce or friendship with that man. The Sultan drenched the land with blood, cut up men, women, and children, spared none, ripped up the womb, bayoneted the babe, and did all manner of hell- ish iniquity. He may have been the Kaiser's friend, but in the name of God, in the name of the Father, and the Son, and the Holy Ghost—speaking of the Sultan, not as an individual, not merely as a man, but speaking of him as the Great Assassin—I say, GOD DAMN THE SULTAN!."*

These words were uttered extemporaneously in righteous indigna- tion and Adamson reports that the audience was stunned and awed. But in seconds they recovered themselves from the shock and broke out in unrestrained applause. This speech was given on 25 April 1899 on behalf of the National Council of Free Churches on the occasion of the tercentenary of the birth of Oliver Cromwell. He chose as his text Ezra 9:3 *"When I heard this thing, I rent my garment and my mantle, and plucked off the hair of my head and of my beard and sat down astonied."* Parker's first words set the tone for the entire message when he said,

"We have lost the genius of indignation; no man is astonished now. When we lose astonishment at moral outrages, sins, crimes, we are no longer worthy to live!"

On another occasion, in reaction to suggestions of Higher Criticism, specifically Professor Cheyne's opinion that Psalm 72 was written in honour of Ptolemy Philadelphus, King of Egypt, Parker reacted with outrage expressed in dramatic speech which also used the literary device of repetition of key phrases. He first noted that Canon Rawlinson had declared that Ptolemy had banished his own wife to Upper Egypt that he might marry his full sister, who had formerly been the wife of his brother-in-law!

"Sorry," Dr. Parker went on to say with passionate earnestness, *"and painful would be the reading of that Psalm in the light of Canon Cheyne's suggestion. Take a few verses in illustration of my meaning.*

'He shall judge thy people with righteousness, and thy poor with judgment.'

'He shall come like rain upon the mown grass, as showers that water the earth.'

Ptolemy Philadelphus, the incestuous beast!

'He shall spare the poor and needy, and shall save the souls of the needy.'

Ptolemy Philadelphus, the incestuous beast!

'His name shall endure forever, his name shall be continued as long as the sun, and men shall call him blessed.'

Ptolemy Philadelphus, the incestuous beast!

No, gentlemen, ten thousand times no! I cannot believe God will divide His throne with the devil!"

William Adamson went on to record,

"When these words were uttered a thrill went through all present, which led them to rise en masse and applaud with an energy very unusual, if not quite unprecedented, in the venerable Assembly, the older and conservative members being as demonstrative as those of younger years."

Another example of the effective use of the repetition of key phrases or sentences is found in Spurgeon's message on *"Elijah Fainting"* from which we quoted previously. Spurgeon was making the point that we have not the faintest idea of what God has in store for us in the future. Elijah's wish to die according to his own time-table and decision was foolish, for it would have caused him to miss out on so much that God had yet in store for him.

> *"Let me die!*
> *But Elijah, would you not like to live until you have veiled your face on Horeb?*
> *O yes, let me live 'till then.*
> *Would you not like to live until you have rebuked Ahab for his sin against Naboth?*
> *O yes, let me live 'till then.*
> *Would you not like to live until you have cast your mantle over that blessed servant of God, Elisha, who is to succeed you?*
> *O yes, let me live 'till then.*
> *And would you not like to see the schools of the prophets raised by your influence…?*
> *O yes, let me live 'till then.*
> *And brother, you do not know how much you have to live for— blessing yet in store for you.*
> *Wait on the Lord and be of good courage!"*

Listen to Alexander Whyte, by the use of repetitive utterances, admonish his Edinburgh congregation about the importance of right choices in life, based upon the account of the disastrous choice Esau made when he sold his birthright:

> *"Choose your reading;*
> *Choose your company;*
> *Choose your husband and your wife.*
> *Choose life, and not death;*
> *Blessing and not cursing;*
> *Heaven and not hell.*
> *You can, if you choose.*
> *You can, if you like."*

Chapter Eighteen

Passionate Intensity

Donald E. Demaray reviewed the preaching of 25 outstanding preachers in his book *PULPIT GIANTS: What Made Them Great* published by Moody Press, Chicago, 1973. He claimed that every one of these 25 preachers was possessed of a *"radioactive earnestness."* He wrote that John Wesley has been called an *"incendiary"* and that Benjamin Franklin went to hear Whitefield preach because *he could watch a man "burn."* He referred to Dr. Paul Rees as a man who is *"on fire."*

It was Richard Baxter who said, *"I preach as never sure to preach again, and as a dying man to dying men."* He preached with passionate intensity.

One common thread between the majority, if not all, of the nine Victorian pulpiteers in our study is that each was possessed of a fiery earnestness, and whether the volume of their voices was either soft or raised, that earnestness carried to every pew in the sanctuary, all the way to the back rows. Even when Jowett whispered in undertones, hearers in every part of the sanctuary were held in the grip of his intensity. Most of the preachers in this study could be classified as "hot communicators" in today's terms, and most certainly, all were possessed by a passionate intensity.

In many circles today it seems to be more in vogue to opt for "cool communicators." These are generally graduates of post secondary institutions such as seminaries and graduate schools attached to colleges or universities. Graduates of these longer streams of education tend to lean heavily in the direction of teaching_from the pulpit, as opposed to preaching/prophesying/heralding, and tend to adopt a more "cerebral" style. Having studied all sides of an issue they often leave the conclusion to the judgment of their hearers after they have been presented with the arguments and counter-arguments of each side of an issue. They appeal primarily to the mind in the endeavour to persuade. With some it is regarded as anti-intellectual to become passionate or emotional about what one is saying…almost a sin which must be confessed on the following Sunday morning! Although I am slightly exaggerating the case, I am convinced that I am not far off the mark. An exception to what I have described is what takes place among Pentecostal and charismatically inclined assemblies.

Whether or not the reader agrees with this generalized characterization is of no consequence to the observation that the nine men in our study were "hot communicators" in the main, but at the same time they were very bright and well-read. They studied broadly and prepared thoroughly but when they preached, they preached earnestly from the heart to the hearts of the people. Even with the brilliance and thoroughness of Liddon's defense of the Gospel, his delivery was passionate.

In a brief sketch of Alexander McLaren which appeared in the *"Freeman"* in 1875, the writer described McLaren's preaching as *"logic on fire,"* and went on to write *"that his words thrill like electricity."*

Rev. T. Harwood Pattison, professor of homiletics in the former Rochester Theological Seminary, wrote to McLaren in 1900, asking him to write an open letter to Pattison's students. McLaren complied with Pattison's request, and in his opening remarks, wrote:

> *"I sometimes think that a verse in one of the Psalms carries the whole pith of homiletics—*
> *'While the fire burned, then spake I with my tongue.' Patient meditation resulting in kindled emotion and the flashing up of truth into warmth and light, and then—and not till then—the rush of speech 'moved by the Holy Ghost'—these are the processes which will make sermons live things with hands and feet, as Luther's words were said to be."*

As already noted, intensity of spirit and fiery disposition are not to be confused with the sheer volume of one's voice. F. B. Meyer was said to be a man "of exceptional power." But W. Y. Fullerton said that he was *"not a passioned orator"* and that he was "rarely carried away by his feelings." But he goes on to say that *"when speaking in the power of the Spirit the very quietness of his style was deeply impressive."* Mann claimed, *"No other man I ever listened to was so completely able to hold my unflagging attention as was F. B. Meyer."* Principal Thomas Phillips of the Baptist

College said that Meyer *"wove a spell over the audience."* Chester Mann said Meyer had *"blood-earnestness"* even though he had a tranquil delivery. *"Meyer felt the truths he uttered."*

We conclude that Meyer's was a quiet, yet *riveting intensity,* which carried people with him as the silent but mighty under-currents of an ocean. Another writer said of him that he possessed *"a yearning earnestness, suggesting the possession of much reserve power."*

Jill Morgan said that G. Campbell Morgan was *"dynamic and virile in the pulpit"* and that there was an *"intangible atmosphere of union between Teacher and taught"* in his meetings. Mr. Atkins described him as having a *"lively personality and explosive method of expressing himself."* A prominent newspaper man wrote of Morgan's ministry in London, Ontario:

> *"Speaking with power that must be akin to that of Peter's on the day of Pentecost, this kindly-looking man becomes a human dynamo, and beyond all else tremendously fervent and deeply in earnest. He is not an apologist, but a trumpeter."*

Another journalist described Morgan:

> *"His pulpit style is animated, his gestures numerous but never exaggerated, and peculiarly graceful. A magnetic man—a man to draw an assembly, and, having drawn it, to hold it prisoner at his will."*

Joseph Parker had a magnetic personality and had a dramatic style of delivery. Rev. Dr. Raleigh said that he never heard Parker preach except it stirred *"the war horse in me and made me more anxious to carry on the warfare against evil."* Albert Dawson described Parker's preaching:

> *"the further away from his manuscript the better he preaches. Usually he covers the ground outlined in his notes, but I have known him to devote practically the whole sermon to the first head. Sometimes he seems to be literally 'possessed'; his voice takes on a peculiar swing, there is a steady, even flow of words, the pauses are few, and he seems to be merely the medium through which a message is being delivered."*

G. Holden Pike described him as *"a preacher of extraordinary power."*

Joseph Parker, in turn, described R. W. Dale as the *"orator of the great occasion."* From the outset of his ministry he was *"a great and commanding power."* In his preaching Parker said Dale had no intermission of force, that *"from first to last the strong man went over rough ground and smooth ground at the same impetuous and irresistible speed."* A. W. W. Dale said of him: *"He gave, and rightly gave, an impression of whole-hearted sincerity."*

John Henry Jowett was like F. B. Meyer, a preacher with a quieter style of delivery but nevertheless earnest and captivating. Frank Morison writes:

> *"You miss the external note of oratorical power usually associated with large gatherings. There is nothing in the manner of the grand port, no highly sustained periods of dramatic power—nothing but an atmosphere of quiet interest as the speaker unfolds his thought which deepens into stillness as he reaches the point to which he has been leading up. Some of his most impressive passages are delivered almost in an undertone which, however, he contrives to make audible throughout the entire building. It is then, apparently that he has the greatest command of his own thoughts."*

And again:

> *"Dr. Jowett's style does not consist so much in the substance of his sermons as in the manner of their delivery. Not a little of his wonderful influence over his congregations is due to the almost hypnotic effect of his personality while preaching. He has a kind of psychological power of thought projection which creates an atmosphere congenial to him. You soon discover that his personality is even more eloquent than his voice. There is a fascination in his manner which enlists your interest even though your judgment pronounce against him. It is this quality which is missed by those who only know him through his printed books."*

Before hastening on, I must comment that anyone who has read Jowett's several published volumes of sermons will have known immediately that Jowett's preaching was much more than mere style. From all first hand accounts of those who heard him preach, his style quite obviously fascinated and captivated their interest, it is true. But the content of his messages bore profound thought, deep spirituality, and refreshing insight.

Henry Parry Liddon was also a man endowed with intensity of spirit. John Octavius Johnston said that preaching had always been a strain on Liddon, and he was always exhausted after preaching. On Sunday he could do little for the rest of the day except read the Lessons at the great evening service. Archbishop Benson described Liddon when in the act of preaching:

> "...all his physical and intellectual structure is quite swallowed up in spiritual earnestness, and he is different to other preachers, in that one feels that his preaching in itself is a self-sacrifice to him— not a vanity nor a gain..."

A journalist in the *Saturday Review* on 24 August 1889, wrote that Liddon's whole argument is steeped in emotion. *"The light is never dry."* Another journalist writing in the *Guardian* on 24 July 1889, tried to account for Liddon's greatness as a preacher. After listing five features, he summed up:

> "Such seem to be some of the elements of Dr. Liddon's power as a preacher. They are qualities of a very fine order; and when they are controlled and animated by an intense conviction of the absolute certainty of the Divine revelation by an absorbing zeal for the salvation of men, by a fearless trust in God and by a constant recollection of our Saviour's Presence, and of the Day of Judgment, it is not strange that they should hold a great place in the life and hope of England."

G. W. E. Russel wrote of Liddon:

> "He was alive all through—vivid, vivacious, sensitive, alert. He seemed surcharged with moral electricity, which tingled and flashed and sometimes scorched." He characterized Liddon's preaching as "a vigorous flow of eloquence."

Rev. Aug. B. Donaldson described Liddon's 1866 Bampton lectures:

"There was a holy vigour and sanguine enthusiasm pulsating through all the lectures, and men felt that a great and gifted champion of the Catholic faith had been given by God to His Church."

In an anonymous biography of Charles H. Spurgeon, written in 1903, the author described Spurgeon's *"manifest zeal and transparent sincerity of heart"* and his *"forcible expression."* A journalist in the *GLOBE* on 22 March 1855, described his preaching as *"fervid and impassioned eloquence."* Spurgeon had an *"intense earnestness"* and was *"possessed by a passion for the souls of men."* *"We have heard his voice break into sobs, and have seen the tears stream down his cheeks, as he pleaded with the unconverted and implored them to be reconciled to God."*

"His earnestness was often terrible. We have seen him preach when in such agony from gout that he could not keep his foot on the ground, but had to kneel on a chair while speaking. But presently as he warmed to his subject, he would spring to his feet and advance to the front of the pulpit and preach with all his old vigour, regardless of the pain that burned like fire in his bones. No wonder that such fervour was potent to persuade men."

"Above all, the blessing of the Holy Spirit manifestly rested upon his ministry. One was conscious while listening, of a power and influence that were not due to the force of his argument or the eloquence of his utterance."

Kathy Triggs said that Alexander Whyte's preaching *"riveted"* the audience's attention. In a book edited by Ralph G. Turnbull, entitled *"The Best of Alexander Whyte,"* Whyte's person and manner in the pulpit are portrayed:

"In the pulpit he was a man of passion. Nobody ever heard from his lips any cold truth. He was never ashamed of getting into a state. His passion ran easily into wildness and it was from him that one learned that a certain amount of wildness and capacity for it is an absolute necessity for all effective preaching."

"His preaching was hot truth let loose, and one hearing him many a time remembered the words of Jesus, 'I am come to send fire on the earth.'...you took your life in your hands when you went to hear him preach." Like Bunyan of old, he *"feared nothing and said*

anything with a courage that made your heart stand still as he preached."

The accumulation and repetition of descriptive phrases sum up this distinctive quality in the preaching of these great men: *"radioactive earnestness" "incendiary" "while I was musing the fire burned, then spake I with my tongue" "kindled emotion and the flashing up of truth into warmth and light" "completely able to hold my unflagging attention" "wove a spell over the audience" "blood earnestness" "dynamic and virile" "a human dynamo" "stirred the war horse in me" "extraordinary power" "an impression of whole-hearted sincerity" "almost hypnotic effect of his personality while preaching" "intensity of spirit" "swallowed up in spiritual earnestness" "the light is never dry" "intense conviction" "absorbing zeal" "surcharged with moral electricity, which tingled and flashed and sometimes scorched" "a vigorous flow of eloquence" "manifest zeal and transparent sincerity of heart" "forcible expression" "possessed by a passion for the souls of men" "his earnestness was often terrible" "riveted the audience's attention" "in the pulpit he was a man of passion" "hot truth let loose" "with a courage that made your heart stand still as he preached" "nobody ever heard from his lips any cold truth."*

Possibly this point of impassioned earnestness is best summed up in the answer Thomas Binney gave to Joseph Parker, previously quoted, when asked what he thought was the best method of preaching. Binney replied, *"Gather your materials, and set fire to them in the pulpit!"*

Chapter Nineteen
Prophets to the Nation and Ministers to the Poor

In addition to their pulpit excellence these men were prophets to their nation and ministers to the nation's poor. They fearlessly spoke out on moral issues of national and international significance, and they engaged in a wide variety of humanitarian projects to lift up the orphan, the poor, the sick, the mentally infirm, and those segments of society which were being abused or disenfranchised. Though their fame is largely due to the impact of their preaching power, their greatness and influence cannot be accounted for fully without acknowledging their practical efforts to reach out, and speak out, in response to their own sensitive social conscience. They cared enough to become involved with social and national issues. They obviously did not regard such actions to be in contradiction to their call to preach the Gospel, but rather a necessary part of carrying out their calling.

On balance we must remember Jowett's admonition to not be so taken up with combating social issues that we fail to evangelize and carry out our spiritual ministry. By becoming so involved trying to transform society, as though we were living in the Old Testament era, we might fail to stick to the centrality of our mission to minister to the awful disorder of the soul. However, by all accounts, these *"men who moved the masses"* appear to have kept these matters in harmony and balance, making the two streams of preaching the Gospel, and of social concern, as one blended watercourse of ministry.

Their congregations were an admixture of people from all walks of life—the gentry, professionals, the growing middle-class, the labouring poor, vacationers in London, clergy from various denominational backgrounds, actors, and students. While the preachers heralded their Biblical message from their pulpits, they were fully aware of the cancer of poverty and vice which ate away at the vitals of British society. They could not stand aloof from such blights upon their nation. When international crimes and atrocities were committed either by their own Britain or by other countries, they were not silent.

G. Campbell Morgan thundered condemnation down upon his own England for the cruel injustice it had committed against China by forcing the Chinese to accept opium imported from India.

Joseph Parker roared damnation against the Turkish Sultan over Turkey's massacre of the Armenians and his censure was echoed in the strong anti-Turkish stand taken by Henry Parry Liddon at St. Paul's Cathedral.

It is also quite interesting to note that when Catherine Booth was reduced to exhausting weakness by cancer, her very last message was delivered from Joseph Parker's pulpit in City Temple on June 21st, 1888. After delivering her message, she had to remain in the pulpit for a full hour before she could be moved. Parker's public support of General and Mrs. Booth is significant in light of the persecution the Salvation Army endured at the hands of the police and the Bishops of the Church of England.

Charles Spurgeon founded his own orphanages and was so involved supporting a wide range of charities it was said he gave away nearly all of his own money. It was Spurgeon who proclaimed, *"The God that answereth by orphanages, let Him be God!"* Parker invited orphans from Spurgeon's Stockwell Orphanage to sing at his Thursday noon meetings to raise money for the institution. He initiated other similar supportive undertakings for the Little Boys' Home, Farningham; The Reedham for Fatherless Children, The Haverstock Hill Orphanage; and The Caterham School for Ministers' Sons. On March 8th, 1884, Charles Spurgeon wrote a thank you letter to Joseph Parker, in which he remarked, *"You have been kindness itself to me. Without solicitation you have aided me in my work, with brotherly kindness."*

F. B. Meyer, while serving as pastor, drove a van around Leicester selling firewood to collect money to assist unemployed, unskilled labourers. On the side of the van, a sign read, *"F. B. Meyer: Firewood Merchant."*

Though not featured in this book, the great Methodist Hugh Price Hughes (1847–1902) inspired the founding of a number of city missions throughout England, and established a *"Sisterhood"* of women drawn from Protestant Evangelical churches called *"Sisters of the*

People" whose mission was *"to come alongside of the sinful and sad."* He also devised a program whereby better-off people in West London could *"patronize"* less fortunate families in East London. Noted for having expanded the ethical side of Christianity, Hugh Price Hughes once said, *"some very earnest Christians are so diligently engaged in saving souls that they have no time to save men and women."* He went on to say:

> *"Of one thing I am profoundly convinced, it will be impossible for us to evangelize the starving poor so long as they continue in a starving condition. I have had almost as much experience of evangelistic work as any man in this country, and I have never been able to bring any one who was actually starving to Christ."*

Over the course of his lifetime of service he became actively involved in a number of moral and social causes, such as, anti-gambling efforts, the temperance movement, spoke out against the persecution of Jews in Armenia and Russia, cruelty to animals, the opium trade, the State regulation of vice, and the "sweating system" in its application to women and children. He realized that the interests and the social needs of the people were an integral part of the ethical teaching of Christ. After chatting with him, Lady Somerset said that she became aware *"that a reformer had come among us who feared no one save God."*

Alexander Whyte was involved in the church's Home Mission work as it sought to care for the physical needs of Glasgow's slum-dwellers. His biggest contribution to this lay in putting pressure on the City Council to provide clean water and proper drains and sewers for slum areas. It was said that *Whyte was always personally drawn to those who combined depth of spiritual life with involvement in social welfare.*

John Henry Jowett struck out against what he called *"strongholds which ought to be pulled down."* They were (1) The British Factory System (2) Money worship (3) Carnality, and (4) International jealousy and ill-will. Jowett had always stood four-square against what Miss Evelyn Underhill called,

> *"devotional basking in the sun while allowing the maiming influence of environment to press myriads of other souls back to the animal levels."*

On 16 January 1908 Mrs. Jowett formally opened the Digbeth Institute which was a centre for holistic ministry to the slum-dwellers of the city of Birmingham. It was the fulfilment of a lifetime dream for Jowett. This facility included a spacious hall capable of accommodating 1,480 people; a billiard room with three full-sized tables; a reading room; games rooms for men and youths; a café which was open at all time to the public; a large and well-equipped gymnasium used alternately by men and women; school rooms; rooms for the Trade Union and other meetings; a wood chopping yard to give temporary assistance to those who were genuinely unemployed.

Dr. R. W. Dale of Birmingham fought for the principle of universal School Boards and free education for children. Not only did he serve on the Birmingham School Board but in 1885 he was appointed to the Royal Commission on the working of the Elementary Education Acts in England.

Thomas Binney, pastor of The King's Weigh House Chapel, London, for forty years, was commonly regarded as *"The Patriarch of Nonconformity."* He established a charity school in the gallery of his church before the Ragged School Union was ever founded. Together with some laymen he founded *"The Colonial Missionary Society"* which became the missionary arm of the Congregational Church. By personal visitation and through the publication of tracts he lent his support to such charitable institutions as the Hospital for the Incurables at Putney, and, Miss Sharman's Orphans' Home in West-square, Southwark, near the "Elephant and Castle."

Summation

The qualities and features of these men of God are not antiquated nor outmoded. They are as perpetual as the sun. Their language may be vintage 19th century, but their lives, preaching, and practical ministries serve as valid models for us today. What we have reviewed is virtually a British case study, but the lessons we can learn from it are universally applicable. The Providence of God introduced these men "to the Kingdom" into the midst of a certain social and historical context, and simultaneously graced them with combinations of gifts, interests and abilities which made them effective to an extraordinary degree. Their preaching and leadership moved the masses. They were certainly centre-pieces in *"The Golden Age of Preaching."* Would to God that He might be pleased to grant us yet another such Golden Age before His Son returns in great glory and splendour!

Bibliography

A Centenary Memoir, by the Rt. Rev. the Lord Bishop of Oxford and Others, London, 1929

A Brief Sketch of the Rev. Alexander McLaren B.A., from the Freeman Office, 21 Castle Street, Holburn, Pewtress Bros. & Gould, London, 1875

Adamson, William, D.D., *The Life of the Rev. Joseph Parker, D.D., Pastor City Temple, London*, Inglis Ker & Co., Glasgow, Cassel & Co. Ltd., London, 1902

Appreciating Literature: MacMillan Literature Series, MacMillan Publishing Company, New York, copyright 1984 and 1987

Bacon, Ernest W., *Spurgeon: Heir of the Puritans*, George Allen & Unwin Ltd., London, 1967

Baker, Sheridan (University of Michigan), *The Practical Stylist (5th edition)* Harper & Row, Publishers, New York, 1981

Barbour, G. F., *Life of Alexander Whyte, D.D.*, Hodder and Stoughton Ltd., London, 1923 (8th edition)

Binney, Thomas, *The Closet and the Church: To the Rising Ministry, More Especially of the Congregational Ministry*, J. Unwin, Gresham Steam Press, London & Bucklersbury, 1849

Binney, Thomas, *King's Weigh-House Chapel Sermons, 1829–1869, Second Series*, edited by Henry Allo, D.D., MacMillan & Co., London 1875 (biographical sketch on Thomas Binney included)

Blench, J. W., (Lecturer in English, University of Aberdeen), *Preaching in England in the Late 15th and 16th Centuries*, Basil Blackwell, Oxford, 1964

Booth, General William, *In Darkest England and the Way Out*, International Headquarters of the Salvation Army, 101, Queen Victoria Street, London, 1890

Booth-Tucker, F. De L., *(The Short) Life of Catherine Booth: The Mother of The Salvation Army (Abridged from the original edition)*, International Headquarters, Publishing Offices on Clerkenwell Road, London, 1893

Brastow, Lewis O., D.D., *Representative Modern Preachers*, The MacMillan Co., London, New York, 1904

Broadus, John A., *A Treatise on the Preparation and Delivery of Sermons*, Hodder and Stoughton, London, 1901

Brooke, Stopford A., *Life and Letters of Fredk. W. Robertson, M.A.*, Henry S. King & Co., 65 Cornhill, London, 1872

Brown, S. J., *An Hour with the Rev. C. H. Spurgeon: The Causes of His Success, Answer to "Why So Popular?"* London, 1856

Bywater, Margaret, *Joseph Parker (A Heritage Biography)*, Independent Press Ltd., London, 1961

Carlile, John C., *Alexander McLaren, D.D.: The Man and His Message*, S. W. Partridge & Co., London, 1901

Chadwick, Owen, *The Victorian Church, Part II, 1860–1901*, SCM Press Ltd., London, 1970, Reprinted in paperback 1987

Charles Haddon Spurgeon: A Biographical Sketch and an Appreciation—By One Who Knew Him Well, Andrew Melrose, London, 1903

Clarke, C. P. S., *The Oxford Movement and After*, A. R. Mowbray & Co. Ltd., London, Oxford, Milwaukee USA, 1932

Cowan, Arthur A., D.D., *The Primacy of Preaching Today (The Warrack Lectures for 1954)*, T. & T. Clark, 38 George Street, Edinburgh, 1955

Daane, James, *Preaching with Confidence: A Theological Essay on the Power of the Pulpit*, William B. Eerdmans Publishing Company, Grand Rapids, Michigan, 1980

Dale, A. W. W., *The Life of R. W. Dale of Birmingham*, Hodder and Stoughton, London, 1898 & 1902

Dale, R. W., *Lectures on Preaching*, Hodder and Stoughton, London, 1877

Dale, R. W., *The Atonemen: The Congregational Union Lecture for 1875*, Congregational Union of England and Wales, Memorial Hall, Farringdon Street, London, 1899

Dale, R. W., *The Evangelical Revival and Other Sermons*, Hodder and Stoughton, London, 1880

Dale, R. W., *Christ and the Controversies of Christendom*, in bound volume called Theological Pamphlets, D. Disraeli, Individual publishing, Hodder and Stoughton, London, 1869

Dale, R. W., *Essays and Addresses by R. W. Dale, L.L.D. (2nd Edition)*, Hodder and Stoughton, London, 1899

Dale, R. W., *The Communion of Saints*, in bound volume called Theological Pamphlets, D. Disraeli, Individual publishing, Hodder and Stoughton, London, 1871

Dale, R. W., M.A., *The Ten Commandments*, Hodder and Stoughton, London, 1871

Dale, R. W., *Week-Day Sermons*, Alexander Straham and Co., London, 1867

Daniels, Rev. W. H., A.M., *D. L. Moody and His Work*, Hodder and Stoughton, London, American Publishing Company, U.S.A., Hartford, 1875

Davies, Horton, *Varieties of English Preaching 1900–1960*, SCM Press Ltd. Bloomsbury Street, London 1963, printed in Great Britain by Western Printing Services Ltd. Bristol

Davis, Henry Grady, *Design for Preaching*, Fortress Press, Philadelphia, 1958

Dawson, Albert, *Joseph Parker D.D.: His Life and Ministry*, S. W. Partridge & Co., London, 1901

Demaray, Donald E., *Pulpit Giants: What Made Them Great*, Moody Press, Chicago, 1973

Donaldson, Rev. August B., M.A., *Henry Parry Liddon*, Rivingtons, London, 1905

Elliott-Binns, L. E., D.D., *Religion in the Victorian Era*, Lutterworth Press, London, 1936

Fasol, Al, *A Guide to Self-Improvement in Sermon Delivery*, Baker Book House, Grand Rapids, Michigan, 1983

Fisher, George Park, D.D., L.L.D., *History of the Christian Church*, Charles Scribner's Sons, New York, 1931

Fitt, Arthur Percy (D. L. Moody's son-in-law and secretary), *(The Shorter) Life of D. L. Moody*, Moody Press, Chicago (no date)

Forman, R. S., *Great Christians*, Ivor Nicholson and Watson, Forty Four Essex Street, London, W.C.2, 1934 (Section on R. W. Dale written by J. K. Mozley)(Section on Hugh Price Hughes written by J. E. Rattenbury)

Forster, Roger, *Ten New Churches*, Marc Europe, The British Church Growth Association, The Chaucer Press, Suffolk, 1986

Forsyth, P. T., *Positive Preaching and the Modern Mind*, Independent Press Ltd., Memorial Hall, London, E. C. 4, 1907

Fullerton, W. Y., *F. B. Meyer: A Biography*, Marshall, Morgan & Scott Ltd., London and Edinburgh, 1929

Gordon, Ernest B., *A. J. Gordon*, Hodder and Stoughton, London, 1897

Gore, Charles, Editor, *Lux Mundi*, November 1889

Hamilton, Walter Kerr, Bishop of Salisbury, *Liddon (Henry Parry) D.D.*, published in "The Guardian," London, 1869

Hammond, J. L. and Barbara, *Lord Shaftesbury*, Constable & Company, Ltd., London, Bombay, Sydney, 1923

Harries, John, *G. Campbell Morgan: The Man and His Ministry*, Fleming H. Revell Co., New York, Chicago, London & Edinburgh, 1930

Hart, Liddell, *History of the First World War*, Pan Books Ltd., London, 1972

Hayden, Eric W., *A Centennial History of Spurgeon's Tabernacle*, Pilgrim Publications, Pasadena, Texas, 77501, 1971

Hogue, Bishop Wilson T., Ph.D., *A Handbook of Homiletics and Pastoral Theology*, Free Methodist Publishing House, Winona Lake, Indiana, 1949

Holloway, David, *The Church of England: Where is it Going?*, Kingsway Publications, Eastbourne, Sussex, 1985

Hughes, Dorothea Price, *The Life of Hugh Price Hughes by His Daughter*, Hodder and Stoughton, London, 1905

Johnston, John Octavius, M.A., *Life and Letters of Henry Parry Liddon, D.D., D.C.L., L.L.D.*, Longmans, Green and Co., London, New York, and Bombay, 1904

Jowett, J. H., *Our Blessed Dead*, Andrew Melrose, London, 1909

Jowett of Balliol and Frederick Temple, *Essays and Reviews*, 1860

Jowett, J. H., M.A., *Apostolic Optimism and Other Sermons*, Hodder and Stoughton, London, 1901

Jowett, J. H., *The Eagle Life and Other Studies in the Old Testament*, Baker Book House, Grand Rapids, Michigan, Paperback edition issued in 1976, Copyright 1922 by George H. Doran Co.

Jowett, J. H., *They That Wait*, James Clarke & Co., 13, 14 Fleet St. E.C., London, 1914

Jowett, J. H., *Thirsting for the Springs, 2nd Edition*, H. R. Allenson Ltd., Racquet Court, Fleet Street, E.C., London, 1907

Jowett, J. H., *From Strength to Strength*, Little Books on Religion, Hodder and Stoughton, 27 Paternoster Row, London, 1902

Jowett, J. H., *The Transfigured Church*, James Clarke & Co., 13, 14 Fleet Street, London, 1910

Jowett, J. H., *The Friend on the Road, and Other Studies in the Gospels*, Hodder and Stoughton Ltd., Toronto, London, New York, St. Paul's House, Warwick Square, E.C.4 (no date)

Jowett, J. H., *The Whole Armour of God*, Baker Book House, Grand Rapids, Michigan,1969; originally Hodder and Stoughton Publishers, London, Copyright 1916 by Fleming H. Revell Company.

Jowett, J. H., M.A., D.D., *The Preacher: His Life and Work—Yale Lectures*, Hodder and Stoughton, London, New York, Toronto, 1912

Jowett, J. H., *Great Pulpit Masters, J. H. Jowett*, Baker Book House, Grand Rapids, Michigan, reprinted 1972, Copyright 1950 by Fleming H. Revell Company

Jowett, J. H., *The First Thing*, The Christian World Pulpit, No. 2,361 Vol. XCI, Wednesday, January 31, 1917

Jowett, J. H., *The Passion for Souls*, James Clarke and Co., London, 1905

Ker, Rev. John, D.D. (Professor of Practical Training in the United Presbyterian Church) 2nd Edition, Hodder and Stoughton, London, 1888

Liddon, H. P., D.D., D.C.L., Canon and Chancellor of St. Paul's, *Christmastide in St. Paul's: Sermons Bearing Chiefly on the Birth of our Lord and the End of the Year*, A.R, Rivingtons, Waterloo Place, London, 1889

Liddon, H. P., D.D., D.C.L., L.L.D., Late Canon and Chancellor of St. Paul's, *Advent in St. Paul's: Sermons Bearing Chiefly on the Two Comings of our Lord*, Longmans, Green, & Co., London, New York, 15 East 16th Street, 1891

Liddon, H. P., *University Sermons*, Rivingtons, London, Oxford and Cambridge, James Parker & Co., Oxford, 1869

Liddon, H. P., *Serkons on Old Testament Subjects*, Longmans, Green and Co., London, New York, 1891

Liddon, H. P., *Easter in St. Paul's*, Longmans, Green, and Co., London and New York,1891

Liddon, H. P., *Sermons at St. Paul's and Elsewhere*, Longmans, Green and Co., London, New York, Bombay and Calcutta, 1907

Liddon, H. P., *Clerical Life and Work: A Collection of Sermons with an Essay (2nd Edition)*, Longmans, Green and Co., London, New York, 1895

Liddon, H. P., D.D., Canon Residentiary of St. Paul's, and Ireland Professor, *Sermons Preached Before the University of Oxford, (Second Series 1868–1880)*, Rivingtons, Waterloo Place, London, Oxford and Cambridge, 1880

Liddon, H. P., *The Contemporary Pulpit Library: Sermons by H. P. Liddon, D.D., D.C.L., Canon of St. Paul's, (2nd Edition)*, Swan Sonnenschein & Co., Ltd., Paternoster Square, London, 1898

Liddon, H. P., *Sermons Preached on Special Occasions 1860–1889*, Longmans, Green & Co., London, New York, and Bombay, 1897

Liddon, H. P., *Forty-One Sermons on Various Subjects*, Charles Higham, London, 1886 (Second Series)

Liddon, H. P., M.A., *The Bampton Lectures: The Divinity of our Lord and Saviour Jesus Christ*, Eight lectures preached before the University of Oxford in the year 1866, on the Foundation of the late Rev. John Bampton, M.A., Canon of Salisbury, by Henry Parry Liddon, M.A., student of Christ Church, and Chaplain to the Bishop of Salibury. Rivingtons, London, Oxford and Cambridge, 1869

Lloyd-Jones, D. Martin, *Preaching and Preachers*, Hodder and Stoughton, London, Sydney, Auckland, Toronto, 1971

Lyman Beecher Lecture on Preaching, Yale University, Hodder & Stoughton, London, 1907

McLaren, Alexander, *Sermons Preached in Manchester (3rd Series) By Alexander McLaren*, MacMillan & Co., London, 1873

McLaren, Alexander, *Expositions of the Holy Scriptures: Volumes 1–17*, Baker Book House, Grand Rapids, Michigan, reprinted 1984

McLaren, Alexander, *Sermons Preached in Manchester (2nd Series) by Alexander McLaren*, MacMillan & Co., London, 1869

McLaren, Alexander, *The Victor's Crowns and Other Sermons*, Christian Commonwealth Publishing Co. Ltd., London, 1898

McLaren, Alexander, *Triumphant Certainties and Other Sermons*, Christian Commonwealth Publishing Co. Ltd., London, 1897

Mann, A. Chester, *F. B. Meyer: Preacher, Teacher, Man of God*, George Allen & Unwin Ltd., London, 1929

McLaren, E. T., *Dr. McLaren of Manchester: A Sketch*, Hodder & Stoughton, London, New York, Toronto, 1911

Meyer, F. B., *From the Pit to the Throne, or, Scenes from the Life of Joseph (A Course of Sunday Evening Sermons Principally Addressed to Young Men and Women, by F. B. Meyer, B.A., Minister of Melbourne Hall, Leicester)*, Elliot Stock, London, 1885

Meyer, F. B., *Expository Preaching: Plans and Methods*, Marshall, Morgan & Scott, London, Edinburgh, 1954

Meyer, F. B., *Jonah: The Truant Prophet*, The Baptist Tract and Book Society, London, 1889

Meyer, F. B., TRACT, W. S. Biggs, New Bond Street, Leicester (1886?)

Meyer, F. B., *Our Daily Homily, 5 Volumes*, Zondervan Publishing House, Grand Rapids, Michigan, 1951

Mitchell, W. Fraser, M.A. (Edinburgh), B.Litt. (Oxon), Lecturer and Tutor, University of Reading, *English Pulpit Oratory from Andrewes to Tillotson*, Russell & Russell, Inc., New York, 1962

Morgan, G. Campbell, *The Analyzed Bible: The Books of the Bible Outlined by the "Prince of Expositors,"* Fleming H. Revell Company, Westwood, New Jersey, 1964

Morgan, G. Campbell, D.D., *Preaching*, Marshall, Morgan & Scott, Ltd., London, Edinburgh, 1937

Morgan, Jill, *A Man of the Word: Life of G. Campbell Morgan*, Pickering & Inglis, Ltd., London, 1951

Morgan, G. Campbell, *The Best of G. Campbell Morgan*, compiled by Ralph Turnbull, Baker Book House, Grand Rapids, Michigan, 1972

Morgan, G. Campbell, *The Westminster Pulpit, Vol. 1*, Hodder and Stoughton, London, 1906

Morgan, G. Campbell, *A First Century Message to Twentieth Century Christians: A Message Based Upon the Letters to the Seven Churches of Asia*, Fleming H. Revell Co., New York, Chicago, Toronto, London and Edinburgh, 1902 (August)

Morgan, G. Campbell, D.D., *The Practice of Prayer*, Hodder and Stoughton, London, 1906

Morgan, G. Campbell, *The Christian World Pulpit*, No. 2,366—Vol. XCI, Wednesday, March 7, 1917 (Price, one penny) & No. 2,368, Wednesday, March 21, 1917, & No. 2,370, Wednesday, April 4, 1917

Morgan, G. Campbell, *Wherein*, James Nisbet & Co. Ltd., London, 1898

Morgan, Kenneth O., *The Oxford Illustrated History of Britain*, Oxford University Press, reprinted 1987

Morison, Frank, *J. H. Jowett, M.A., D.D.: A Character Study*, James Clarke & Co., London, 1911

Muirhead, J. H. L. L. D., *Nine Famous Birmingham Men*, Lectures delivered in the University of Birmingham, Cornish Brothers Ltd., Birmingham, 1909 (Section on R. W. Dale, written by Rev. Charles Silvester Horne, M.A. (Born 1 Dec. 1829, died 13 March 1895)

Murray, Harold, *Cambell Morgan: Bible Teacher, A Sketch of the Great Expositor and Evangelist*, Marshall, Morgan & Scott Ltd., London and Edinburgh, 1938

Orr, J. Edwin, *The Fervent Prayer: The Worldwide Impact of the Great Awakening of 1858*, Moody Press, Chicago, 1974

Parker, Joseph, *Missionary Sermons 1812–1924*, The Carey Press, 19, Furnival Street, E.C., London, 1929 (Parker's message, "The Measure of the Altar" preached in the Town Hall, Reading, 3 October 1893) (Spurgeon's message "Preparing the Way" preached at The Music Hall, Royal Surrey Gardens, London, on 28 April 1858)

Parker, Joseph, *The City Temple Pulpit*, Hodder and Stoughton, London, 1899

Parker, Joseph, *The Gospel of Jesus Christ: Sermons by Joseph Parker*, Arthur H. Stockwell, London, 1903

Parker, Joseph, *The City Temple Pulpit, Vol. VI*, Hodder and Stoughton, London, 1902

Parker, Joseph, *Ad Clerum: Advices to a Young Preacher*, Hodder and Stoughton, London, 1870

Parker, Joseph, *The City Temple Pulpit, Vol. IV*, Hodder and Stoughton, London, 1901

Parker, Joseph, *The People's Bible*, Published in five sets, 25 volumes in total, Hazell, Watson & Viney, Ltd., Hodder & Stoughton, London, 1905

Pattison, T. Harwood, *The Making of the Sermon: For the Classroom and the Study*, The American Baptist Publication Society, Valley Forge, Chicago, Los Angeles, 1941

Peel, Albert, *A Hundred Eminent Congregationalists*, The Independent Press Ltd., London, 1927

Pike, G. Holden, *Dr. Parker and His Friends*, T. Fisher Unwin, London, 1904

Pike, G. Holden, *Seven Portraits of the Rev. C. H. Spurgeon with Reminiscences of His Life at Waterbeach and London*, Passmore and Alabaster, London, 1879

Porritt, Arthur, *John Henry Jowett, C.H., M.A., D.D.*, Hodder and Stoughton, London, 1924

Qualben, Lars P. (St. Olaf College), *A History of the Christian Church*, Thomas Nelson and Sons, New York, 1942

Quayle, Bishop William A., *The Pastor-Preacher*, Jennings & Graham, Cincinnati, Eaton & Mains, New York, 1910

Railton, George S., "His First Commissioner," *General Booth*, (With A Preface by General Bramwell Booth), Hodder and Stoughton, London, New York, Toronto (2nd edition) 1912

Robertson, F. W., *Sermons Preached at Brighton by Rev. Frederick W. Robertson*, Kegan Paul, Trench & Co., London, 1884 (Sermons preached between Aug. 15, 1847 and Aug. 15 1853)

Robinson, Haddon W., *Expository Preaching: Principles & Practice (A Unique How-to Book)*, Inter-varsity Press, Leicester, and Baker Book House Co., U.S.A., 1980

Russell, George W. E., *Leaders of the Church 1800-1900*: Article on Dr. Liddon by G. W. E. Russell, A. R. Mowbray & Co., London, Oxford, 1905

Russell, George W. E., *Dr. Liddon*, A. R. Mowbray & Co. Ltd., London, Oxford, Milwaukee, 1905

Ryle, John Charles, Bishop of Liverpool, *The Upper Room: Being A Few Truths for the Times*, The Banner of Truth Trust, Edinburgh, Carlisle, PA, 1970; first published in 1888 by Wm. Hunt & Co.

Seaward, James, *A Chat About Spurgeon in a Railway Train*, London, 1867

Seeley, Sir J. R., K.C.M.G., Litt. D., *Ecce Homo: A Survey of the Life and Work of Jesus Christ*, MacMillan and Co. Ltd., St. Martin's Street, London, 1916

Shindler, Rev. R., *From the Usher's Desk to the Tabernacle Pulpit: The Life and Labours of Pastor C. H. Spurgeon*, Passmore and Alabaster, London, 1892

Smith, George Adam, *The Life of Henry Drummond*, Hodder and Stoughton, London, MCMX

Smyth, Charles, *The Art of Preaching: A Practical Survey of Preaching in the Church of England 747–1939*, Society for Promoting Christian Knowledge, Northumberland Ave., WC2, MacMillan Co., London, New York, 1940

Spurgeon, C. H., *12 Sermons of the Resurrection*, Baker Book House, Grand Rapids, Michigan, 1968

Spurgeon, C. H., *12 Sermons on the Second Coming of Christ*, Baker Book House, Grand Rapids, Michigan, 1976

Spurgeon, C. H., *Lectures to My Students*, Marshall, Morgan & Scott, London, 1954

Spurgeon, C. H., *An All-Round Ministry: Addresses to Ministers and Students*, The Banner of Truth Trust, 78b Chiltern Street, London, W.1, 1960, second impression 1965 (First published 1900)

Spurgeon, C. H., *Messages to the Multitudes*, Sampson Low, Marston & Co., London, 1892

Spurgeon, C. H., *The Passion and Death of Christ*, William Eerdmans Publishing Company, Grand Rapids, Michigan, 1973

Spurgeon, C. H., *C. H. Spurgeon's Fifty Most Remarkable Sermons*, Passmore and Alabaster, London, 1908

Spurr, Frederic C., *Charles Haddon Spurgeon 1834–1892*, from Great Christians, edited by R. S. Forman, Ivor Nicholson and Watson, London, 1934

Stewart, James S., *Heralds of God (The Warrack Lectures)*, Hodder and Stoughton, Ltd., London, 1946

Stewart, James S., D.D., *A Faith to Proclaim: The Lyman Beecher Lectures at Yale University*, Hodder and Stoughton, London, 1953

Tewinkel, Joseph M., *Built Upon the Cornerstone: A Brief History of the Christian Church*, Christian Publications, Inc., Harrisburg, PA, 1980

Toon, Peter & Smout & Michael, *John Charles Ryle: Evangelical Bishop*, James Clarke & Co. Ltd., Cambridge, 1976

Triggs, Kathy, *Alexander Whyte: The Peacemaker*, Pickering Paperbacks, 1984 (Basingstoke, Hants.)

Unstead, R. J., *England: Book 4, A Century of Change*, A. C. Black Ltd., London, reprinted with corrections, 1964

Wagner, Don M., *The Expository Method of G. Campbell Morgan*, Fleming H. Revell Co., 1957

Walker, Williston (Titus Street Professor of Ecclesiastical History in Yale University), *A History of the Christian Church*, Charles Scribner's Sons, New York, 1950

Walker, Andrew, *Restoring the Kingdom the Kingdom: The Radical Christianity of the House Church Movement*, Hodder and Stoughton, London, Sydney, Auckland, Toronto, 1985

Watson, Angus, *Joseph Parker, 1830–1902*, From Great Christians, Edited by R. S. Forman, Ivor Nicholson and Watson, London, 1934

Whyte, Alexander, *The Walk, Conversation and Character of Jesus Christ Our Lord*, Oliphant, Anderson and Ferrier, Edinburgh, 1905

Whyte, Alexander, *Bible Characters Volumes 1–6*, Oliphants Ltd., London and Edinburgh, 1896, 1898, 1899

Whyte, Alexander, *The Best of Alexander Whyte*, Edited by Ralph G. Turnbull, Baker Book House, Grand Rapids, Michigan, Reprinted in 1968, copyright 1953 by Fleming H. Revell Co.

Whyte, Alexander, *That They All May Be One: A Reunion Sermon by Alexander Whyte, D.D.*, J. M. Dent & Co., Bedford St. W.C., London, 1906

Whyte, Alexander, *Lord, Teach us to Pray: Sermons on Prayer*, Doubleday, Doran & Company, Inc., Garden City, New York, 1929

Wymer, Norman, *Father of Nobody's Children: A Portrait of Dr. Barnardo*, Hutchinson, Stratford Place, London, 1954

Chart

London	Denom.	Ministry #	Born	Began	Church	Finished	No. of yrs	Died	Age
H. P. Liddon	C. of E.		1829	1870	St. Paul's Cathedral	1890	20	1890	61
Joseph Parker	Congreg.	2	1830	1869	Poultry Chapel/City Temple	1902	33	1902	72
C. H. Spurgeon	Baptist		1834	1854	New Park St./Metropolitan Tab.	1891	37	1892	57
G. Campbell Morgan	Congreg.	2	1863	1897	New Court, Tollington Park	1901	4	1945	81
	Congreg.	3	1863	1904	Westminster Chapel	1917	13	1945	81
	Congreg.	4	1863	1933	Westminster Chapel	1943	10	1945	81
John Henry Jowett	Congreg.	4	1863	1918	Westminster Chapel	1922	4	1923	60
F. B. Meyer	Baptist	3	1847	1888	Regent's Park Church	1892	4	1929	81
	Baptist	4	1847	1892	Christ Church, Westmin. Bridge	1909	17	1929	81
	Baptist	5	1847	1909	Regent's Park Church	1915	6	1929	81
	Baptist	6	1847	1915	Christ Church, Westmin. Bridge	1921	6	1929	81
Manchester									
Alex. McLaren	Baptist	2	1826	1858	Union Chapel	1903	45	1910	84
Joseph Parker	Congreg.	1	1830	1858	Cavendish Chapel	1869	11	1902	72
Birmingham									
R. W. Dale	Congreg.		1829	1852	Carr's Lane Chapel	1895	43	1895	65
John Henry Jowett	Congreg.	2	1863	1895	Carr's Lane Chapel	1911	16	1923	60
G. Campbell Morgan	Congreg.	1	1863	1893	Westminster Road	1897	4	1945	81
Southampton									
Alex. McLaren	Baptist	1	1826	1846	Portland Chapel	1858	12	1910	84
Edinburgh									
Alex. Whyte	Free Pres		1836	1870	Free St. George's	1916	46	1921	84
Leicester									
F. B. Meyer	Baptist	1	1847	1874	Victoria Rd. Church	1878	4	1929	81
Newcastle -on-Tyne									
John Henry Jowett	Congreg.	1	1863	1889	St. James Congregational Ch.	1895	6	1923	60
New York, U.S.A.									
John Henry Jowett	Congreg.	3	1863	1911	Fifth Ave. Presbyterian	1918	7	1923	60

Index: Victorian Age Preachers

Index Supplement

Airedale College, Yorkshire, 87

Australia, x, 7, 40-41, 47-48, 68-69, 92

Barnardo, Dr. Thomas John, 20

Brighton College, 185

Cambridge University, 233

Cambridge Seven, 189

Carr's Lane Chapel, Birmingham, 63, 301

Cavendish Street Chapel, Manchester, 119, 131

Christ Church Chapel, Oxford, 95, 301

Christ Church College, 95, 99

Christ Church, Westminster Bridge Road, 192, 301

Church of England, 11-13, 17, 35, 68, 97, 100-101, 105, 111, 280, 289, 297

City Temple, 47, 51, 121-127, 130, 133, 137, 168, 218, 231, 236, 280, 285, 295, 301

Crystal Palace, 7, 153, 160-161

Cuddesdon Diocesan Training College for the Clergy, 97

Digbeth Institute, 202, 282

Essays and Reviews, 13, 68, 99, 290

Fifth Avenue Presbyterian Church, New York, 202

Keswick Conferences, 13, 190

978-0-595-36222-6
0-595-36222-2

Printed in the United States
34022LVS00003B/100-120

9 780595 362226